D0887014

Wallace Stevens and Modern Art

Wallace Stevens and Modern Art

From the Armory Show

to Abstract Expressionism

Glen MacLeod

Yale University Press

New Haven and London

Designed by Sonia L. Scanlon.
Set in Sabon type by The Composing Room of
Michigan, Inc.
Printed in the United States of America by Vail-
Ballou Press, Binghamton, New York.

Library of Congress Cataloging-in-Publication Data
MacLeod, Glen G.
    Wallace Stevens and modern art : from the
    Armory Show to abstract expressionism /
    Glen MacLeod.
      p. cm.
    Includes bibliographical references and index.
    ISBN 0-300-05360-6
    1. Stevens, Wallace, 1879–1955—
    Knowledge—Art. 2. Art and
   literature—United States—History—20th
   century. 3. Art,
   Modern—20th century. I. Title.
   PS3537.T4753Z6775   1993
   811'.52—dc20
   92-25358
    CIP

A catalogue record for this book is available from
the British Library.

The paper in this book meets the guidelines for
permanence and durability of the Committee on
Production Guidelines for Book Longevity of the
Council on Library Resources.

10 9 8 7 6 5 4 3 2 1

For James L. Steffensen, Jr.

Contents

Illustrations

Acknowledgments

I began the research for this book with the help of a six-month National Endowment for the Humanities Fellowship for College Teachers. A year-long J. Paul Getty Fellowship in the History of Art and the Humanities allowed me to undertake the extensive research in art history that was necessary to complete it. A fellowship from the Huntington Library permitted me to examine the Wallace Stevens Archive there, and a number of smaller grants from the University of Connecticut Research Foundation have enabled me to make steady progress on this project. I am very grateful to all these institutions.

Two scholars of Wallace Stevens have been particularly helpful to me. A. Walton Litz encouraged me to undertake this study and has supported it faithfully along the way. I count myself lucky to be able to rely on his generous criticism and sound advice. Milton J. Bates has cheerfully answered my queries and corrected my errors over the years. He has also rescued me from a number of scholarly predicaments, for which I am happily in his debt.

I want to thank especially several art historians whose guidance has made this book possible. Francis Naumann's contagious enthusiasm for art history, and his spirit of scholarly cooperation, made this interdisciplinary project seem less daunting to me; his detailed knowlege of Marcel Duchamp in particular supplied the substance of my first chapter. Dore Ashton has helped me in several important ways. Her excellent *The New York School: A Cultural Reckoning* gave me the idea for this book and proved a handy guide in my early research. She discussed the book with me at length during its formative stages, giving me the benefit of her first-hand knowledge of the New York art world and of her astute observations on both art and literature. It is a privilege to acknowledge her generous assistance.

I owe a very large debt of gratitude to Francis V. O'Connor, who took an early interest in my research and has taught me more about art in conversation than I would ever have learned from books. His special knowledge of American art from the 1930s through the 1950s, together with his genuine interest in poetry, made him the ideal adviser for this project. He has read several drafts of the manuscript and is responsible for numerous improvements. He not only pointed out errors of fact but also suggested larger changes that have clarified the book's organization and strengthened its argument.

A number of other scholars have contributed substantially to this project. For their interest in my work from its early stages, and for their continued support, I am grateful to Clarence Brown, Garnett McCoy, the late James Baird, and the very much alive Roy Harvey Pearce. The late Peter Brazeau first suggested to me that Stevens' relation to surrealism was a topic in need of investigation; his hint led me in directions neither of us could have foreseen, and I wish he were here to see the results. Thanks to William Burney for many stimulating discussions about the relations between poetry and painting in general, and about Stevens and Klee in particular. And thanks to Charles Berger for his generous help while I was at work on *The Man with the Blue Guitar.*

I am grateful to the late Holly Stevens for her fine editing of *Letters of Wallace Stevens* and *The Palm at the End of the Mind,* for her thoughtful consideration of her father's early life in *Souvenirs and Prophecies,* and for her cooperation at various stages during my research for this book. I remember her friendship with pleasure.

For their kind assistance over the years, I would like to thank the staffs of the following institutions: the Yale University Libraries; the New York Public Library; the Archives of American Art; Martin Ridge, Daniel Woodward, and Sara Hodson of the Huntington Library; Cathy Henderson of the Harry Ransom Humanities Research Center, University of Texas at Austin; John Teahan of the Wadsworth Atheneum, Hartford; Susanne Javorski of the Wesleyan University Art Library; Susan Thebarge, Sheila Lafferty, and especially Janet Swift of the Waterbury Campus Library of the University of Connecticut.

The research for this book has taken ten years and has often led me into unexpected areas of art history, some of which have regretfully been omitted from the final text. In the process of correcting my ignorance about modern art, I have benefited from the kind cooperation of so many people in the art world that it is impossible to thank them all individually. I wish especially to acknowledge the following people, each of whom was exceptionally helpful in some way: Elise Asher, Sally Avery, Jennifer Bartlett, Ethel Baziotes, Bill Berkson, Louise Bourgeois, the late Nicolas Calas, Barbara Cavaliere, Robert Dash, Richard Diebenkorn, Ann Gibson, John Gruen, Mona Hadler, David Hare, Mary Emma Harris, Ward Jackson, Armistead Leigh, Cathy Levesque, Ouida Lewis, Loren MacIver, Musa Mayer, William McNaught, George McNeil, Diana Menkes, the late Robert Motherwell, Jesse Murry, Annalee Newman, Elaine O'Brien, Philip Pavia, Stephen Polcari, Anne Porter, Martica Sawin, the late Prescott Schutz, Charles and Lenore

Seliger, David Shapiro, Rose Slivka, Rachel Tworkov, Jane Wilson, and Don Wyckoff.

Finally, I want to thank a number of friends, relatives, and fellow scholars for their part in the making of this book: my parents, William and Laura MacLeod, for seeing me through countless rough spots; Robert Pattison, Douglas Brenner, and Marion Meilaender for their companionship and wise counsel; Delia Duty and my brother, Bruce MacLeod, for reading and commenting on the manuscript; Rachael Lynch for proofreading; Brendan Lynch for his expertise with computers; and Harold Steever for his patience.

Portions of this book have appeared, in somewhat different form, in the *Archives of American Art Journal,* the *Journal of Modern Literature, American Literature,* and the *Wallace Stevens Journal.*

For permission to quote from unpublished writing by Wallace Stevens, I am grateful to Peter R. Hanchak. Stevens' poetry is reprinted with the permission of Alfred A. Knopf, Inc., and Faber & Faber Ltd.

This book is dedicated to James L. Steffensen, Jr., whose genius for teaching, scholarship, and friendship has inspired me more than I can say.

Abbreviations

CP *The Collected Poems of Wallace Stevens* (New York: Alfred A. Knopf, 1954).

L *Letters of Wallace Stevens,* ed. Holly Stevens (New York: Alfred A. Knopf, 1966).

NA *The Necessary Angel: Essays on Reality and the Imagination* (New York: Alfred A. Knopf, 1951).

OP *Opus Posthumous: Poems, Plays, Prose,* ed. Milton J. Bates (New York: Alfred A. Knopf, 1989).

SP Holly Stevens, *Souvenirs and Prophecies: The Young Wallace Stevens* (New York: Alfred A. Knopf, 1976).

Introduction

I pay just as much attention to painters as I do to writers because, except technically, their problems are the same. They seem to move in the same direction at the same time.
—L, 593

Wallace Stevens' relation to modern art may seem, at first glance, a narrow focus for a book-length study of the poet. On the contrary, I mean to show that this subject is crucial to understanding Stevens' poetry; that it largely explains the unusual character of his poetic development; and that it accounts for his peculiar position in the field of modern poetry. To understand Stevens' relation to modern art is to grasp one of the central currents in American cultural history.

For those who know Stevens' reputation as a recluse who kept aloof from the latest trends in art and literature, it may come as a surprise to discover that he followed the contemporary art world intently throughout his mature career. This preoccupation is everywhere evident in his writing—in his letters telling of trips to galleries in New York and elsewhere; in his essays, which often draw analogies between poetry and painting; and in the notebooks where he jotted down favorite passages from current books and articles about the visual arts. Stevens' interest in the world of art was deep and continuous. It helped to determine the character of his poetry in many ways, from the choice of subjects for particular poems to the comprehensive organizing concepts of his poetic theory.

Stevens' poetic development closely parallels the development of modern art in America from the 1910s through the 1950s. This not only helps to explain his anomalous position in modern poetry, it also suggests why his poetry speaks more directly to visual artists than that of any other modern poet in English. Viewed in this context, Stevens is not the isolated and peculiar figure he often seems when compared only with his poetic contemporaries. Rather, he is perhaps the most central and representative American poet of his time.

To suggest that there is a direct relation between Stevens' poetry and the *contemporaneous* development of the visual arts in the United States challenges the prevailing view. Stevens' interest in "the relations between poetry and painting" has never been questioned. His 1951 essay of that title is only the most sustained treatment of a theme that occupied him throughout his career. But most critics have focused on Stevens' relation to impressionism, fauvism, and cubism—the major French movements that antedated his mature poetic utterances. The most thorough study of this subject is still that of Michel Benamou, who interprets Stevens' poetry in terms of a conflict between impressionist (romantic) and cubist (modern) aesthetics.[1] Without taking issue with this view, Robert Buttel and James Baird have contributed substantially to our understanding of Stevens' close relation to the visual arts.[2] Recently, Charles Altieri has analyzed Stevens' aesthetics in the context of what he calls "painterly abstraction" in twentieth-century art. But his broadly speculative approach finally has more to do with philosophy than with art history, and he does not address the question of Stevens' relation to the contemporary art world.[3] There seems to be general agreement that—after *Harmonium,* at least—Stevens was simply out of touch with the avant-garde art movements of his time.

One factor contributing to this critical consensus is Stevens' own art collection. Composed mainly of small canvases by minor artists who had some reputation in Paris during his lifetime, the collection seems to represent a very conservative taste. The works are mostly landscapes, and have been described as "paintings that, in a quiet way, protested against Cubism, Fauvism, abstraction, harkening back to Impressionism or returning to Barbizon 'reality.'"[4] (A checklist of the collection is given in the appendix.) Stevens bought many of these works sight unseen, entrusting nearly all his purchases first to Anatole Vidal, a Parisian bookseller, and then, after Vidal's death during World War II, to his daughter, Paule Vidal.[5] Stevens showed no interest in collecting American art even when, by the end of the war, the vital center of Western art had shifted from Paris to New York.

The evidence of Stevens' art collecting has made it seem reasonable to assume that such a man had little concern for contemporary developments in the visual arts. The chief problem with this assumption is that Stevens' art collection is not a valid register of the full range of his artistic interests. The works of art a man chooses to *live* with are not necessarily those he most admires. Stevens liked the paintings of Georges Rouault, for example; his library included a number of books about or illustrated by the artist.[6] He could have afforded to buy one of Rouault's paintings, but in 1938 he declined to do so, explaining that Rouault's "tragic and overpowering things are a little more than I want, except on particularly bad days." In the same way, although he admired Joan Miró, he did not want to buy any of his paintings: "We have had rather a deluge of surrealist things recently and, while I think that the work of Miro in particular is miraculous, still I have no particular desire to own any of it."[7] Again, Stevens never acquired even a small work by Paul Klee, although it was within his means to do so and Klee was his favorite painter.[8] James Johnson Sweeney, the director of the Guggenheim Museum when Stevens knew him, recalls that Stevens was often genuinely interested in contemporary art despite—or even, perhaps, because of—its foreignness to him: "When he talked to me [about painting], I thought he looked at contemporary painting much as he looked at French poetry, not as something native to him but which attracted him. I found it was always what was interesting to him as a stimulant."[9] To the extent that Stevens experienced contemporary art as alien he could welcome it as a stimulant. But this same strangeness and vitality, which attracted him and stimulated his imagination, also made such art inappropriate to the familiar, comfortable atmosphere he desired at home.

Stevens' remarks about modern art were sometimes quite dismissive.[10] Consider this passage from a letter to Ronald Lane Latimer in 1936 about the landmark exhibition "Fantastic Art, Dada, Surrealism" at the Museum of Modern Art: "When I was in New York last week I thought of going to the exhibition at the Modern Museum, but having to make a choice because of the shortness of time, I went to the Morgan Library instead (the exhibition room on the corner). Better fifty minutes of the Morgan Library than a cycle in the Surrealist Exhibition. The metaphysics of Aristotle embellished by a miniaturist who knew the meaning of the word embellishment knocks the metaphysics of Dali cold" (L, 315). This seems, on the face of it, a fairly straightforward declaration that Stevens had no sympathy with Surrealism, which was, during the 1920s and early 1930s, the most visible and influential avant-garde movement in Western art. In a general way, therefore, it seems to corroborate the standard view—supported by other passages in Stevens' letters and essays—that Stevens had little interest in the course of modern art after impressionism and cubism. But this statement, like much of what Stevens had to say about art, cannot be taken at face value. His apparent dismissal of Surrealism must be seen in the context of his conscious dialogue with Surrealist art theory in 1936–1937, which culminated in his major poem "The Man with the Blue Guitar" (see chapter 3). Nor did his apparent scorn of Salvador Dalí in 1936 prevent Stevens from acquiring the lengthy catalogue of Dalí's one-man show at the Museum of Modern Art in 1941.[11] The attitude expressed in Stevens' letter has more to do with Dalí's already well-established reputation as a shameless popularizer than with Dalí's painting, and it reflects Stevens' boredom with the relentless promotion of Surrealism rather than a contempt for Surrealist art. He is not adopting the pose of an aesthetic reactionary who prefers medieval to modern art; rather, he is taking satisfaction in being so well informed and up-to-date that the latest New York craze is already old hat to him.

This example illustrates the importance of interpreting Stevens' references to art in context. This applies not only to his comments about contemporary artists and movements but also to his frequent allusions to figures from art history. Take, for instance, his mention of van Gogh in a letter to Robin Lane Latimer: "The fundamental source of joy in life is the instinct of joy.[12] If that is true, and a little difficult to realize in life, it is infinitely more true in poetry and painting, and much more easy to realize there. Van Gogh painted to indulge the instinct of joy" (L, 296). Stevens' reference to van Gogh is entirely unprompted; the rest of the letter contains no allusion to him. Reading this passage on its own, we may suppose that Stevens simply needed to illustrate what he meant by "the instinct of joy," that he thought of van Gogh because he was a fellow Dutchman and because the painter's colorful, boldly expressionistic manner made him in some ways a kindred spirit. But we miss the essence of Stevens' allusion if we think of it as having no particular historical context. In fact, this reference is specific and timely. In November 1935, when Stevens wrote the letter, the Museum of Modern Art had just opened a one-man exhibition of van Gogh. The artist's work did not then enjoy the nearly universal esteem it does today. In fact, the museum had been doubtful of the exhibition's prospects. The American press and public had simply ignored the van Gogh paintings at the Armory Show in 1913, and an exhibition at the Montross Gallery in 1920 had not attracted a single buyer.[13] The museum's Advisory Committee had opposed the show on the grounds that van Gogh's paintings were too similar to make an interesting one-man show and that he had had little influence on contemporary painting. In the event, however, the show was overwhelmingly successful with both the critics and the public, who crowded into the museum in record numbers. Although we have no record of it, it seems likely that Wallace Stevens was among the visitors.[14]

The nationwide publicity surrounding this exhibition first established van Gogh's enormous popularity in the United States. The legend of van Gogh as a neglected genius creating images of transcendent beauty amid a sordid and tormented existence captured the imagination of a nation in the midst of the Depression. As Russell Lynes puts it: "It was as though in the depths of the Depression . . . a bright and cheerful light had been let in. No matter that it came from a dark soul and an often deranged mind. Wasn't everybody's soul feeling somewhat dark and his mind somewhat off its track then?"[15] Stevens' characterization of van Gogh as the embodiment of "the instinct of joy" springs directly from this context. His seemingly hermetic allusion to the nineteenth-century Dutch artist actually reflects Stevens' lively engagement with events in the contemporary art world.

The pattern of such references in Stevens' letters and poems maps a continuing dialogue with the contemporary art world that can also serve as a mirror of Stevens' development as a poet. His only other reference to van Gogh in the *Letters,* for instance, demonstrates how his view of artistic creation changed during the 1930s. In 1943 he described for Henry Church his reactions to a van Gogh exhibition at Wildenstein's: "The word for all this is *maniement*: I don't mean a mania of manner, but I mean a total subjection of reality to the artist. It may be only too true that Van Gogh had fortuitous assistance in the mastery of reality. But he mastered it, no matter how. And that is so often what one wants to do in poetry: to seize the whole mass of everything and to squeeze it, and make it one's own" (L, 459).[16] In this passage van Gogh serves once again as a kind of alter ego for Stevens, but now instead of the "instinct of joy" he represents a "mastery of reality." This implies a more active, forceful view of art that reflects Stevens' changing response to the "pressure of reality" between the Depression and the Second World War. During this transitional period in his career, he shifted to a more aggressive conception of poetry as "the act of the mind."

Often when Stevens refers to the visual arts in his poetry or letters, he is testing his own artistic identity against the "reality" of the contemporary art world. Thus even historical art exhibitions could take on contemporary significance in terms of Stevens' poetic development. A small but well-conceived show like "The Painters of Still Life" at the Wadsworth Atheneum in 1938 could have great impact despite its modest scale, as its influence on Stevens' *Parts of a World* demonstrates. (See chapter 4.) Although Stevens, unlike his friend William Carlos Williams, did not visit artists' studios, his poetic growth is, in its own way, just as closely linked to the contemporary art world.

The comparison with Williams is useful in clarifying Stevens' relation to the visual arts. Bonnie Costello has stated what seems to me the crucial distinction: "All the studies of Williams agree that he takes the analogy with painting literally and strives for an equivalency of effect in words. Stevens' relation to painting is a far more figurative and conceptual one."[17] For Stevens, the important relations between poetry and painting were in the realm of theory, not technique. This helps to explain why few books have been written about Stevens and painting, but many about Williams and painting.[18] The Western tradition of *ut pictura poesis* has conditioned us to expect that analogies between poetry and painting will involve direct comparisons between particular paintings and poems, usually in terms of their common iconography or technique. In this sense, it is illuminating to compare Williams' poem "The Rose" with Juan Gris' cubist collage *Roses* (1914) or his painting *The*

Open Window (1921).[19] But such comparisons rarely work in the case of Stevens, whose inspiration came less from individual paintings than from what he called "the literature of painting": "To a large extent, the problems of poets are the problems of painters and poets must often turn to the literature of painting for a discussion of their own problems" (OP, 187). So Stevens' essay "The Irrational Element in Poetry" was inspired by an art review in the *New Statesman and Nation*; "The Man with the Blue Guitar" sprang from Stevens' reading of a special Picasso issue of *Cahiers d'art;* his 1938 "Canonica" series owes its conception to the catalogue of the "Painters of Still Life" exhibition at the Wadsworth Atheneum; and the first section of "Notes toward a Supreme Fiction" reflects Stevens' reading of an essay by Piet Mondrian.

As these examples illustrate, by "the literature of painting" Stevens generally meant not the weighty tomes of art history but current books and periodicals. His knowledge of the art world is that of a well-read gallery-goer and has little to do with scholarly art historians like Erwin Panofsky and E. H. Gombrich, whose influence dominated the academic journals during his lifetime. Indeed, one constant difficulty in trying to sort out Stevens' idiosyncratic views of art is the need to see *through* the prevailing biases of art history, to avoid attributing to Stevens historical perspectives that he did not share. To take one example: Panofsky's iconological method has so deeply influenced twentieth-century views of Dutch painting that we now see *vanitas* symbolism even in the most innocent-seeming still-lifes. In this context, Stevens' remark that "there is nothing in any one of these [Dutch] pictures . . . suggestive even of the existence of evil" (L, 852) may seem either ignorant or provocative. But in fact it is neither. Stevens' view was formed without help from Panofsky and conforms to the standard interpretation prior to the twentieth century—what is still probably the layman's view—that seventeenth-century Dutch paintings are exactly what they seem: pure, realistic visual description; celebrations of normal everyday life.

For his knowledge of art Stevens tended to rely on relatively popular, ephemeral publications rather than sturdier academic ones. On the face of it, this practice seems to prove him a dilettante rather than a serious student of art. Most critics have refrained from comment on this tendency, probably out of the same embarrassment they feel in discussing Stevens' art collection. The assumption seems to be that, if only Stevens had had more time, if he had not been a busy insurance executive, he naturally would have sought out a more intellectually rigorous understanding of art history. Perhaps this is true. But if so, I am not at all sure Stevens' poetry would have been the better for it. Stevens did not read current reviews and articles by default, but by choice. Especially in the 1930s, when he no longer had personal contact with the artistic avant-garde, reading current periodicals was one way he could keep his finger on the pulse of the art world. It allowed him to feel that he was in touch with the vital issues of the day, at least as they affected the visual arts. His reading of current articles and books about art was only one aspect—though a centrally important one—of his larger effort to establish his "relation to contemporary ideas" (L, 340).

Stevens was more successful in this endeavor than his critics have allowed. In some surprising ways, his experience often closely parallels that of the avant-garde artists of the New York School. One striking example is the fact that Stevens was interested in the Dutch artist Piet Mondrian in 1942. In that year Stevens' interest in his own Dutch heritage, combined with his close attention to events in the New York art world, made him aware of the significance of Mondrian's presence in Manhattan at a time when few others could have appreciated it. As Robert Motherwell has remarked, in the early 1940s very few people knew of Mondrian at all, and the number of those who took him seriously as an artist and theorist was smaller still: "There could only have been a few dozen such people around. At least a third of them were painters and were deeply influenced by Mondrian."[20] Other such examples form a pattern linking Stevens' poetry to contemporary developments in the visual arts throughout his career.

This pattern was recognized by Hayden Carruth when he reviewed Stevens' *Collected Poems* in 1955. Observing that "in point of time, Stevens' career as a writer has been co-extensive with the development of modern art, at least as it has occurred in this country" he finds in the *Collected Poems* a poetic record of this development: "I was continually impressed, as I wandered—no other word will do—among the hundreds of poems in this volume, by the way in which they present to us the whole movement of this century in art."[21] To be more specific, Stevens' mature career (1913–1955) exactly spans the period from the Armory Show (1913), which introduced the American public to post-impressionism and cubism, to the ascendancy of abstract expressionism in the 1950s.

The chief focus of my research has been Stevens' transitional period during the 1930s and early 1940s, when he developed his own poetic theory in response to the highly politicized atmosphere of the time and, in the process, deliberately transformed himself from the aesthete of *Harmonium* to a poet of "the act of the mind" (CP, 240). My thesis is that he performed this self-transformation with the opposing art movements of surrealism and abstraction in mind. To the literary critic, this probably sounds as if I am merely substituting two different art-historical terms for the ones usually applied to Stevens' poetry (impressionism and cubism). On the contrary, the opposition between surrealism and abstraction was a historical fact during the 1930s and early 1940s. I mean to show that Stevens was closely aware of this vital theoretical opposition in the contemporary art world, and that this awareness helped to determine the development of his own poetry and poetic theory.

Because my primary field of interest is literature rather than art, I had no idea, when I began the research for this book, that the battle lines had ever been so clearly drawn between surrealism and abstraction. Only after several years did I realize that my study of Stevens could be organized according to these two categories. At first I thought of this organization as a working hypothesis, a theoretical imposition necessary to give coherence to a mass of "squirming facts" (CP, 215). But it soon became apparent that, to

some extent, Stevens himself had thought in precisely these categories. Moreover, the abstraction/surrealism debate turned out to be
not simply an invention of the critics but a historical fact. What had
taken me years to "discover" was, in fact, something so well known
in the art world that histories of modern art scarcely bother to
mention or explain it.

The true irony of this situation is best illustrated by an episode in
my research. Shortly after the theoretical usefulness of the ab-
straction/surrealism polarity became apparent to me, I called to
arrange an interview with the Surrealist writer and art critic Nicolas Calas. Flushed with the sense of discovery, I began by explaining my thesis. I expected him to react with polite incredulity, and I
was prepared to answer his objections with the factual evidence I
had been gathering. His response took me entirely by surprise.
Almost before I had finished, he broke in impatiently: "Oh, but it's
such a cliché!" I didn't know whether to rejoice that my thesis had
been confirmed, or to despair that it had turned out to be so
commonplace. Never has the gap separating the fields of literature
and the visual arts been clearer to me than at that moment.

In this book, I have tried to bridge that gap. Chapter 1 focuses
briefly on Stevens' relation to the New York avant-garde during his
Harmonium period (1913–23).[22] His friendship with Walter Conrad Arensberg, the patron of avant-garde artists and pioneering
collector of modern art, placed Stevens at the very heart of early
modernist experimentation in the arts in America. The stimulating
effect of the Armory Show of 1913, and the heady atmosphere of
the Arensberg salon that flourished in its wake, account in large
part for the extraordinary energy and inventiveness of *Harmonium*. Some of Stevens' most characteristic poems from this period
bear comparison with the art of Marcel Duchamp, the leading
figure of New York Dada and of the Arensberg salon. His experience during these years established the pattern of close interaction
with the world of contemporary art that became essential to his
creative process. Chapter 2 considers Stevens' return to writing
poetry in the 1930s after a long period of silence. In the politically

charged atmosphere of that time, the poet consciously sought a new and empowering sense of self, and he did so in the context of the art world. His idiosyncratic "mythology of self"[23] that evolved during these years was partly shaped by two personal factors to which I devote special attention: his pride in his Dutch heritage (including the tradition of Dutch painting) and his fascination with the figure of the art collector.

Chapters 3–6 trace Stevens' dialogue with the theories of surrealism and abstraction, from "The Man with the Blue Guitar" (1937) through "Notes toward a Supreme Fiction" (1942). Chapters 7 and 8 consider his relation to Abstract Expressionism, the first American art movement of international importance. The painters of the New York School developed their new art, by their own account, out of the combined influences of surrealism and abstraction. The common background in art theory explains why the evolution of Stevens' poetry and poetic theory from the 1930s through 1955 so closely parallels the development of Abstract Expressionism. Stevens' declaration in 1942 that his supreme fiction "must be abstract" coincides with an increasing devotion to abstraction among the avant-garde artists of the New York School. His most abstract, difficult late poems (like "The Auroras of Autumn" and "An Ordinary Evening in New Haven") were written at the same time that artists like Jackson Pollock and Willem de Kooning were taking the final step into pure nonobjectivity. The critical discourse that accompanied this new painting—both the artists' own comments on their work and the critics' more elaborate formulations—often bears a striking resemblance to Stevens' writing, both in its vocabulary and in its predominant categories of thought. For example, Abstract Expressionist art theory often appeals to concepts of the noble or the sublime; to the notion of the artist as an existential warrior engaged in violent confrontations with reality; and to the artistic act as a series of circuitous, indirect approaches to a central but unstated subject. This helps explain why critics have long found it convenient to quote Stevens' poetry and essays to elucidate aspects of Abstract Expressionism. My final chapters explore Stevens' relation to the art world from this perspective.

Stevens' relation to the contemporary art world is a subject centrally important to understanding the man and his work. The chief advantage we gain from viewing his achievement in this context is the ability to see the poet actively engaged with the advanced art of his time. Stevens' awareness of contemporary issues in the art world helped to determine the subjects and the critical vocabulary he chose to use or avoid, the ways of thinking he explored in both his poetry and his essays. Stevens speaks the dialect of the art world. When we view his thought in that context, his point of view seems less peculiar, more a part of the living critical discourse that is at the heart of American art and literature in the twentieth century.

Part **One**
Early Stevens and Modern Art

Chapter 1
Harmonium and the
Arensberg Circle

The story of Wallace Stevens' relation to modern art begins with the
Armory Show of 1913. From that
date we can trace the development
of modernism in all the arts in
America, and more particularly the
rapid growth of the New York
avant-garde of which Stevens was
part. It was soon after the Armory
Show that Stevens began writing his
first mature poems. He recognized
that there was a significant connection between these two events, stat-
ing it simply in an essay of 1948:
"In recent years, poetry began to
change character about the time
when painting began to change
character" (NA, 124). His poetic
transformation in the wake of the
Armory Show established a pattern
of close parallels with events in the
art world that would characterize
his poetic process for the rest of his
life.

It was a fortunate combination of
circumstances that allowed Stevens

to respond so productively to the sudden impetus of the Armory Show. In the first place, he had been conscientiously developing his interest in the visual arts during the preceding decade. When he left Harvard in 1900 and moved to New York City, he had a dual purpose: to make his way as a "man of the world"—perhaps as a journalist or as a "money-making lawyer" (L, 32)—and to devote himself to art by becoming a poet. As he set out on a career first in journalism (1900–1901) and then in the law, he also made a point of keeping his eye on what he called the "summum bonum" of beauty (L, 44). One of the ways he did this was by studying the visual arts. His journal records frequent visits to museums and galleries—the Metropolitan Museum of Art, the Brooklyn Museum, the National Academy of Design, the American Art Gallery, and so on. His letters to his fiancée, Elsie Viola Kachel, whom he met in 1904 and married in 1909, often describe these visits. Although Stevens admitted to being an "ignorant and untutored amateur" (SP, 200) in the realm of the visual arts, he was taking steps to improve his knowledge and appreciation of it. When the Armory Show suddenly brought the fresh discoveries of modern painting to America, Stevens was well prepared to engage in the lively debate that ensued.

At the same time, however, Stevens had already developed the shy, solitary habits in his personal life that would later become part of his literary legend. He generally made his visits to galleries alone, for instance. His reserved temperament would probably have kept him from becoming involved with the avant-garde activities that flourished in New York after 1913 if it had not been for one other fortunate coincidence: he had a close friend, Walter Conrad Arensberg, who came to play a central role in the development of the New York avant-garde during the 1910s. Stevens' involvement with Arensberg and his circle was essential to the creation of *Harmonium*.[1]

Arensberg (1878–1954) was a wealthy poet and art collector whose famous collection is now part of the Philadelphia Museum of Art.[2] Stevens got to know Arensberg at Harvard, where they

1. The Armory Show, New York, Feb. 17–March 15, 1913.

became friends, took several courses together, and were both active on literary magazines: Arensberg on the *Harvard Monthly* and Stevens on the *Harvard Advocate* (L, 820). When Stevens left Harvard, they seem to have fallen out of touch (although his journal records a lunch with Arensberg at the Harvard Club in 1906 [L, 92]). But in 1914, Arensberg moved to New York and the two men resumed their college friendship. "Walter and I were good friends over a long period of years and I saw a lot of him and his wife," Stevens wrote. "I liked them both" (L, 850). It was the Armory Show that brought about the flowering of this friendship.

The Armory Show appeared in New York from February 17 through March 15, 1913.[3] Held in the Sixty-ninth Regiment Armory, which still stands at Lexington Avenue and Twenty-fifth Street, it was an enormous exhibit of both American and European art (see fig. 1). The show is chiefly remembered because it introduced the visually uncultivated American public to post-impressionism and cubism, and it was this aspect of the show that attracted Arensberg, who traveled from Boston to see it. "I don't suppose there is anyone to whom the Armory Show of 1913 meant more than it meant to him," Stevens recalled (L, 821). According to the most dramatic version of the story, "Walter visited the exhibition, was transfixed by it, and actually forgot to go home for several days."[4] Arensberg purchased at the Armory Show the first of the paintings that would grow into his collection of modern art, to which he would devote a major part of his life and fortune. Shortly thereafter, he and his wife moved to New York in order to be at the heart of the new art movement in America.

A chief agent in this remarkable conversion was the American painter Walter Pach (1883–1958), one of the main figures involved in putting together the Armory Show. Pach, who had lived in Paris for years, had an "intimate knowledge of the current Parisian art tendencies" as well as important connections in the Parisian art world.[5] He was the European representative of the Association of American Painters and Sculptors, which organized the Armory Show; and when the show opened in New York, he became by default a "spokesman for modernism," the "chief defender of European art to the American public."[6] As Milton Brown puts it, "Pach at least had an understanding of what was happening and could supply the facts as well as the standard premises of the new art which, although fairly current abroad, were not well known here, except in the Stieglitz circle."[7] Arensberg met Pach at the time of the Armory Show, and the two men were soon spending long hours together discussing the new art.[8]

Stevens recognized the importance of Pach's proselytizing talents in the conversion of Arensberg: "Probably Pach helped this [the Armory Show] to take the extraordinary hold on him that it took in fact" (L, 821). Through his own friendship with Arensberg, Stevens also came to know Pach well. It was Pach who designed the set for Stevens' play *Bowl, Cat, and Broomstick* when it was performed in 1917, and who illustrated Stevens' "Earthy Anecdote" and "Moment of Light." They became lifelong friends. Pach's persuasive interest in the avant-garde must have played an important part in Stevens' own appreciation of modern art (fig. 2).

2. Wallace Stevens, ca. 1940. Photograph by Pach Bros., New York, the family firm of Stevens' friend Walter Pach.

It is significant that Stevens' primary connection to the Armory Show should be through these two people, Arensberg the art collector and Pach, who is best known as an art critic and for his role in organizing that celebrated exhibition. Throughout his career, Stevens tended to know art collectors, gallery directors, and museum administrators rather than artists. This means that his relation to painting is often mediated by his awareness of the complexities involved in the acquisition and display of art objects. Some effects of this tendency on his poetry and poetic theory are explored in greater detail in chapter 2.

The most publicized attraction of the Armory Show was a cubist painting entitled *Nude Descending a Staircase* (fig. 3). The newspapers singled out the *Nude* for ridicule—one critic called it "an explosion in a shingle factory"—and it soon became a symbol in the American press for all modern art. Its creator was a young Frenchman named Marcel Duchamp, who did not attend the Armory Show and had never been to the United States. But it seems inevitable, in retrospect, that Duchamp, who seemed to embody the very spirit of the Armory Show, should have met Arensberg, whose life was changed and given direction by the show.

In June 1915, Duchamp sailed from Paris to New York to escape World War I. There to greet him was Arensberg (together with their

3. Marcel Duchamp, *Nude Descending a Staircase, no. 2* (1912).

4. The *Others* group, 1916. Front row, l. to r.: Alanson Hartpence, Alfred Kreymborg, William Carlos Williams, Skip Cannell. Back row: Jean Crotti, Marcel Duchamp, Walter Arensberg, Man Ray, R. A. Sanborn, Maxwell Bodenheim.

mutual friend Walter Pach, who had arranged the meeting). Duchamp was taken directly to Arensberg's apartment on West Sixty-seventh Street, and the two men soon became close friends. They appear arm in arm in the last row of the well-known photograph of the group associated with *Others* (fig. 4), a little magazine financed by Arensberg that began publication in the summer of 1915.

During that same summer, Arensberg introduced Duchamp to Stevens, who recorded the event in a letter to his wife on August 3: "Walter Arensberg telephoned yesterday afternoon and asked me to take dinner with him at the Brevoort with Marcel Duchamp, the man who painted *The Nude Descending a Staircase*. . . . After dinner, we went up to Arensberg's apartment and looked at some of Duchamp's things. I made very little out of them. But, naturally, without sophistication in that direction, and with only a very rudimentary feeling about art, I expect little of myself" (L, 185). This was the first of many such visits for Stevens during the 1910s.

Arensberg was in the habit of inviting friends to the apartment to share his enthusiasm for modern art, and in order to accommodate his widening circle of acquaintances he eventually began holding "open house" in the apartment several nights a week. Stevens was a frequent guest at this artistic "salon," where he saw a good deal of Duchamp over the next few years.

The interior of the Arensberg apartment as Stevens knew it is recorded in a group of photographs taken by the artist Charles Sheeler in 1918. Figures 5–8 show the walls of the main studio crowded with paintings by Matisse, Duchamp, Picabia, Picasso, Cézanne, Braque, and others. Most of the artists represented in his collection were French, and this Gallic emphasis was typical of the Arensberg salon. The war had forced many European artists abroad, and they found a warm reception at 33 West 67th Street. Among the frequent visitors, in addition to Duchamp, were Francis Picabia and his wife, Gabrielle Buffet-Picabia, Albert Gleizes and Juliet Roché, Jean and Yvonne Crotti, Henri-Pierre Roché, and the composer Edgard Varèse.[9] French was often spoken in the apartment, which made some American guests uncomfortable. William Carlos Williams, for one, sometimes felt ill at ease at the Arensbergs' because "we weren't, or I wasn't, up to carrying on a witty conversation with the latest Parisian arrivals."[10] Others resented what seemed to them the special attention given to these foreigners. "One day one of [Arensberg's] very oldest friends spoke with some soreness to the effect that Walter was giving a lot of time to these Frenchmen and neglecting others," wrote Stevens. But he hastened to add, "I myself had not noticed this" (L, 850).

As his addendum suggests, the impact of this foreign invasion on Stevens was almost entirely positive. It stimulated his imagination, as would the even larger migration of European artists and intellectuals to the United States at the beginning of World War II. Although he never traveled to Europe, Paris remained throughout his life the vital center of his imagination. He must have been very pleased to find the artistic ferment of the French capital suddenly available to him on West Sixty-seventh Street. He knew and loved

French so well that he considered it and English "a single language" (L, 699). The cosmopolitan atmosphere of the Arensberg salon provided Stevens a rare opportunity to practice speaking French "for the pleasure that it gives" (L, 792). He recorded of one conversation he had with Arensberg and Duchamp, "When the three of us spoke French, it sounded like sparrows around a pool of water" (L, 185).

It was cubism that made the strongest impression on Arensberg at the Armory Show, and it soon formed the largest part of his collection. Sheeler's photographs document the predominance of cubist works on the walls of his apartment. Stevens was attracted to cubism, too, and his interest was probably nursed during his frequent visits to his friend's apartment. When, in later years, he admitted to "a taste for Braque but a purse for Bombois" (L, 545), he may well have been comparing his own very small collection of paintings with his memories of the Arensberg salon.[11]

Critics have often discussed Stevens' poetry in terms of cubism.[12] The analogy is appropriate if we think of cubism in general terms as the crucial break with the Western tradition of painting. Viewed from this perspective, it is the watershed of modernism because it abandoned standard notions of perspective and spatial orientation. It is typically "modern" because it is experimental, radically self-questioning. So generalized an analogy, however, is not very helpful in defining Stevens' particular poetic qualities. We may be more specific and note the common use of multiple perspectives in cubism and Stevens—most obviously in a poem like "Thirteen Ways of Looking at a Blackbird," whose separate, haiku-like stanzas suggest a variety of possible viewpoints like those in a cubist painting. In the same way, Stevens' characteristic manner of organizing long poems into separate but related stanzas might be thought of as cubist. One often gets the feeling in reading Stevens' longer poems—"The Man with the Blue Guitar," for instance—that the individual stanzas are not conceived as part of a conventional narrative or dramatic sequence; instead, they are juxtaposed in varying relations of similarity and contrast like the

5. Walter Conrad Arensberg's apartment, 33 W. 67th St., New York, ca. 1918. Photograph by Charles Sheeler. The paintings, listed from top to bottom beginning at the upper left, are: Marcel Duchamp, *Chocolate Grinder, no. 1* (1913); Francis Picabia, *Physical Culture* (1913); Marcel Duchamp, *Yvonne and Magdeleine Torn in Tatters* (1911); Paul Cézanne, *Landscape with Trees* (1890–94). Above the mantel: Henri Matisse, *Mlle. Yvonne Landsberg* (1914); Cézanne, *Still Life with Apples* (ca. 1880–85); Cézanne, *Group of Bathers* (1892–94). To the right of the mantel: Georges Braque, *Musical Forms* (1913); Charles Sheeler, *Barn Abstraction* (1918). On the right-hand wall: Braque, *Still Life* (1913); Braque, *Musical Forms (Guitar and Clarinet)* (1918); Duchamp, *The Sonata* (1911).

elements of a cubist painting. Their relation to one another is primarily spatial rather than temporal.

A closer look at Duchamp's *Nude Descending a Staircase*—the most famous cubist painting in Arensberg's collection—will highlight a particular affinity between Duchamp's use of cubism and the poetry of Stevens.[13] We may begin by asking why Duchamp's *Nude* should have seemed so shocking in 1913. The cubist style— which suggested the figure's body by an arrangement of geometrical planes—is not enough to explain it, since many other cubist

6. The Arensberg apartment, ca. 1918. Photograph by Charles Sheeler. The paintings, listed from top to bottom beginning at the upper left, are: Pablo Picasso, *Violin* (ca. 1912); Marcel Duchamp, *The Chess Players* (1911). The two large pictures above the piano: Duchamp, *Portrait* (1911); Duchamp, *King and Queen Surrounded by Swift Nudes* (1912). The smaller pictures above the piano: John R. Covert, *Hydro Cell* (1918); Henri Rousseau, *Village Street Scene* (1909); Rousseau, *Landscape with Cattle* (ca. 1906). To the right of the piano: Duchamp, *Chocolate Grinder, no. I* (1913); Francis Picabia, *Physical Culture* (1913); Duchamp, *Yvonne and Magdeleine Torn in Tatters* (1911); Paul Cézanne, *Landscape with Trees* (1890–94). Collection of Whitney Museum of American Art. Gift of James Maroney and Suzanne Fredericks (80.30.2).

pictures in the Armory Show did not achieve such notoriety. Probably the futurist aspects of the canvas—its emphasis on the kinetic motion of the figure—contributed to its strangeness. Duchamp himself admitted that there were both cubist and futurist influences in this work: "I felt more like a cubist than a futurist in this abstraction of a nude descending a staircase: the general appearance and the brownish coloring of the painting are clearly cubistic even though the treatment of the movement has some futuristic overtones."[14] But Man Ray is surely right, it seems to me, in

7. The Arensberg apartment, ca. 1918. Photograph by Charles Sheeler. The paintings are listed from top to bottom, beginning at the left. Above the chest of drawers: Joseph Stella, *Landscape* (1914); André Derain, *Nude* (ca. 1909). Above the sofa: Georges Braque, *Fox* (drypoint, 1912); Pablo Picasso, *Violin and Guitar* (1913); Marcel Duchamp, *Nude Descending a Staircase, no. 3* (1916); Pierre-Auguste Renoir, *The Bather* (ca. 1917–18); Picasso, *Still Life: Bottle* (drypoint, ca. 1912); Picasso, *Female Nude* (1910-11). On right-hand wall: Morton Schamberg, *Mechanical Abstraction* (1916); Charles Sheeler, *Barn Abstraction* (1917); Sheeler, *L'hasa* (date and present location unknown).

locating the principal public offense in the painting's title: "If the picture, 'Nude Descending a Staircase,' had not had that title, it would not have attracted any attention at all. It was the title. Let's face it."[15]

One of Duchamp's contributions to modern art was his use of odd titles that seem at first to bear only a tangential relation to the works they describe. He began experimenting with the significant interplay between an artwork and its title in 1911, when he titled a study of two nude figures in a landscape *The Bush*. He recalled of that painting, "The presence of a non-descriptive title is shown

8. The Arensberg apartment, ca. 1918. Photograph by Charles Sheeler. The paintings, listed from top to bottom beginning at the upper left, are: Georges Braque, *Still Life* (1913); Braque, *Musical Forms (Guitar and Clarinet)* (1918). Above door: Marcel Duchamp, *The Sonata* (1911). Above chair: Braque, *Still Life* (1913); Duchamp, *Chocolate Grinder, no. 2* (1914). Above wooden figure: André Derain, *Woman* (ca. 1914); Paul Cézanne, *View of the Cathedral of Aix* (1904–06). Small painting to right of wooden figure: Joseph Stella, *Chinatown* (ca. 1917). Above cabinet: Duchamp, *Nude Descending a Staircase, no. 3* (1916).

here for the first time. In fact, from then on, I always gave an important role to the title, which I added and treated like an invisible color."[16] The title became an integral part of the artwork; he even went so far as to paint the title on some of his "readymades."

The title *Nude Descending a Staircase* is deliberately indecorous. A painted nude is traditionally placed in a situation in which nudity may be imagined to be appropriate: a bedroom, a seraglio, an artist's studio, an Eden-like outdoor setting. Duchamp's nude, on the contrary, shamelessly walks downstairs; she negotiates a public passageway in a very private state of undress. There is a kind of bawdy humor in this conception. But there is also a humorous disjunction between this titillating title and the actual painting, in which the naked female anatomy is hardly recognizable amid the geometric patterns of the composition. The title deliberately arouses expectations which the painting itself frustrates. This effect also describes many of Stevens' most characteristic titles, like "The Man Whose Pharynx Was Bad," "Tea at the Palaz of Hoon," or "Le Monocle de Mon Oncle." Perhaps the most familiar example is "The Emperor of Ice Cream," a favorite puzzle for beginning students of poetry because the poem apparently has nothing to do either with emperors or with ice cream. Titles were very important to Stevens, as he himself admitted: "Very often the title occurs to me before anything else occurs to me." He kept lists of possible titles, many of which later became complete poems.[17] And he sometimes worried that his titles were too oblique, as he once confessed to Ronald Lane Latimer: "Possibly the relation [between the titles and the poems] is not as direct and literal as it ought to be" (L, 297).

The idea of a nude in motion appealed to Duchamp, for he completed in the same year, 1912, *King and Queen Surrounded by Swift Nudes,* which, together with a copy of *Nude Descending a Staircase,* hung in Arensberg's apartment throughout the 1910s. Stevens must have responded to this motif, for he employed it in his poem of 1919, "The Paltry Nude Starts on a Spring Voyage." But the aesthetic affinities between these two men extend deeper than their similar use of titles. Duchamp explains the conception of *King and Queen Surrounded by Swift Nudes* as follows:

Done immediately after the "Nude Descending a Staircase" in the spring of 1912, this oil painting called "King and Queen Surrounded by Swift Nudes" is a development of the same idea. The title "King and Queen" was . . . taken from chess but the players . . . have been eliminated and replaced by the chess figures of the king and queen. The swift nudes are a flight of imagination introduced to satisfy my preoccupation of movement still present in this painting. . . . It is a theme of motion in a frame of static entities. In other words the static entities are represented by the king and queen, while the swift nudes are based on the theme of motion.[18]

The interplay of imagination and reality, figured in an aesthetic treatment of motion and stasis, is also one of the principal themes of *Harmonium*. As Michel Benamou has observed, Stevens tends to present "conflicts of ideas as conflicts of forms and shapes."[19] "Earthy Anecdote," for example, the first poem of *Harmonium* (and also the first of Stevens' *Collected Poems*), is a parable about "bucks" clattering over Oklahoma but swerving to avoid a "fire-cat" that opposes their movement:

Every time the bucks went clattering
Over Oklahoma
A firecat bristled in the way.

Wherever they went,
They went clattering,
Until they swerved
In a swift, circular line
To the right,
Because of the firecat.

Or until they swerved
In a swift, circular line
To the left,
Because of the firecat.

[CP, 3]

As Milton Bates has remarked, this poem might be explained simply "in terms of its objective, spatial relationships," in which case Stevens' conception is very close to Duchamp's in *King and Queen Surrounded by Swift Nudes*—"it is a theme of motion in a frame of static entities."[20]

When Duchamp painted the *Nude* and *King and Queen* he was

already moving beyond the narrow confines of cubist theory. His *Bride,* also painted in 1912, marked a further step in this direction: "Abandoning my association with Cubism and having exhausted my interest in kinetic painting, I found myself turning towards a form of expression completely divorced from straight reality. . . . This is not the realistic interpretation of a bride but my concept of a bride expressed by the juxtaposition of mechanical elements and visceral forms."[21]

Duchamp's final break with cubism came with his *Chocolate Grinder* of 1913, two versions of which hung in Arensberg's apartment (see figs. 5, 6, and 8). Duchamp recalled of this work: "Through the introduction of straight perspective and a very geometrical design of a definite grinding machine like this one, I felt definitely out of the Cubist straitjacket."[22] It is important to bear in mind that by the year of the Armory Show, Duchamp had already, in his own view, exhausted the possibilities of cubism and abandoned it. Although the cubist movement itself remained a vital force in Western art till about 1925, Duchamp had tired of its self-imposed limitations twelve years earlier. Stevens therefore saw regularly, throughout the 1910s, not only the stimulating cubist paintings (many by Duchamp) displayed in Arensberg's apartment, but also the living presence of Duchamp himself, who considered them, ultimately, a dead end. We would do well to recall the irony of this situation when we ponder Stevens' many ambivalent statements about modern art.

The sort of art Duchamp created during Stevens' *Harmonium* years may be conveniently represented by the second (and last) issue of his publication *The Blind Man.* This magazine was founded as the official organ of the Society of Independent Artists, which was conceived and organized in the Arensberg apartment, and which held its First Annual Exhibition in the Grand Central Palace on April 10, 1917, four days after the United States entered World War I. The "Indeps," as it was called, was to be a thoroughly democratic exhibition. It would be open to anyone who could pay the five-dollar entry fee, and there would be no jury. In order to test the sincerity of the hanging committee (of which he was the head) in making this high-minded claim, Duchamp entered a work pseudonymously. Called *Fountain* and signed "R. Mutt," it was an ordinary porcelain urinal, placed on its side on a pedestal. The work was rejected, and Duchamp (together with Arensberg) resigned in protest from the committee.[23]

The second issue of *The Blind Man* discussed this exhibition, and we know that Stevens read it: Pitts Sanborn sent him a copy on May 23, 1917.[24] On its cover is a reproduction of Duchamp's *Chocolate Grinder*. The context brings out the image's significance as an autoerotic motif, alluding to the French saying, "The bachelor grinds his chocolate by himself."[25] By placing the *Chocolate Grinder* on the cover of this issue, Duchamp is protesting the rejection of *Fountain* from the exhibition. The image questions the sincerity of the hanging committee's professed commitment to uninhibited artistic creativity.

The main feature of *The Blind Man*, no. 2, is introduced on page 4 by a full-page photograph captioned "Fountain by R. Mutt," taken by Alfred Stieglitz (fig. 9). *Fountain* is the most famous of Duchamp's readymades, an art form he invented in 1913, though the term was not coined until 1915. His first readymade, *Bicycle Wheel*, consisted of a bicycle wheel mounted upside-down on top of a four-legged stool. Over the next decade the artist created a number of these works. In each of them he took an ordinary mass-produced object—a hat rack, a snow shovel, a bottle rack—and displayed it as an art object. The concept of a readymade naturally raises the most fundamental aesthetic questions. The viewer's initially puzzled query, "Is it art?" must soon lead to the complex philosophical issue, "*What* is art?" As Duchamp explained, "I was interested in ideas—not merely in visual products. I wanted to put [art] once again at the service of the mind."[26]

Fountain calls into question, for one thing, the traditional role of the artist as craftsman. It is the concept of the readymade, and not the object itself, which is of primary aesthetic interest. This is the point made by an article entitled "The Richard Mutt Case," which

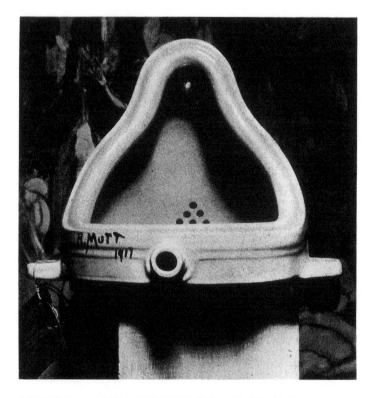

9. Marcel Duchamp, *Fountain by R. Mutt* (1917). Photograph by Alfred Stieglitz.

appeared on page 5 of the second issue of *The Blind Man*. In this article, the artist is defined not as a craftsman, but simply as one who chooses: "Whether Mr. Mutt with his own hands made the fountain or not has no importance. He CHOSE it. He took an ordinary article of life, placed it so that its useful significance disappeared under the new title and point of view—created a new thought for that object."[27]

It is not the execution but the idea behind the work that makes the readymade interesting. In the creation of a readymade, emphasis is thrown upon the object itself, placed in a strange environment and divorced from its practical function, so that it is viewed solely as a "thing" without relation to its use. As Duchamp put it, "functionalism was . . . obliterated by the fact that I took it out of the earth and onto the planet of aesthetics." And equal emphasis is placed upon the artist, not as craftsman, but as gifted perceiver whose *choice* of an object is seen as a creative act. The act of choosing a readymade allowed Duchamp, in his own words, to "reduce the idea of aesthetic consideration to the choice of the mind."[28] The parallel with Stevens' later definition of poetry as "the act of the mind" is obvious.[29] The readymade thus becomes the focus of a meditation on the relation between external things and our perception of them, or—to use the terms Stevens would later employ to describe the same effect in his own poetry—a self-conscious meditation on the relation between reality and the imagination.

Stevens' poem "Anecdote of the Jar," written in 1919, bears a close family resemblance to Duchamp's readymades.

I placed a jar in Tennessee,
And round it was, upon a hill.
It made the slovenly wilderness
Surround that hill.

The wilderness rose up to it,
And sprawled around, no longer wild.
The jar was round upon the ground,
And tall and of a port in air.

It took dominion everywhere.
The jar was gray and bare.
It did not give of bird or bush,
Like nothing else in Tennessee.

The enigmatic gesture which is the subject of this poem might well describe the creation of a readymade. The speaker selects an ordinary object, and places it in a strange context: "I *placed* a jar in Tennessee, / And round it was, upon a hill." In doing so, he "creates a new thought for that object"—as *The Blind Man* said of Duchamp's *Fountain*—so that the new arrangement is unique: "Like nothing else in Tennessee."

Characteristic of both "Anecdote of the Jar" and Duchamp's *Fountain* is an essential ambiguity. To place a jar on a hill in Tennessee, and to place a porcelain urinal on its side atop a pedestal, are both ambiguous (as well as strange) gestures. In each case the nature of the object itself is also ambiguous: Is it to be considered as a machine-made object, without aesthetic value in itself, an instance of anti-art? Or is it, on the other hand, to be considered a worthy example of utilitarian design? It is the nature of a readymade to inspire these questions without resolving them. Duchamp's *Bottlerack,* for instance, mass-produced in dull metal, is unquestionably "gray and bare," like Stevens' jar; but it has also been praised by Robert Motherwell as "a more beautiful form than almost anything made, in 1914, as sculpture."[30] In the same way, Stevens' jar has been endlessly discussed as an "artifact," but whether its significance as such in the poem is negative or positive is the subject of a critical controversy that testifies to its essential ambiguity. As Stevens once wrote, "One of the essentials of poetry is ambiguity. I don't feel that I have touched the thing until I touch it in ambiguous form."[31]

If we are willing to consider "Anecdote of the Jar" as a readymade, then Roy Harvey Pearce may well have discovered the particular mass-produced object Stevens had in mind when he wrote the poem (fig. 10). This fruit jar was in use in Tennessee in 1918, when Stevens traveled there prior to writing "Anecdote of the Jar."[32] It is specially designed to take "Dominion" everywhere; and it is unquestionably "gray and bare." In meditating on such an object, Stevens was adapting Duchamp's enigmatic art form to his own poetic purposes. And this meditation resulted in one of his most successful and popular poems. That fact alone suggests the importance of Duchamp to Stevens' poetic development.

Duchamp and the other writers and artists of the Arensberg circle are generally referred to as the New York Dada movement.

10. "Dominion" canning jar. Photograph by David Crowne.

Unlike Dada artists in Europe, the New York group "did not distribute revolutionary pamphlets at factory gates, they did not provoke large audiences in concert halls or cabarets, they did not even write manifestos."[33] The artistic character of New York Dada is well summarized by William Innes Homer: "If European Dada had a destructive, even self-destructive, character, New York Dada was almost playful. In political terms, the difference was similar to that between the committed revolutionary and the adherent of 'radical chic.'"[34] The playful, provocative, cerebral art of Marcel Duchamp is the most characteristic product of New York Dada, and we have seen that it has much in common with the poetry of *Harmonium*.

It is useful to think of *Harmonium* in terms of Dada for several reasons. Because Dada refers to an attitude or way of life rather than to any particular artistic style, it is more appropriate to the remarkably various *Harmonium* than any more narrowly defined stylistic category such as impressionism, cubism, or fauvism. The place of Dada in art history also makes it a fitting analogy for Stevens' *Harmonium* period. In the 1920s the anarchic energy of Dada was subsumed by the Surrealist movement, with its more coherent theoretical foundation and more positive aesthetic program. In the same way, in the 1930s, Stevens set out to formulate his own poetic theory; and in so doing his poetry changed character, from the exuberant variety of *Harmonium* to the theoretical coherence and stylistic virtuosity of his later years. As Dada relates to Surrealism, so *Harmonium* relates to the rest of Stevens' career.

Chapter 2

Stevens in the 1930s

Stevens' close friendship with Arensberg came to an abrupt end in 1921, shortly before Arensberg and his wife moved permanently to California. Stevens described the incident that caused this break in a "confidential" letter to Weldon Kees in 1954 (L, 849–51). Briefly, the quarrel began when Stevens tried to intercede on behalf of a mutual friend who had fallen into Arensberg's disfavor. "Walter froze up when I spoke to him and when he froze up, I froze up too . . . . [We] remained on our high horses. I never saw him again. Shortly after that he left for the coast." Not long after Arensberg's departure, Stevens ceased writing poetry altogether and did not take it up again for nearly seven years.

A number of elements contributed to Stevens' silence from 1924 to about 1930, particularly his new familial responsibilities with the birth of Holly in 1924 and his desire to secure for himself a "seat on the front bench" in the insurance field, as his father had always exhorted him to do (L, 20). But it is not merely coincidental, I think, that Stevens' *Harmonium* period corresponds almost exactly to the years in which the Arensberg circle flourished in New York. That circle disintegrated when Arensberg left, and its leading artist, Duchamp, gave up painting entirely in 1923, a renunciation legendary in the art world. Stevens' lapse into poetic inactivity parallels this disintegration. The loss both of his friendship with Arensberg and of his privileged access to the contemporary art world dealt a blow to Stevens' creative powers. The remarkable inventiveness and self-assurance of *Harmonium* had been nurtured by his direct, personal relation to the New York avant-garde. The "art crowd," as Stevens called the Arensberg group, had provided the "radiant and productive atmosphere" (NA, 57) that allowed his poetic gifts to flourish. Once he lost that stimulus and support, poetry no longer came so easily, if at all.[1]

When Stevens took up writing poetry again the situation in which he found himself was vastly different from the days of *Harmonium*. There could hardly be an atmosphere less hospitable to Stevens' ideal of "pure poetry" than the world-wide economic crisis and the politically charged atmosphere of the 1930s.[2] No thoughtful person could have remained aloof from the often bitter ideological battles that characterized the intellectual life of that decade. Writers and artists were under constant pressure to justify their devotion to art at a time when so many urgently "real" problems seemed to threaten civilization itself. Stevens in particular found himself on the defensive because of his early critical reputation as a poetic dandy or hedonist. He knew well what it was to be "A most inappropriate man / In a most unpropitious place" (CP, 120). One result of this experience was that he developed a growing respect for art theory as the artist's chief line of defense. His impatience, in later life, with "the many minor artists who do not communicate any theory that validates what they do and, in consequence, impress one as being without validity" (L, 763) grew directly out of his embattled situation during the 1930s.

In these circumstances, Stevens' chief concern as a writer was to create a secure sense of his own poetic identity. In large part this meant consciously trying to reestablish the empowering sense of self he had enjoyed, fortuitously, during his *Harmonium* years within the sympathetic artistic community of the Arensberg circle. He began a deliberate and systematic effort to piece together, imaginatively, the parts of a world that would provide the stimulation and support, the sense of belonging that had allowed his poetic muse to flourish in the 1910s. One way of doing this was to address contemporary issues in his poetry, in order to establish, as he wrote to Henry Church in 1939, his "relation to contemporary ideas" (L, 340). This new aesthetic attitude was far removed from that of *Harmonium,* whose poems had, he freely admitted, "nothing to do with the ideas of the day in which they were written" (L, 340). The series of long poems entitled "Owl's Clover" (1935–36), for example, deals with such issues as the Depression, Marxism, fascism, and Mussolini's invasion of Ethiopia. More often, Stevens tried to work out his "relation to contemporary ideas" in the context of the art world. For just as he often looked to the "literature of painting" for a discussion of his own problems as a poet (OP, 187), so he habitually thought of the contemporary art world as an analogue through which he could understand his situation as a poet.

Although Stevens was no longer personally involved with the artistic avant-garde in the 1930s, he kept abreast of the latest artistic developments in several ways. He read widely in British, French, and American periodicals—not only art magazines like *Apollo* and *Cahiers d'art* but also newsweeklies like the *New Statesman and Nation* and *Figaro,* whose essays about art and reviews of exhibitions sometimes inspired his own essays or poems. He also visited galleries and museums in New York on a regular basis. Living in Hartford, Connecticut, was in some ways an obstacle to following the latest trends in the art world, but it also provided one enormous advantage that Stevens could hardly have foreseen when he moved there in 1916. During the 1930s, the Wadsworth Atheneum in Hartford was the most modern museum in the United States, presenting the latest European movements even before they appeared in the New York art galleries or in the Museum of Modern Art. Under the direction of A. Everett ("Chick") Austin, the Atheneum presented the first Surrealist show in America ("Newer Super-Realism," 1931), for example, and the first retrospective of Picasso (in 1934). It also sponsored the gala world premiere of the Gertrude Stein–Virgil Thomson opera *Four Saints in Three Acts* (1934), which Stevens attended; regularly presented programs of the most advanced work in dance, film, and music; and brought to Hartford such major figures in the arts as Salvador Dalí, Le Corbusier, Walter Gropius, Gertrude Stein, George Balanchine, Aaron Copland, Paul Bowles, Nadia Boulanger, and Lincoln Kirstein. Quite by chance, Stevens found himself once again in close proximity to the most vital center for advanced art in America. To visit the Wadsworth Atheneum in the 1930s, as Stevens often did, was by no means a dry exercise in antiquarianism; it meant, rather, stimulating encounters with the avant-garde.

Because Stevens' exposure to advanced thinking occurred so often in the context of the art world, it is perhaps not surprising to discover that even "Owl's Clover"—his most extended effort to relate his daily experience directly to the political and social issues of the day—was inspired by a visit to an art gallery. Here is Stevens' description of the genesis of "The Old Woman and the Statue," the first poem of the series: "The subject I had in mind was the effect of the depression on the interest in art. . . . If I dropped into a gallery I found that I had no interest in what I saw. The air was charged with anxieties and tensions. . . . I wanted to deal with exactly such a subject and I chose that as a bit of reality, actuality, the contemporaneous" (OP, 225–26). This passage shows Stevens focusing on an incident in an art gallery *not* in order to evade reality through art, but in order to ground his poetry in the reality of his personal experience. The distinction is important. Because we tend to think of the art gallery as being at several removes even from the "reality" of artistic creation, Stevens' choice of subject here and elsewhere has seemed to many critics to confirm his reputation for ivory-tower escapism. The poet's intention, however, was quite other-wise: "I chose that as a bit of reality, actuality, the contem-poraneous." Stevens' visits to galleries were part of his everyday life, and he did not consider his own experience less "real" than that of his less privileged "old woman." In fact, the old woman represents, metaphorically, that part of Stevens' own psyche that sometimes caused him to lose interest in art during the Depression.

Stevens' purpose in writing a poem based on such a "bit of reality" was to relate that reality to his own "sensibility" and thereby to clarify, for himself, his own sense of identity: "I wanted to apply my own sensibility to something perfectly matter-of-fact. The result would be a disclosure of my own sensibility or individu-ality . . . certainly to myself" (OP, 226). Stevens thought of the art world as a fruitful context for self-exploration. This was a regular habit of mind with him, and it became particularly important in the 1930s and 1940s as he gradually transformed himself from a poet of perception into a poet of "the act of the mind." More often than not during this period, Stevens derived his image of himself, and through himself of his poetry, from his encounters with the art world. This pattern is clearest in his complex responses to the opposing artistic movements of surrealism and abstraction, the subject of chapters 3–6. In the remainder of this chapter, I want to explore two more general aspects of Stevens' personal "mythology of self" that occupied his mind during the 1930s and that helped to determine, in various ways, his response to events in the contempo-rary art world: 1) his idealization of the life of the connoisseur/art collector; and 2) his pride in his Dutch heritage, including the legacy of seventeenth-century Dutch painting.

Connoisseur of Chaos

These are the works and pastimes
Of the highest self: he studies the paper
On the wall, the lemons on the table.
—CP, 280

The point of view of the aesthete or connoisseur was always important to Stevens. Whether or not we share his interest in such a privileged point of view, we must not assume that the life of the connoisseur represented—for him—a literary pose or a merely imaginary mode of existence. The dominance of the connoisseur's point of view in *Harmonium* is not simply a relic of the fin de siècle. It is grounded in the everyday reality of Stevens' experience of the Arensberg salon during the 1910s.

The title of Stevens' poem "Connoisseur of Chaos" (1938) epitomizes his self-image in the 1930s: the word *chaos* summing up the political and economic crises of the time, and the word *connoisseur* serving as shorthand for the poetic outlook to which Stevens aspired. That Stevens liked to imagine the life of a connoisseur—particularly that of the wealthy art collector—is clear from his letters. Here is an excerpt from one addressed to Barbara Church in 1949: "Early in the summer I wrote to the Villa Favorita at Castagnola, which is either in or about Lugano for material concerning a collection of pictures, etc. formed by one of the Thyssens. They sent me a catalogue and a lot of reproductions and postcards. It must have been an extraordinary experience to live in Lugano and to collect these things and have them about one. Unfortunately, they did not send me a photograph of the Villa itself, but I have found a substitute in a photograph of Lugano with the palms, or perhaps I ought to say palmettos, on the shore of the lake, and distant mountains" (L, 645). Here we see Stevens consciously trying to summon up, for his own enjoyment, a complete sense of the life of a wealthy collector—to imagine what it would be like "to collect these things and have them about one."

The art collector represented for him not simply a man of keen sensibility and discriminating taste; any ineffectual aesthete might be that. He was also a man who was capable of acting on his perceptions, and whose intellectual choices therefore had tangible consequences. Stevens was acutely aware, as he put it, of "the difference between the theorist and the technician, the difference between Hamlet and Horatio, the difference between the man who can talk about pictures and the man who can afford to buy them" (OP, 285). As a businessman he appreciated how much knowledge of the marketplace, willingness to take risks, and shrewd judgment are necessary to acquire a great art collection. The wealthy art collector represented, for Stevens, a "figure of capable imagination" whose character combined the aesthetic refinement of an artist with the practical intelligence of a businessman. In Stevens' own words, "More often than the satirists admit, the man who can afford to buy pictures is entirely competent to take their measure and at the same time to take the measure both of the artist and of the dealer" (OP, 286). The collection of such an individual was tangible evidence of his personal integrity. It meant, for Stevens, one of the highest forms of self-expression. "After all," he wrote in 1940, "in the case of a collector, his intelligence and his sensibility are the same thing as his honor: they involve everything he is."[3]

Stevens had similar respect for museum directors, who must have many of the same qualities of character a collector has. He was proud to know personally the directors of the Fogg Museum in Cambridge, the Wadsworth Atheneum in Hartford, the Guggenheim and Frick museums in New York; to correspond with the director of the Irish National Gallery in Dublin; and to be acquainted with upper-level administrators at the Museum of Modern Art and other institutions. In Stevens' time it was expected that a museum director would be an expert in art, a connoisseur, and a competent administrator. This may be less true today, when museum directors are sometimes better trained in business than in art. But John Russell's recent assessment of the kind of personality that is required to direct London's National Gallery still seems closely attuned to Stevens' view of the art collector: "It has nothing to do with exalted interior decoration. It is a human and moral task, as much as an aesthetic one, and it calls for a daunting combination of qualities."[4]

During the 1930s, Stevens began to buy as many paintings as he could afford. His letters record the pleasure he got from his small collection, to which he devoted considerable time, effort, and money. The experience of forming his own collection helped him to imagine more fully the pleasures involved in selecting and displaying great works of art, and it was partly this practice that brought him into contact with another art collector who would play an important role in his imaginative life: Henry Church. As coeditor (with Jean Paulhan) of *Mesures,* a journal of art and literature published in Paris, Church had contacted Stevens early in 1939, asking permission to publish translations of several poems from *Harmonium* (see L, 338). Stevens, who had subscribed to *Mesures* from its first issue several years before, was happy to oblige. They were still corresponding about the translations when war broke out in Europe in September 1939, and Church (an American by birth) returned to the United States. Soon thereafter, the two men met for the first time in New York. As a prelude to that meeting, Stevens wrote to Church (on November 3, 1939) on the topic of art collecting: "I have been in New York the last several Saturday afternoons, and shall be coming again before long, when I shall be glad to look you up and make your acquaintance. . . . I have been buying a picture or two once a year or thereabouts through Mr. Vidal and, while I have no thought of making any change, still it is difficult to keep in touch with what is going on or, at least, to single out the vital figures at a distance or through a bookseller. It is about that sort of thing that I thought possibly I might find out something useful from you" (L, 343).

Stevens liked the fact that Church was a connoisseur and art collector, and Church must have lived up to his expectations. The two men got along well at that first meeting, and their friendship grew over the next few years. To Stevens, Church represented a real "man of art," an independently wealthy American who lived— with his wife, Barbara—much of his life in Paris and moved easily in the international art world. "I think Stevens felt very much at home with them," Frederick Morgan remembers. "They shared a whole milieu, this art world, this Paris cultural thing, which Stevens adored and was deep into and knew so much about."[5] He clearly idealized Church, dedicating two long poems to him—

"Notes toward a Supreme Fiction" (1942) and "The Owl in the Sarcophagus" (1947)—and admitting with exceptional candor in a letter to him that "you have so thoroughly lived the life that I should have been glad to live" (L, 401).

It seems clear in retrospect that Stevens responded so warmly to Church at least partly because Church filled the special place in Stevens' imaginative life that Arensberg had vacated in 1921: the role of a close friend with whom Stevens could identify and whose privileged existence fired the poet's imagination. The reality of Church's charmed life expanded, for Stevens, the range of human possibility far in the direction of the ideal. By identifying with Church, Stevens was able to achieve the empowering sense of self his poetry required. His friendship with this wealthy connoisseur– art collector encouraged in him a tendency already well developed— to imagine his ideal self in terms of the traits he associated with the art collector.

The Noble Art Collector

A common theme of Stevens' poetry in the 1930s and early 1940s is the idea of the hero. In 1940 he copied into his commonplace book these words of Henry Adams: "I need badly to find one man in history to admire. I am in near peril of turning Christian, and rolling in the mud in an agony of human mortification."[6] He put the same idea into his own words in a letter to Henry Church in 1945: "What is terribly lacking from life today is the well developed individual, the master of life, or the man who by his mere appearance convinces you that a mastery of life is possible" (L, 518). If such men were absent in the 1930s and 1940s, they had nevertheless existed during Stevens' lifetime. There had been heroic artists like Vincent van Gogh, for example, who embodied, for Stevens, "the mastery of reality" (L, 459). And there had been wealthy, expansive men whose lives seemed to achieve a kind of mythic stature. Such powerful figures had been common—or so it seemed to Stevens—before World War I. His nostalgia for that period is clear in this passage from an essay of 1936: "The pressure of the contemporaneous from the time of the beginning of the World War to the present time has been constant and extreme. No one can have lived apart in a happy oblivion. For a long time before the war nothing was more common. In those days the sea was full of yachts and the yachts were full of millionaires. It was a time when only maniacs had disturbing things to say. The period was like a stage-setting that since then has been taken down and trucked away" (OP, 229).

Despite the imputation of escapism in Stevens' description of the millionaires "liv[ing] apart in a happy oblivion," his admiration for these figures is obvious. They were the wealthy industrialists whom boys of Stevens' generation were taught to emulate. We no longer admire so uncritically these "robber barons"; nor, in all likelihood, did Stevens when he was writing this passage in 1936. But he looked back fondly on the time before the war when it was possible to believe (as he knew from his own experience) that these seemingly larger-than-life individualists represented the noble flowering of American idealism: lofty ambition wedded to practical intelligence; power concentrated in the most capable hands. Modern historians have discredited the Victorian willingness to believe in "great men," but they have discovered nothing to take the place of such once credible heroes. As Stevens realized, the absence of such living models of human excellence, whether or not we are conscious of it, weakens our confidence in our own capabilities.

A great part of the appeal these nineteenth-century figures had for Stevens was that, in addition to being shrewd businessmen, they were, almost as a rule, devoted to art. For the time of yachts and millionaires was also the golden age of American art collecting. As one historian describes that colorful period: "A swarm of American millionaires ransacked Europe for masterpieces. . . . This new surge of the collectors gathered momentum during the eighteen-nineties, rushed at full tilt from 1900 to 1914, and continued, though at a less sensational pace, after the First World War. It resulted in such extraordinary concentrations of fine objects from abroad as the Gardner, Huntington, Mellon, and Frick collections, to say nothing of those of John G. Johnson, Folger, Bliss, Altman, Havermeyer, Widener, Nelson, Lewisohn, Bliss, Hearst, Bache, and a cluster of others."[7]

What is unique in this trend, apart from its unprecedented scope, is that most of these private collectors eventually donated their treasures to public institutions—a fact that accounts for the greatness of America's museums. This pattern had never existed in Europe, where the great collections generally stayed in private hands.[8] The American collector wanted to feel that his activities were ultimately philanthropic and public-spirited, making available to the average citizen the riches of world culture without the necessity of a trip to Europe. Indeed, so successful were the combined efforts of these millionaire collectors that, by the mid-twentieth century, cultured Europeans found it necessary to travel to America to complete their education. As one British writer remarked in 1940: "Nothing impresses the visitor to the States more than the immense wealth of its museums and art collections. America is, in fact, to the modern traveler what Italy was to his predecessors of a hundred years ago."[9] Few people have been in a better position to appreciate this fortunate state of affairs than Stevens, the avid museum-goer, who made a lifelong study of art without ever traveling to Europe.

One man stands out as the virtual epitome of the American art collector: "At the head and front of the company of American purchasers was [J. Pierpont] Morgan, the pace-setter for them all."[10] Descriptions of his contribution to the history of art collecting almost invariably resort to superlatives: he was "the leading art collector of his time," "the most prodigious private art collector of all time," "the greatest figure in the art world that America has yet produced."[11] Stevens had, in addition, many more personal reasons to be interested in Morgan. The millionaire was a legendary presence in New York when Stevens lived there. The appearance of Morgan's yacht, the *Corsair,* in the waters around Manhattan was the surest sign that the great man was in town, and may account for

Stevens' fond memories of "yachts . . . full of millionaires." Morgan was president of the Metropolitan Museum of Art, which Stevens visited often, from 1904 to his death in 1913. When the Morgan Collection was exhibited there posthumously in 1914—an exhibition Stevens is unlikely to have missed, though we have no record of his attending it—the catalogue described it as "probably without parallel in the history of collecting."[12]

Stevens' awareness of Morgan's activities is evident in a letter he wrote to his wife in 1911. By that time, Stevens had spent more than a decade in New York trying to establish himself in a secure, well-paying career. He had promised his wife when they married in 1909 that he would arrange a life that would make her happy. But she did not like New York, and she soon began spending long periods away from him, visiting her family in Reading, Pennsylvania, or vacationing in the country. During one such absence, Stevens sent Elsie a letter describing some beautiful "Chinese and Japanese jades and porcelains" he had recently seen in the American Art Gallery, lamenting as he did so his own colorless circumstances: "I wish, intensely, that I had some of those vivid colors here. When connois[s]eurs return from the pits of antiquity with their rarities, they make honest, everyday life look like a seamstress by the side of Titian's daughter" (L, 169). Stevens contrasts his dull life in New York, made to seem even more unbearable because of his wife's dissatisfaction, with the romantic existence of "connoisseurs" who can explore the "pits of antiquity" for "rarities." The connoisseur Stevens probably had in mind was Morgan who, as president of the Metropolitan Museum of Art, was directing the excavations in Egypt that were bringing back many priceless artifacts for the museum's collections. The fact that Stevens does not explain this allusion probably indicates that he expected Elsie to understand it and to appreciate how much Morgan's example meant to him as he struggled to create a beautiful life for both of them.

If Morgan's presence often touched Stevens' life in New York, Morgan's spirit was ubiquitous in Hartford, where Stevens moved in 1916. Morgan was born and raised in Hartford, and he was buried there in 1913. One of the first sights Stevens went to see in Hartford when he visited there briefly in 1914 was Morgan's grave in the Cedar Hill Cemetery. (This was the same cemetery in which, more than forty years later, Stevens himself chose to be buried; see L, 182.) Morgan was the greatest benefactor of the Wadsworth Atheneum, paying for the construction of the Morgan Memorial (completed in 1916) to house the magnificent collection he donated to it. The example of Morgan could not have been far from Stevens' thoughts whenever he considered the achievements of American art collectors.

Morgan's reputation as a collector is problematic. Despite the unrivaled scope of his acquisitions, there have always been critics to accuse Morgan of confusing quantity with quality, of being "a 'checkbook collector' with some knowledge and little 'eye'."[13] They are the same kind of critics who are uncomfortable with the fact that Stevens was both a poet and a businessman. A case in point is Randall Jarrell, who expressed dislike for Stevens' later poetry in a telling comparison: "His poetry is obsessed with lack, a lack at last almost taken for granted, that he himself automatically supplies; if sometimes he has restored by imagination or abstraction or re-creation, at other times he has restored by collection, almost as J. P. Morgan did—Stevens likes something, buys it (at the expense of a little spirit), and ships it home in a poem."[14] Jarrell thinks of this as a disparaging comparison because he makes the common assumption that Morgan was a collector with a lot of money and little taste. This alone shows his inability to share Stevens' point of view. But far more revealing in this passage is his obvious lack of respect for art collecting as an adventure of the imagination. In attempting to define what bothers him about Stevens' poetry, Jarrell has unwittingly betrayed a fundamental lack of sympathy with the collecting impulse that plays such an important part in Stevens' poetic world. No wonder he cannot enjoy the later poems.

Stevens himself would surely have been flattered to be compared to Morgan. He had dedicated his life to demonstrating that there is no contradiction between business and art, that they are simply two different aspects of everyday life. "It is odd that people should think business and poetry incompatible," he wrote, "and yet accept business and almost anything else as all in a day's work" (L, 612). A figure like Morgan proved this point by his extraordinary success in both fields. Stevens' genuine respect for the legendary collector is evident in this passage of a letter to Henry Church: "I believe that both you and Mrs. Church would enjoy seeing the [Pierpont Morgan] Library. . . . This was Morgan's *soledad,* and it is worth looking at as a relic. It is a way of getting into the mind of a man whose mind was worth getting into. The room that was once his study and where, in better times, there were a number of Memlings, and then the main room of the Library, several stories high, will give you something to think about" (L, 459). The great collection of rare books in the Morgan Library surely reinforced Stevens' own interest in fine bindings and in books as art objects. He delighted in the special editions of his works published by fine printers like the Cummington Press; and he had copies of each of his own books specially bound for his personal library.[15]

Stevens was probably encouraged to form his high opinion of Morgan by the testimony of his good friend Walter Pach. Pach's father did photography for Morgan, and as a boy Walter had met the great man numerous times when helping to deliver photographs. His personal memories of the millionaire art collector were wholly admiring, and his eyewitness testimony must have encouraged Stevens to interpret Morgan's achievement in the same sympathetic spirit. Stevens' tendency to idealize the figure of the art collector is perfectly in tune with Pach's summary of Morgan's character:

"Everything about Mr. Morgan's thought and action was marked by the same largeness, and so when he came to indulge the passion for art-collecting that had been developing in him since his student days in Europe, he did so with the vision of a Medici. . . . Only those who saw Mr. Morgan's possessions as they were shown at the Metropolitan in the years just after his death in 1913, and who can supplement that memory by a knowledge of the treasure in his library, are able to appreciate the imperial scope of his collecting."

Pach's emphasis on the "largeness" of Morgan's vision and on his "imperial scope" clearly fits the heroic mold. Contrary to suspicions that Morgan's success as a collector had more to do with the crude values of the marketplace than with any real aesthetic sensibility, Pach affirmed Morgan's true connoisseurship, both intuitive and intellectual: "The old collector did have that sense of quality. He applied it to bronzes, to faiences, to paintings, and so there were but few things which he passed upon and which afterward turned out to be 'wrong ones.' This faculty of his had a curious minor application to his smoking; by smelling a tobacco leaf he could tell just where it came from and of what quality it was. But far more important than his sensuous response to things was his intellectual grasp. That was what gave to the various groups of collections he owned their almost uniformly high level, despite their wide range."[16]

I think Stevens shared this vision of the noble art collector who has "the vision of a Medici" and an "imperial scope." It was partly his imaginative identification with such heroic spirits that made him think of museums as "place[s] of enchantment" (L, 691). In considering Stevens' poetry and poetic theory, therefore, we should not lose sight of how closely such important concepts as nobility and the idea of the hero are related to his experience in the art world.

Associational Value

Stevens' imaginative engagement with the world of the art collector helps us to understand another important aspect of his poetry that otherwise seems peculiar and troubling. I mean his deep interest in what William Carlos Williams referred to, disparagingly, as the "associational" value of objects. A clear example of this tendency occurs in Stevens' description, in a letter to his wife-to-be, of a visit to the National Academy of Design in 1909:[17] "One of the pictures yesterday had been exhibited in Paris. It had the number of the Paris exhibition on its frame and bore the 'Medaille' mark—an honor picture. By looking at that, and at nothing else I could imagine myself in Paris, seeing just what any Parisian would see— I laughed in my sleeve at New York, far out on the bleak edge of the world" (L, 117). Here Stevens is far more interested in the painting's romantic associations than in the painting itself, which he does not even bother to describe. He looks at the token "Médaille" instead. The work of art hardly exists as a thing in itself, but becomes an occasion for the poet to daydream of far-away places.

Another aspect of this tendency is Stevens' liking or disliking a work of art because of its personal associations. Writing to a friend about Giorgione in 1948, Stevens remarked, "What particularly interested me in him was the fact that for a good many years my wife has had a photograph of one of his portraits hanging up at home and this of itself made me want to know more about him" (L, 608). Here, as Alan Filreis has noted, Stevens is not interested in any particular painting but in "the context a painting gains as an object within his personal idea of order."[18]

Williams, who also tended to think in terms of analogies between poetry and the visual arts, disagreed sharply with Stevens about this aspect of poetry. As he wrote in 1918: "The true value is that peculiarity which gives an object a character in itself. The associational or sentimental value is the false. . . . Here I clash with Wallace Stevens. . . . It is easy to fall under the spell of a certain mode, especially if it be remote of origin. . . . But the thing that stands eternally in the way of really good writing is always one: the virtual impossibility of lifting to the imagination those things which lie under the direct scrutiny of the senses, close to the nose."[19] From Williams' point of view, the modern artist's chief task was to strip away all personal and conventional associations, any vestiges of fin-de-siècle dreaminess that could stand in the way of direct perception of the thing itself. To a great extent, Stevens sympathized with this project, and his poetry often stressed—like Williams' poetry or like Marcel Duchamp's readymades—fresh encounters with the objects of everyday life. But he was not willing to make this the exclusive aim of his poetry, or to deny entirely the importance of "associational" value. It played too great a role in his own imaginative life.

This tendency in Stevens can often appear to be mere exoticism. He delighted in postcards from strange places, for instance; he collected small curios from around the world; and he loved to sample rare teas and wines and cheeses gathered on his trips to New York. These parts of his life often became parts of his poems. To Williams, on the other hand, a taste for such things seemed beside the point. The real task of the modern poet, as he saw it, was to restore freshness to ordinary, everyday things. To seek out, instead, rare and exotic items in order to daydream about their places of origin seemed to him easy and self-indulgent. He was right, in one sense. Stevens indulged these appetites simply because it gave him pleasure to do so. But such concrete pleasure was one of the things Stevens had in mind when he insisted that "the imagination must not detach itself from reality" (OP, 187).

The two poets were in agreement that the focus of poetry ought to be "not ideas about the thing but the thing itself," as one of Stevens' titles has it. Williams insisted on the objective "otherness" of the thing itself. So did Stevens in many poems. But unlike Williams, Stevens also insisted that the poet's subjective response was *part* of the thing itself: "What our eyes behold may well be the text of life, but one's meditations on the text and the disclosures of these meditations are no less a part of the structure of reality" (NA, 76). In writing about a thing, the poet necessarily changes it. His words become part of its "associational" value. Stevens welcomed this idea because it supported his Shelleyan precept that the poet creates "our present conception of reality" (NA, 176). As he put it once in a letter, "The power of literature is that in describing the world it creates what it describes" (L, 495).

Stevens' respect for "associational" value is perhaps best understood in the context of the art world, where it is simply taken for granted. Associational value often constitutes a great part of the real market value of an artwork. For instance, a work's historic significance may give it a value above and beyond its purely aesthetic interest. (Such distinctions also apply in the realm of literature, but there they are strictly academic because literary value is not tied in the same way to the concrete art object.) The problem of attribution illustrates this point even more clearly. If an established authority—a Bernard Berenson, say—declares that a formerly obscure painting is the work of a great master, its market value suddenly soars. The actual painting has not changed at all, but its *value* has, by association with a great artist. Such value, from Stevens' point of view, is just as real as aesthetic value.

Stevens' respect for art collectors itself may be taken as another example of this kind of "associational" value. Consider his comment on the well-known collector Jakob Goldschmidt: "The mere fact that a picture is owned by this man is a token of its quality. I have never seen any of Goldschmidt's pictures that were not superb."[20] This brief statement shows, first of all, that when Stevens visited galleries, he took note of the *owners* of paintings, as any serious student of art must. Over the years, he had noticed Jakob Goldschmidt's name affixed to a number of "superb" paintings in different loan exhibitions, and he had remembered these occasions. His conclusion that Goldschmidt's ownership of a painting is a "token of its value" is quite accurate. Provenance—the record of ownership—is extremely significant both in art history and in the art marketplace. The designation "Ex. Coll. J. P. Morgan," for instance, raises the value of a painting automatically. The Morgan name connotes quality; it confers value by associating the object with the man himself.

To Williams' objection that such values are "false," Stevens might simply have replied that they are nonetheless *real*. One proof of their reality is that they can readily be translated into money. Stevens was too much of a realist to discount such considerations. His saying that "money is a kind of poetry" (OP, 191) was not meant ironically.[21] It was his realistic acceptance of the advantages of wealth that made it possible for him to idealize the life of the art collector. Money is like poetry because it is a *means* to freedom and power. The wealthy art collector, like the poet, is a man of "*capable* imagination" (CP, 249) because he has the means to realize his ambitions.

Straight out of Holland

A man's sense of the world is born with him and persists, and penetrates the ameliorations of education and the experience of life.—NA, 120

Among the associations that most mattered to Stevens when he sought to establish his personal "relation to contemporary ideas" were any having to do with his Dutch ancestry. Stevens was proud that he came from a "family of Dutch farmers" (L, 431). His consciousness of his Dutch heritage was part of his attachment to New York, which was founded as the Dutch colony of New Netherland in 1614. He liked to imagine (with only a little exaggeration) that he was "descended from the first white child born in New Netherland."[22] Thus, in 1904, when he found himself living alone and in poor circumstances in New York City, he contrasted his situation ironically with that of his prosperous, sociable Dutch forebears: "Here I am, a descendant of the Dutch, at the age of twenty-five, without a cent to my name, in a huge town, knowing a half-dozen men and no women. God bless us, what a lark!" (L, 69).

Stevens considered his own character essentially Dutch. Writing to Elsie in 1909, he attributed his moodiness to heredity: "I am pretty grumpy now and then . . . . The Dutch are all like that—as weird as the weather" (L, 146). He gave the same explanation to Holly in 1942: "My own stubbornness and taciturn eras are straight out of Holland and I cannot change them any more than I can take off my own skin" (L, 422). His interest in all things Dutch naturally affected his poetic explorations of self during the 1930s and 1940s, most obviously after 1941, when he undertook the genealogical research that would occupy him for many years.[23] It seems clear that he allowed to develop freely those aspects of his character he thought of as typically Dutch, and that this habit of mind determined, to some extent, his interests in art and art theory. Knowing this helps to explain certain aspects of his life and poetry.

Any consideration of the Dutch national character inevitably turns to the seventeenth century—the golden age of Dutch history during which the Dutch character achieved its fullest expression. It is not surprising, then, to find that Stevens had a particular interest in that era. In 1912 he wrote to Elsie about a visit to the Metropolitan Museum of Art: "My hobby just now is the 17th Century, a very remarkable period in modern history. Fancy my pleasure then in realizing that *all* the pictures in the Flemish room and in the Dutch room were 17th Century pictures" (L, 176).

It was natural for Stevens to make a trip to an art museum in order to study the history of seventeenth-century Holland, for our knowledge of this period depends, to a great extent, on our knowledge of seventeenth-century Dutch painting. This was the great age of realism. As a rule, Dutch painters avoided the conventional, elevated treatment of scenes from the Bible, mythology, or history. They depicted, instead, the ordinary life around them, recording their careful observations of everyday people and objects in meticulous detail and often in a nearly photographic style. It is said that Vermeer was the first painter to use a camera obscura in order to attain the closest possible approximation of visual reality. The work of the Dutch painters therefore has a documentary value that historians have not failed to appreciate.

That Stevens sometimes measured his own achievement against the art of seventeenth-century Holland is clear from a letter he wrote to the poet Mona Van Duyn in 1954, responding to a special Wallace Stevens issue of *Perspective* that she had edited:

> One of the contributors speaks of the generalized attitude towards evil [in my work]. It so happens that I have recently visited the exhibition of Dutch paintings at the Metropolitan

in New York. This covers the period, say, from the middle of the 16th century to the middle of the 17th century. Certainly the ordinary Dutchman had every possible experience of evil in that century. But there is nothing in any one of these pictures, which represent the "Golden Age of Dutch painting", suggestive even of the existence of evil. I speak of this because I gather that you are of Dutch descent, as I am, and I thought it might be of interest to you. (L, 852)

Here Stevens invokes the achievement of Dutch painting as an analogy for his own poetic practice. He did this, to some extent, throughout his career. Two key instances will be considered in later chapters: his interest in Dutch still life as he was beginning to write the poems of *Parts of a World* (chapter 4), and his engagement with the work of Piet Mondrian while he was writing "Notes toward a Supreme Fiction" (chapter 5). In this chapter I want to suggest some more general ways that Dutch painting seems to have served Stevens as a model for his own art.

The letter quoted above is a good starting point. Stevens' comment that "the ordinary Dutchman had every possible experience of evil in that century" asserts that he has some knowledge of the history of that period; it refers particularly, I think, to Stevens' awareness of how great a part *war* played in that history. Stevens may well have thought of seventeenth-century Dutch painting as a paradigm of artistic greatness achieved through courageous resistance to the violence of war. Consider this passage from Thomas Craven's *Treasury of Art Masterpieces,* a book Stevens knew: "The most independent and completely nationalistic outburst of painting in history is the Dutch school, which began with Frans Hals and passed out of existence in the seventeenth century . . . . The impetus to a self-sufficient art appeared with the struggles of Holland against Spanish oppression: a part of her energy and unparalleled powers of resistance was diverted into painting. The final peace with Spain was not signed until 1648; all the important artists were born before that date, and all painted to the roar of the cannon and the marshaling of troops. It takes courage to paint in such circumstances."[24] This notion, that it can be courageous to devote oneself to art in times of violence, appealed deeply to Stevens. It became a central part of his own poetic theory when he formulated the idea that life in our own century is lived "in a state of violence" (NA, 21). To write poetry, under these circumstances, is a form not of escape but of resistance—the noble resistance of "the imagination pressing back against the pressure of reality" (NA, 36).

Neither the art of seventeenth-century Holland nor Stevens' poetry typically depicts the horrors of war. On the contrary, in Stevens' words, there is "nothing in any one of these pictures . . . suggestive even of the existence of evil." The leading characteristic of Dutch art is, in the words of Madlyn Kahr, its "impression of good cheer and tranquillity."[25] In a time of nearly continuous warfare, Holland's painters depicted an everyday life that was remarkably free of disturbance. Their still-lifes and interiors celebrate, in particular, the quiet and comfortable life of the home. This tendency may be considered typical of the Dutch character: "The Dutch citizen closes his house against the tumult, the noise, the restlessness of human action; he recuperates by contemplating the things that belong to him, are there for his use and enjoyment."[26] The Dutch imagination "presses back against the pressure of reality" with images of the quiet and comfort of ordinary home life.

The sense of the external world as a "warlike whole" (NA, 21), combined with an imagination that proposes a version of bourgeois comfort as the highest ideal, marks the point of closest affinity between Stevens' poetic outlook and Dutch art. In this way of thinking, the home becomes a place to which the artist retreats, not as a form of escape, but in order to fortify his spirit for his daily struggles against the "pressure of reality." This view of the relation between art and life amounts to a kind of secular mysticism, as Stevens was well aware: "The poet who wishes to contemplate the good in the midst of confusion is like the mystic who wishes to contemplate God in the midst of evil" (OP, 230). The mystic retires to his cell, the poet to his home. This Dutch sense of the dwelling-place as a center of revivifying meditation and a source of spiritual strength appears often in Stevens' work: in such titles as "The Hermitage at the Center" and "The House Was Quiet and the World Was Calm"; and in many poems, from "Sunday Morning" (1915)—whose profound meditation takes place in a very comfortable bourgeois setting:

> Complacencies of the peignoir, and late
> Coffee and oranges in a sunny chair,
> And the green freedom of a cockatoo
> Upon a rug . . . .
>
> [CP, 66]

—to the beautiful conclusion of "Final Soliloquy of the Interior Paramour" (1950), where a scene of simple, domestic fellowship becomes a metaphor for spiritual fulfillment:

> Out of this same light, out of the central mind,
> We make a dwelling in the evening air,
> In which being there together is enough.
>
> [CP, 524]

The love of painting was itself, according to Stevens, one of "the simple pleasures of life" (SP, 212). When he bought a reproduction to decorate his sparsely furnished room in New York in 1907, his choice was revealing. To Elsie, whom he would not feel able to marry for another two years, he wrote: "At noon today, I ran up-town and (to do what I could) bought a large photograph of one of Rembrandt's paintings. It is a portrait of himself and of his wife, Saskia—*and she is sitting in his lap!* I might just as well have chosen a Madonna, but now I am glad I chose this, because it is just what I needed" (SP, 178).

What Stevens "needed" in his loneliness was the feeling of comfort he got from Rembrandt's vision of the artist and his wife living together in easy domestic intimacy. Characteristically, it was a Dutch painting that most directly answered his imaginative desire.[27]

Another aspect of the Dutch love of bourgeois comfort is central to Stevens' world view: a wholehearted appreciation of purely sensual pleasure. Erasmus in his *Adagia*—a book Stevens knew and liked (L, 409)[28]—defined the Dutch character as follows: "They are straightforward, scorning trickery and all make-believe, and *offend by no serious vices except a propensity to good living*"[29] (my italics). This describes Stevens' character fairly well. His outwardly conventional life as a Hartford businessman was certainly "straightforward" enough; and his one indulgence was a "propensity to good living," especially a predilection for the tangible pleasures of food and drink. He shared the Dutch passion for flowers, too, and enjoyed having weekend lunches of wine and cheese in his well-tended garden, surrounded by color and fragrance (fig. 11).[30] As he wrote to Henry Church, "Moderately high living of that sort goes well with an effort to think plainly and is incomparably better than the old plain living and high thinking" (L, 453). He thought of this as a typically Dutch approach to life.

This attitude toward sensual enjoyment is one we also associate with impressionism, as in Kenneth Clark's description of that movement: "Impressionism is the perfect expression of democratic humanism, of the good life which . . . [is] thought to be within the reach of all. . . . What pleasure could be simpler or more eternal than those portrayed in Renoir's *Déjeuner des Canotiers;* what images of an earthly paradise more persuasive than the white sail in Monet's estuaries, or the roses in Renoir's garden?"[31] Critics have often noted Stevens' connection to impressionism, which he called "the only really great thing in modern art" (OP, 241). But we are sometimes liable to misread Stevens' intent if we ignore his interest in Dutch art. Aspects of his poetry that seem peculiar in the context of impressionism—like Stevens' focus on the object (rather than effects of light), or his frequent use of interiors (rather than outdoor scenes)—are quite at home in the Dutch tradition of painting.

11. Snapshot of Wallace Stevens in his garden. Courtesy of the Huntington Library.

A keen appreciation of simple, sensual pleasures is central to Stevens' poetic outlook.[32] His description of the Canon Aspirin's sister is entirely approving: "in what a sensible ecstasy / She lived in her house" (CP, 401–02). To cultivate such a domestic "sensible ecstasy" represented, to him, not frivolous self-indulgence but a healthy appreciation of the goodness of concrete reality. This is the subject of his poem "Anything Is Beautiful if You Say It Is" (1938). Here Stevens contrasts two attitudes toward life that correspond to two different types of art. The first four stanzas depict an overly refined atmosphere of roses and marble, inhabited chiefly by women of disreputable or frivolous character (the "concubine," the denizens of the "demimonde," the "parrots"—from the French *perruche,* slang for a chatty, forward young woman). Their "fretful," finicky tastes reflect their vapidity. In utter contrast to this enervated, Frenchified scene, the last two stanzas open with a hearty, masculine, Dutch outburst:[33]

The Johannisberger, Hans.
I love the metal grapes,

The rusty, battered shapes
Of the pears and of the cheese

And the window's lemon light,
The very will of the nerves,
The crack across the pane,
The dirt along the sill.

[CP, 211]

The abrupt energy of this ending is refreshing, and there is no doubt that it expresses Stevens' own delight in the uncomplicated life of the senses: the unpretentious comfort of the room, the plain but delicious natural foods, and the kind of robust appetite that can savor even the cracked pane and the dirty sill. Although he is drinking Johannisberger, a German wine, the speaker is an essentially Dutch character. (So, most likely, is the servant "Hans.")[34] Stevens' point is to contrast southern European refinement with northern heartiness; the whole poem elevates to the level of an artistic ideal the "propensity to good living" that he thought of as typically Dutch.

As an example of the kind of art Stevens hoped to create at this time, these stanzas represent what he called "the normal." As he later explained in a letter to Hi Simons: "I have been interested in what might be described as an attempt to achieve the normal, the central. . . . For instance, a photograph of a lot of fat men and women in the woods, drinking beer and singing Hi-li, Hi-lo convinces me that there is a normal that I ought to try to achieve" (L, 352).[35] Those fat men and women are enjoying the same "normal" pleasures Stevens celebrated in "Anything Is Beautiful if You Say It Is"—the simple, animal satisfactions that all men share. He has in mind the same kind of scene when he praises routine existence as "a final good / The way wine comes to a table in a wood" (CP, 405). And his ode to the "central poem," "A Primitive Like an Orb," describes life at the "center" as follows:

What milk there is in such captivity,
What wheaten bread and oaten cake and kind,

Green guests and table in the woods and songs
At heart . . . .

[CP, 440]

This concept of "the normal" was a major concern of his mature poetry, as is clear in this letter of 1946 to Henry Church: "For myself, the inaccessible jewel is the normal and all of life, in poetry, is the pursuit of just that" (L, 521). Stevens describes as "a photograph" the picture of relaxed pleasure he uses to illustrate "the normal." But the scene depicted—"a lot of fat men and women in the woods, drinking beer and singing Hi-li, Hi-lo"—seems far better suited to a seventeenth-century Dutch genre painting—particularly the pictures of wine, women and song known as "Merry Companies."[36] Scenes of social gatherings by Willem Buytewech, Esais van de Velde, and Jan Steen are examples of such paintings that commonly hung in Dutch middle-class homes.[37] Whether or not Stevens was consciously recalling such paintings, this is another instance in which the quality of his imagination seems to be essentially Dutch.

Perhaps the most fundamental parallel between Stevens' poetry and seventeenth-century Dutch painting is their similar treatment of the human element. The Dutch tend to focus on description rather than narrative, to use Svetlana Alpers' useful distinction. They "present their pictures as describing the world seen rather than as imitations of significant human actions."[38] Instead of depicting a dramatic scene, the Netherlandish painter (as another writer puts it) "often gave more attention and applied more tender care to the accessories and attributes characterizing and enriching his theme than to dramatic representation."[39] In this sense, still-life painting is the most characteristic genre of Holland's golden age. This interesting fact has had some unfortunate consequences for the critical assessment of Dutch painting. According to traditional standards, derived primarily from the example of Italian painting, the greatest art must present significant human actions. Because still-life painting ignores human action entirely, it is ranked "at the lowest echelon in the hierarchy of painting."[40] For the same reason, Dutch art as a whole is often considered minor, or "merely" descriptive.

The same criticism is often made of Stevens' poetry. Unsympathetic readers deplore his tendency to write poems about the perception of objects rather than about "real" human problems. It is common to contrast the absence of human drama in Stevens' poems with the real characters and situations in the poems of Robert Frost. Frost's own comment that Stevens' poetry is "about bric-a-brac" neatly summarizes this view: it implies not only a comparison of Stevens' poetry with still-life painting, but also the judgment that such art is trifling, that such an artist is afraid or unable to tackle human subjects.[41] Even so generally sympathetic a critic as Randall Jarrell has made essentially the same point: "As a poet Stevens has every gift but the dramatic. It is the lack of immediate contact with lives that hurts his poetry more than anything else, that has made it easier and easier for him to abstract."[42] The absence of fully dramatized human characters in Stevens' poetry is taken to indicate a failure of feeling on his part, and Stevens' dictum "It must be abstract" is turned accusingly against him.

The proper response to such criticism is suggested by the analogy of Dutch art. To eliminate narrative and drama is not necessarily to de-emphasize the human element. On the contrary, it is possible to argue, as Madlyn Kahr has done, that the chief contribution of Dutch painting to Western culture is precisely its *humanization* of art. She describes one aspect of this humanization in her discussion of Rembrandt's *Holy Family with Painted Frame and Curtain* (1646):

> Merely to compare this interpretation with any traditional depiction of the Madonna and Child is to see at a glance the revolutionary achievement of the Dutch humanization of art. Of the humanization of religious themes, Rembrandt was the prime exponent. He represents sanctity not by a regal, remote, aloof image of the ideal beauty, but by an ordinary, familiar mother fondling her infant. This intimate conception

of the revered figures brings them so close to us that we can identify with them, while at the same time it enhances the essential human relationships that structure family life and underlie all social functioning.[43]

What makes Rembrandt's achievement typically Dutch in this painting is that he has secularized and domesticated religious feeling. He has translated the religious perspective into a correspondingly intense way of looking at the real world. The true subject of Dutch art is this new way of looking.

Stevens seldom includes in his poetry even so undramatic a human scene as that in Rembrandt's painting. (In this respect, he is more typical of Dutch art than Rembrandt.) But his central concern throughout his career, from "Sunday Morning" (1915) through such late poems as "To an Old Philosopher in Rome" (1952), was humanization in precisely the sense I have just described. If the Dutch artists communicated their new way of looking through the manipulation of paint on canvas, Stevens' medium was language, with its inevitable connection to the human voice:

> To say more than human things with human voice,
> That cannot be; to say human things with more
> Than human voice, that, also, cannot be;
> To speak humanly from the height or from the depth
> Of human things, that is acutest speech.

[CP, 300]

There is much in Stevens' poetry of the 1930s and 1940s that is acutest speech "straight out of Holland."

Part **Two**

Surrealism and Abstraction

Chapter **3**

"The Man with the Blue Guitar" and Surrealism

Stevens' determination to establish his "relation to contemporary ideas" during the 1930s is most evident in "Owl's Clover," which he labored over from the spring of 1935 through the spring of 1936. The last poem in that series, "Sombre Figuration," focuses on the artistic implications of Freud's exploration of the unconscious. The spread of Freud's ideas in America accelerated rapidly in the 1930s, so that, by 1940, it would be generally recognized that "the center of world psychoanalysis had shifted to the United States."[1] The subject was much in the air in the art world of 1936, chiefly because it was the basis of the Surrealist movement, which was then a vital force in the realm of "contemporary ideas." Indeed, Stevens' letters show that he was conscious of certain surrealist aspects of "Sombre Figuration." Glossing one section of that poem, he wrote: "In the camera of the subconscious, things are not (may not be) what they are in the consciousness. The locust may titter. The turtle may sob. Surrealism" (L, 375).

"Owl's Clover" is generally considered a poetic failure, a judgment Stevens himself confirmed by excluding it from his *Collected Poems*.[2] But in December 1936, he began writing what would become his most successful long poem to date, "The Man with the Blue Guitar." This sudden and remarkable advance can be traced to Stevens' interest in surrealism.

Surrealism had been the most publicized avant-garde art movement in Paris since the mid-1920s, and Stevens had surely been aware of it even then. Despite his own poetic inactivity between 1924 and 1930, he had continued to read widely and was acquainted with other American writers like William Carlos Williams who were interested in the Surrealist movement during those years. Stevens was predisposed to appreciate the spirit of surrealism because of his association in the 1910s with the Arensberg circle and particularly with Marcel Duchamp. But surrealism did not become well known in America until the mid-1930s, when Stevens began to exhibit interest in it. Surrealist art theory is the unstated subtext of his correspondence with Ronald Lane Latimer, for example. Latimer was director of the Alcestis Press, which published two of Stevens' books: *Ideas of Order* (1935) and *Owl's Clover* (1936), and whose magazine *Alcestis* published a number of Stevens' poems in 1934–35. Stevens' letters to Latimer between 1934 and 1938 contain some of his most revealing comments on his own poetry.[3] Latimer once asked Stevens whether he felt that "there is an essential conflict between Marxism and the sentiment of the marvellous." Stevens responded in a letter of November 5, 1935: "Marxism may or may not destroy the existing sentiment of the marvellous; if it does, it will create another" (L, 291–92). As both writers certainly knew, the phrase "the marvellous" was virtual shorthand for surrealism at the time. André Breton had enshrined the term in a much-quoted passage of the *Manifesto of Surrealism* (1924): "Let us not mince words: the marvelous is always beautiful, anything marvelous is beautiful, in fact only the marvelous is beautiful."[4] In asking Stevens' opinion about the relation between surrealism and Marxism, Latimer was referring to the most serious crisis the Surrealist movement had weathered during the late 1920s, when Breton's growing insistence on doctrinaire Marxism had given rise to intense theoretical disputes and resulted in the expulsion of many artists and writers from the movement. Stevens' knowing use of the loaded term "the marvellous" demonstrates his familiarity with the theoretical issues that concerned the Surrealists. He was well prepared to appreciate the significance of events in the art world the following year.[5]

The peak of surrealism's popular appeal in America occurred during the 1936–37 art season in New York. Few people could have been unaware of surrealism during that season. In November 1936, *Harper's Bazaar* accurately predicted: "One sure thing, you aren't going to find a solitary place to hide from surrealism this winter. . . . Department stores have gone demented on the subject for their windows. Dress designers, advertising artists and photographers, short stories in the *Saturday Evening Post,* everywhere, surrealism."[6] The cause of this upsurge of publicity was the Museum of Modern Art's much heralded exhibition "Fantastic Art, Dada, Surrealism," which opened on December 9, 1936. That Stevens was well aware of this exhibition is clear from his prose essay "The Irrational Element in Poetry." Stevens delivered this paper at Harvard on December 8, 1936, and his opening remarks were a timely reference to the MOMA show: "We are at the moment so beset by the din made by the surrealists and the surrationalists, and so preoccupied in reading about them that we may become confused by these romantic scholars and think of them as the sole exemplars of the irrational today. Certainly, they exemplify one aspect of it" (OP, 224).

"The Irrational Element in Poetry" is the first of the essays in which Stevens would clarify and develop his own poetic theory over the next decade; it marks the formal beginning of his conscious attempt to establish his "relation to contemporary ideas." It is particularly significant, therefore, that Stevens conceived this essay in response to surrealism. The title alone would have suggested surrealism to Stevens' audience in 1936, even if he did not intend a direct allusion to Salvador Dalí's *Conquest of the Irrational,* published in New York the previous year. And Stevens' claim to have been "preoccupied in reading about" surrealism would have conveyed a further meaning to any Anglophiles in his Cambridge audience. There had been a major International Surrealist Exhibition in London the previous summer (June 11–July 14), so that British periodicals, too, had been full of surrealism. Stevens himself subscribed to *Contemporary Poetry and Prose,* published by the English Surrealist group (see L, 334), and had published his poem "Farewell to Florida" in its July 1936 issue. The London Surrealist Exhibition had naturally received much attention in this magazine. Stevens also read, with even greater interest, Peter Quennell's review of the exhibition in the *New Statesman and Nation* (a periodical of which he claimed proudly to have been "a reader from #1" [L, 575]). This particular review, in fact, seems to have suggested to Stevens both the specific topic of "the irrational element in poetry" and his general approach to it.

Like Stevens' essay Quennell's review begins with the observation that surrealism represents only one aspect of a universal human experience: "We are most of us Surrealists in some degree— that is to say, we are familiar with the experiences that the Surrealist painter, writer or sculptor sets out to reproduce." Quennell then shifts his attention to the long history of "surreal" art: "It seems a pity that some kind of historical introduction could not have been arranged; for thus the uninstructed visitor might be brought to realize that what he or she may perhaps consider a recent and entirely gratuitous form of intellectual vagary is as old as the creative impulse itself, and that the love of the fantastic, singular and terrible, has its roots in the deepest recesses of the human spirit. Did not Fuseli—to go back only a hundred years— devour raw beef before retiring to bed that his nocturnal visions should be the more highly coloured?"[7]

In the same way, Stevens turns from his introductory comments to address the "history of the irrational element in poetry," borrowing Quennell's example of Fuseli and putting it to his own use: "There is, of course, a history of the irrational element in poetry, which is, after all, merely a chapter in the history of the irrational in the arts generally. . . . Fuseli used to eat raw beef at night before going to bed in order that his dreams might attain a beefy violence otherwise lacking" (OP, 225). Stevens' conclusion, too, follows closely Quennell's judicious summing up of the Surrealist Exhibition. Quennell concludes his review by lamenting "the poverty of much official Surrealist art" but praising the movement generally as a welcome "stimulant": "The disadvantage of official Surrealist art is that, although Surrealism may be interesting and valuable as a tendency, its deliberate manifestations are apt to be dull. . . . Nevertheless, if the Surrealist movement had performed no other service, it could at least be recommended as a stimulant to sluggish systems—a spiritual cathartic of which modern art . . . stands very much in need."[8] Stevens concludes "The Irrational Element in Poetry" in the same way, by criticizing the narrowness of official surrealist art but welcoming the "dynamic quality" of the movement as a whole: "They concentrate their prowess in a technique which seems singularly limited but which, for all that, exhibits the dynamic influence of the irrational. They are extraordinarily alive and that they make it possible for us to read poetry that seems filled with gaiety and youth, just when we were beginning to despair of gaiety and youth, is immensely to the good" (OP, 232).

That he relied so heavily on Quennell's authority in composing "The Irrational Element in Poetry" is ample proof that Stevens was uncertain of his own aesthetic stance at this time. His starting point, like Quennell's, is surrealism; and his basic approach is the same as Quennell's: to set surrealism in a broad context that will point out both its general value and its specific limitations. But unlike Quennell, Stevens is also concerned to place his own poetry in that broader context, and he is clearly determined to avoid being labeled a surrealist.[9] So where Quennell speaks of the long tradition of "surrealism" in Western art (using the lower-case "s" to distinguish it from the official Surrealist movement), Stevens substitutes the rather awkward phrase "the irrational element." The inadequacy of this phrase, which Stevens acknowledges in his first sentence, typifies the inadequacy of the essay as a whole: it is "much too general to be serviceable" (OP, 224). At various points in his essay he uses "the irrational" to signify the individuality of the poet, "pure poetry," any emotional response to reality, spiritual freedom, and the entire poetic realm. His use of the term acquires the breadth, but not the coherence, of his later use of the term "imagination." The same lack of precision is evident in his inconsistent use of other key terms. The phrase "true subject," for example, is used in two contradictory senses: in one place it is opposed to "the poetry of the subject," and in another to "the nominal subject" (OP, 227, 229). As a result, the whole essay is haphazardly organized and vague in its point of view. It is the prose equivalent of "Owl's Clover," and as Stevens excluded that poem from his Collected Poems, so he omitted this essay from The Necessary Angel.

"The Irrational Element in Poetry" represents Stevens' failed attempt to define his exact relation to surrealism. Only a few weeks later, however, in writing "The Man with the Blue Guitar," he would succeed at last in resolving this issue. The inspiration for that poem came—once again—from the art world. The other main attraction of the 1936–37 art season, in addition to the "Fantastic Art" exhibition, was the first major New York showing of Picasso. Picasso "is quite the kingpin of this surprise attack that has put so inescapable a Parisian stamp upon the first weeks of our present art season," reported the New York Times. "You encounter him at almost every turn."[10] This interesting circumstance is not likely, taken by itself, to explain Stevens' allusion to Picasso in "The Man with the Blue Guitar." Stevens had, after all, known Picasso's work well at least since the 1910s. And he had had the opportunity two years before to consider that artist's entire achievement at the first major Picasso retrospective in America, held at the Wadsworth Atheneum in 1934.[11] But Stevens' knowledge of Picasso was not confined to events this side of the Atlantic. An article by Clive Bell, entitled simply "Picasso," in the *New Statesman and Nation* of May 30, 1936, provides the key to Stevens' thinking about Picasso in that year. Bell is reporting on the recent celebration of Picasso in Paris: "Whether Picasso is the greatest visual artist alive is an open question, that he is the most influential is past question. Something like a recognition of this was celebrated, more or less accidentally, about three months ago; and for a fortnight at the end of February and beginning of March, until Herr Hitler gave us something else to talk about, all Paris was talking of Picasso. [Here he lists all the exhibitions] . . . and *Cahiers d'Art* produced a special number, devoted to Picasso 1930–1935, in which, for the first time, the public was given a sample of the painter's poetry."[12] Bell devotes most of his article to this special issue of *Cahiers d'art*, particularly to Picasso's poetry, which is its main feature. It seems likely that Stevens read this article with great interest and was inspired by it to acquire his own copy of the special Picasso number.

As critics of Stevens have long been aware, this particular issue of *Cahiers d'art* is the source of the quotation from Picasso that Stevens includes in "The Man with the Blue Guitar":

Is this picture of Picasso's, this "hoard
Of destructions," a picture of ourselves,

Now, an image of our society?
[xv][13]

"Hoard of destructions" is Stevens' translation of "une somme de destructions," a phrase gleaned from "a group of dicta by Picasso," as he later remembered (L, 783), in an article by Christian Zervos entitled "Conversation avec Picasso."[14] As Susan Weston was the first to point out, it is not only this one "group of dicta" but the entire issue of *Cahiers d'art* that lies behind Stevens' conception of "The Man with the Blue Guitar."[15] Here we may also observe what no one has yet noted: that this issue is devoted entirely to surrealism.

Cahiers d'art had a special relation to Picasso. Zervos, its editor, had been a close friend of Picasso since he founded the magazine in 1926, and since that time he had virtually dedicated his life to documenting Picasso's career. When he was not editing *Cahiers d'art,* he was compiling the Picasso catalogue raisonné (also published under the imprint of Cahiers d'Art) that appeared in twenty-two volumes between 1932 and Zervos' death in 1970. *Cahiers d'art* never shifted its focus from Picasso for long, and since Picasso was closely associated with the Surrealist group in Paris from the mid-1920s through the 1930s, the magazine naturally acquired a surrealist bias during those years. The issue immediately preceding the Picasso number, for instance, was a special Surrealist number; and the same figures dominated both issues, among them André Breton, Benjamin Péret, Paul Eluard, Georges Hugnet, Salvador Dalí, and Man Ray. The Picasso Stevens encountered in *Cahiers d'art* was the surrealist Picasso.

It is important to recognize that Stevens' inspiration for this poem came primarily from what he called "the literature of painting" (OP, 187), rather than from any particular work of art. It is true that his descriptions of the guitarist "bent over his guitar / A shearsman of sorts" (i) and "hunched / Above the arrowy, still strings" (ix) echo the posture of *The Old Guitarist* (1903) from Picasso's blue period. But that painting bears little relation to the rest of the poem, and Stevens stated quite clearly that he "had no particular painting of Picasso's in mind" (L, 786). Critics have also discussed "The Man with the Blue Guitar" in terms of the aesthetics of cubism,[16] and the phrase "a hoard of destructions" does suggest the cubist elements of fragmentation and multiple perspectives. But it seems unlikely that Stevens would have been suddenly inspired by cubism in 1937, since he had been familiar with it since the 1910s and it had ceased to be a vital movement by the late 1920s. The whole of "The Man with the Blue Guitar" is described more accurately by the term *surrealism* because it is a literary as well as an artistic movement, and because it signifies an approach to life rather than any particular style. Thus André Breton considered Picasso essentially surrealist even in his earlier blue and cubist periods.

That Picasso had a surrealist period is so well known it is surprising Stevens criticism has never acknowledged it. He was well represented in the Museum of Modern Art's "Fantastic Art" show, for example—with thirteen works—and the catalogue's capsule biography noted simply: "Surrealist period begins c. 1925."[17] Although Picasso himself never officially joined the Surrealist group, he began exhibiting with them regularly in 1925, accepted their official homage, and counted several of the Surrealist poets among his closest friends.

Picasso's peculiar position in regard to the Surrealists helps to explain Stevens' conception of him in "The Man with the Blue Guitar." He was, in a word, the Surrealists' hero. They praised the qualities in his work they recognized as surreal, but they also praised his divergences from Surrealist doctrine as evidence of his preeminent stature among them. Breton's major essay "Surrealism and Painting" (1928) summarized Picasso's position as hero of the movement: "We claim him unhesitatingly as one of us, even though it is impossible and would, in any case, be impertinent to apply to his methods the rigorous system that we propose to institute in other directions. If surrealism ever comes to adopt a particular line of conduct, it has only to accept the discipline that Picasso has accepted and will continue to accept. . . . I shall always oppose the absurdly restrictive sense that any label (even the 'surrealist' label) would inevitably impose on the activity of this man from whom we confidently expect great things."[18] Breton repeats this conception of Picasso in the special issue of *Cahiers d'art,* referring to him with emphasis as "une personnalité *héroique*" (Breton's italics).[19] This thoroughly romantic conception of the artist as hero, sustained on the one hand by Picasso's unflagging creative energy, and on the other by Breton's confident theorizing, surely lies behind Stevens' idea of the hero in "The Man with the Blue Guitar." His guitarist is preoccupied with trying to create a hero who is both real and ideal, both Picasso himself (we might say) and Breton's heroic conception of him: "I sing a hero's head, large eye / And bearded bronze, but not a man" (ii); "Ah, but to play man number one" (iii).

The idea of Picasso not simply as hero, but as surrealist hero, led Stevens to the satisfactory formulation of his own relation to surrealism that had eluded him in "The Irrational Element in Poetry." As he was well aware, non-Surrealist critics regularly used the example of Picasso to point out the limitations of surrealism. James Thrall Soby, for example, had written in 1935: "The limitations of the Surrealist movement are never so apparent as when the name of the movement is applied to Picasso. . . . He towers above the Surrealists in every way."[20] Peter Quennell echoed this view in his 1936 review already cited, describing Picasso as "a talent impossible to confine within the somewhat narrow sectarian limits that its high-priest has laid down."[21] Thus, by identifying with Picasso in "The Man with the Blue Guitar," Stevens was, in effect, asserting his own superiority to the narrow restrictions of surrealism. He was adopting an aggressive stance toward surrealism, reversing the defensive posture that had weakened "The Irrational Element in Poetry." No longer would he worry about distinguishing his own practice from that of the Surrealists. Instead, he would simply take upon himself the air of unquestioned preeminence for which Picasso was famous, in full confidence that any similarities between his own aesthetics and those of surrealism would only throw into relief the limitations of that movement. This single, bold imaginative act—identifying himself with Picasso, the unquestioned leader of modern art—set loose in Stevens the sudden access of creative power that resulted in "The Man with the Blue Guitar," his first major poetic advance since *Harmonium*. And his experience in writing this poem therefore became the paradigm, I think, for his later definition of what modern poetry must be: "the poem of the act of the mind."

Ironically, Stevens achieved this remarkable advance primarily by giving free rein to those tendencies in his poetry that were closest to surrealism, tendencies that he must also have recognized in Picasso (for instance) but that he nevertheless seems to have held in check out of fear of being labeled a surrealist. It will be easiest to see what those tendencies are if we focus our attention on the surrealist version of Picasso as Stevens found it in *Cahiers d'art* in 1936. The Picasso of 1936 was, first of all, the foremost living exemplar of the "pure" artist. He had never shown any interest in socially "engaged" art. We must therefore avoid the anachronism of associating "The Man with the Blue Guitar" with the kind of art Picasso produced in *Guernica*. Picasso's first politically inspired art, the series of etchings entitled *Dreams and Lies of Franco,* did not appear (in *Cahiers d'art*) until the summer of 1937, after Stevens had completed "The Man with the Blue Guitar."[22] Thus, in the special Picasso number of the magazine, Zervos' article "Social Fact and Cosmic Vision" (from which Stevens quotes in "The Irrational Element in Poetry" [OP, 230]) sets out to defend Picasso against the criticism—common in the 1930s—that his allegiance to "l'art pur" (Zervos' phrase) is out of date.[23] Zervos uses the typically surrealist argument that Picasso's psychological explorations are actually revolutionary activities, serving humanity's struggle for freedom in the realm of the spirit. He concludes rhetorically, "Can we say that he has less social conscience because he devotes his attention to the conquest of the unconscious?" This basic line of reasoning, asserting the spiritual efficacy of "pure art," and therefore its social relevance, would also characterize Stevens' developing aesthetic theory in 1930s and 1940s. "Poetry is the subject of the poem," he would assert in "The Man with the Blue Guitar" (xxii), explaining in his *Letters* that "here poetry is used as the poetic, without the slightest pejorative innuendo. I have in mind pure poetry" (L, 363).[24]

The Surrealist version of Picasso is conveniently epitomized by an article in this same issue of *Cahiers d'art* entitled "Picasso poète," by the high priest of Surrealism himself, André Breton. Breton's purpose in this essay is to place Picasso's poetry in relation to his painting. Because Breton is a poet himself, his article is appropriately poetic—condensed and allusive in style, and conceived as a variation on the theme of stringed instruments. He begins with the observation that Picasso's poetry might easily be mistaken for a "violon d'Ingres," a French idiom for a hobby. (The phrase is especially appropriate in this context, since it refers to the painter Ingres, who liked to think of himself as a musician in his spare time.) Then, taking this phrase literally, he cites a scientific article about a real violin: When a fine old violin is opened up, the interior is found to contain countless tiny pieces of wood, fragments that the violin has rejected over the years; thus, the violin improves its tone as if by an "unconscious intelligence" (a notion that naturally delights the Surrealist Breton). By analogy, Breton then asserts that Picasso himself is this violin, that "perfects itself by means of interior fingers."[25]

Already Breton's playful analogical method, comparing first Picasso's poetry and then Picasso himself to a violin, suggests in a general way the atmosphere of "The Man with the Blue Guitar." This parallel becomes quite specific, however, when we encounter the centerpiece of Breton's article: an anecdote about a guitar. This anecdote is the donnée, I think, of Stevens' guitar image, and it suggests the specific ways in which "The Man with the Blue Guitar" relates to Surrealism. The passage has never, to my knowledge, been translated into English:[26]

> Pour qui, vraiment épris de ce que l'oeuvre picturale de Picasso nous propose comme revalorisation constante du concret, pourrait craindre qu'il ne sacrifiât à la poésie la part magnifique de ce concret même dont il dispose—la poésie, qui a d'autres pouvoirs, n'a pas celui de mettre l'objet sous nos yeux—je me hâterai de citer une anecdote. Elle m'a instruit tout le premier de la situation des poèmes de Picasso *dans l'espace* où j'ai besoin, comme quiconque, de les voir s'inscrire parce qu'il m'a accoutumé à cette forme de reconnaissance particulière envers les créations qui sont les siennes. J'ai vu, il y a quelques jours, Picasso apporter en présent à une dame qui venait d'accoucher une petite "guitare d'accompagnement" puis, seulement ensuite, projeter d'écrire un poème qu'il pût épingler sur cette guitare. Ainsi en allait-il pour lui, à

cet instant, d'un tel poème avant qu'il n'eût pris forme: l'important est qu'il le concevait comme devant très précisément s'insérer entre ce qui n'avait que l'apparence d'un jouet et ce qui était le commencement de la vie.

For those who, truly loving the way Picasso's work constantly gives fresh value to the concrete, might fear that he could sacrifice to poetry the magnificent part of that same concreteness that is the material of his art—since poetry, which has other powers, has not that of putting the object before our eyes—let me hasten to tell an anecdote. It taught me first of all about the placement of Picasso's poems *in the particular place* where I, like anyone else, must see them inscribed because he has accustomed me to this form of particular perception toward his creations. Several days ago I saw Picasso give, as a present to a woman who had just given birth, a miniature guitar; then, only after he had given it to her, he had the idea of writing a poem that he could pin on this guitar. At that instant, this is how he conceived of such a poem, before it had taken shape; the important thing is that his conception required that the poem be placed very precisely between what looked like a toy and what was the beginning of life.[27]

That Picasso himself, in this anecdote, uses the guitar as a symbol of his entire work—presenting it as a gift to the new mother, from one "creator" to another—probably identifies this gesture as the germ of "The Man with the Blue Guitar."[28] Certainly the idea of a poem "placed very precisely between what looked like a toy and what was the beginning of life" anticipates exactly the "placement" of Stevens' poem, which celebrates the incessant conjunctions between "things as they are" and "the blue guitar," between reality and imagination, between life and art. Breton's special emphasis on seeing Picasso's poems *in the particular place* ("*dans l'espace*") where they are inscribed is the essence of Stevens' meditation in canto vi:

A tune beyond us as we are,
Yet nothing changed by the blue guitar;

Ourselves in the tune as if in *space,*
Yet nothing changed, except the *place*

Of things as they are, and only the *place*
As you play them, on the blue guitar,

Placed so, beyond the compass of change,
Perceived in a final atmosphere;

For a moment final, in the way
The thinking of art seems final when

The thinking of god is smoky dew.
The tune is *space.* The blue guitar

Becomes the *place* of things as they are,
A composing of senses of the guitar.

Since the French *espace* can mean both "space" and "place," it
seems likely that Stevens here is composing a paradoxical meditation on the phrase Breton used to capsulize the main point of his
anecdote. Returning to the spatial metaphor in canto xxxii, his
conception is again close to Breton's:

Throw away the lights, the definitions,
And say of what you see in the dark

That it is this or that it is that,
But do not use the rotted names.

How should you walk in that space and know
Nothing of the madness of space,

Nothing of its jocular procreations?

Stevens' "dark" corresponds to Breton's reference in "Picasso poète" to the "profound and magnificent night of our age."[29] The
essential poetic response Stevens describes here is close to what
Breton later called "black humor"[30]: it is funny ("jocular") but
also has an edge of "madness." And, like Breton, Stevens saw this
response as the very key to modern poetry: "The point of the poem

is, not that this can be done, but that, if done, it is the key to poetry, to the closed garden, if I may become rhapsodic about it, of the fountain of youth and life and renewal" (L, 364). As Breton continues his meditation on the guitar anecdote, he too becomes unequivocally "rhapsodic":

Le frêle instrument, que j'ai tenu sans songer à le faire résonner, m'a paru muet de l'attente de ce poème même, comme inversement il me semble que j'aurais moins bien compris, sans ce que le peintre disposait jadis auprès d'eux, tout ce qui peut s'attacher de valeur émotionnelle à la reproduction d'un titre de journal ou d'un bout de chanson des rues. Cette guitare prenait figure de support idéal en la circonstance: c'était bien le même que celui de tant de tableaux, de sculptures. Le poème en puissance se déroulait contre cette guitare à la façon de la banderole-oriflamme qui, dans un portrait ancien, met—comme le rossignol dans la romance française du romarin—un brouillard de mots latins sur les lèvres fermées de Raymond Lulle.

The frail instrument, which I held without even thinking of making it play, appeared to me mute with the hope of this very poem, as inversely it seemed to me that I would less well have understood all the emotional value that can attach itself to the reproduction of a newspaper title or to a snatch of a street song, without that which the painter once placed around them. This guitar assumed the appearance of an ideal support in those circumstances. It was certainly the same kind of support as that of so many paintings and sculptures. The potential poem was unfolding itself against this guitar in the manner of a flamelike pennant that, in an ancient portrait, put—like the nightingale in the French romance of Rosemary—a mist of Latin words on the closed lips of Raymond Lulle.[31]

Breton interprets Picasso's gesture as thoroughly surrealist. The poem is not intended to be read aloud or to be sung to the accompaniment of a guitar; it is, rather, to be *pinned* to the guitar. The oddness of this conception causes Breton to view the guitar itself strangely, without regard to its proper function: "I held [it] without even thinking of making it play." Picasso's inspired conjunction of guitar and poem has created a surrealist object. He has divorced the guitar from its usefulness by putting it in a strange context, thereby disturbing the perceptions of the viewer and bringing into play spontaneously the powers of his unconscious. There is an obvious similarity between such an object and Marcel Duchamp's readymades, the art form Stevens had put to his own use in "Anecdote of the Jar." Indeed, we may now observe that many of the qualities that aligned Stevens with Duchamp and New York Dada in the 1910s are also characteristic of surrealism: it is cerebral, playful, and delights in disturbing the habitual expectations of the public. It is hardly surprising that the Surrealists claimed Duchamp as one of their own. His readymades in particular were shown at the Exposition Surréaliste d'Objets in Paris in 1936, and Breton counted them as a special class of surrealist objects.[32]

In the paradoxical meditation that follows, Breton finds that, while Picasso's poem is only "potential" (and in fact is never written), it takes on fully the significance of a concrete object, unfolding almost tangibly like a "flamelike pennant." The actual guitar, on the contrary, loses its particularity under the circumstances and becomes an "ideal support" for the poem, taking on an abstract significance, an "emotional value." Such transformations of reality into imagination, and of imagination into reality, are the essence of "The Man with the Blue Guitar." Stevens' note on canto iv, for example, might describe Breton's meditation as well as his own: "In this poem, reality changes into imagination (under one's very eyes) as one experiences it, by reason of one's feelings about it" (L, 793).

The function of surrealist objects is described in more detail in Breton's important essay "Crisis of the Object," published in Cahiers d'art in 1936: "In 1924 . . . when I suggested that objects seen in dreams should be manufactured and put into circulation, I

envisaged the assumption of concrete form by such objects . . .
dream-engendered objects representing pure desire in concrete
form . . . the objectification of the very act of dreaming, its transformation into reality."[33] Stevens echoes Breton's very language
when he brings up the same idea of "dream-engendered objects" in
"The Man with the Blue Guitar":

> A dream (to call it a dream) in which
> I can believe, in face of the object,
>
> A dream no longer a dream, a thing,
> Of things as they are.
>
> [xviii]

Even more essentially Surrealist in Breton's meditation on Picasso's guitar/poem, however, is his fascination with the fundamental
interrelations between poetry and painting. Later in "Picasso poète" Breton points to Picasso's poetry, with enthusiastic approval,
as evidence of his need for "total expression," his desire to remedy
the insufficiency of one art form by means of another.[34] The Surrealists insisted on the fundamental relations between the arts.
Their habit of thinking in terms of inter-art analogies is so all-
pervasive that it virtually defines the Surrealist outlook, and the
two chief art forms in which they concentrated their efforts were
poetry and painting. This deliberate and impassioned confusion of
different art forms put them in direct opposition to the proponents
of abstraction—the other vital artistic movement of the time—
who were committed to maintaining the basic purity of each individual art form. On this score, Stevens found himself squarely in
the surrealist camp. In 1939 he summarized his objectives as a poet
in terms that reveal the deep connection he assumed between poetry and painting: "My own way out toward the future involves a
confidence in the spiritual role of the poet, who will somehow have
to assist the painter, etc. (any artist, to tell the truth) in restoring to
the imagination what it is losing at such a catastrophic pace, and in
supporting what it has gained" (L, 340). "The Man with the Blue

Guitar" gains its charm in large part from its witty and playful variations on the guitar image, which Stevens uses as a figure for the interrelations between poetry and painting, just as Breton did in "Picasso poète." In this crucial respect, "The Man with the Blue Guitar" is thoroughly compatible with surrealism.

Breton's meditation on Picasso's guitar continues in this ecstatic vein:

> Et cette guitare avait au-dessus d'elle toute la hauteur des balcons espagnols d'où l'on écoute, des fenêtres croulantes de géraniums et de capucines, que l'on entr'ouvre dans la nuit et par lesquelles se concluent les seuls marchés de la vie qui en vaillent la peine. Ces fenêtres, j'ai compris que, quoi qu'il fasse, c'est vers elles que, non seulement pour tout un pays mais pour tout un monde, Picasso lève les yeux, c'est vers elles que, du départ au dernier retour, il usera à l'envi tous les artifices de la séduction.

> And this guitar had above it all the haughtiness of the Spanish balconies from which one listens, from windows overflowing with geraniums and nasturtiums, which one opens a little at night and from which one concludes the only bargains of life that are worth the trouble. I understand that whatever may come to pass, it is toward these windows that, not only for a whole country but for an entire world, Picasso raises his eyes; it is toward these windows that, from the outset to the last return, he will use in concert all the artifices of seduction.[35]

This image of the artist as guitarist/lover surely relates to Stevens' conception of his own guitarist *serenading* an unidentified audience at the beginning of "The Man with the Blue Guitar." As Breton presents it, Picasso's impassioned serenade, aimed at seducing his audience into accepting his gorgeous inventions as real, is not less worthwhile for being imaginary: if one is to make compromises (or "bargains") in this life, as one surely must, then it is with such elevated visions in mind that "one concludes the only bargains of life that are worth the trouble." Stevens makes the same point:

> If to serenade almost to man
> Is to miss, by that, things as they are,
>
> Say that it is the serenade
> Of a man that plays a blue guitar.
>
> [ii]

In Breton's final transformation of the guitar anecdote, the "Spanish balconies" become a bullfighting arena and Picasso becomes a matador saluting his adoring audience. The image alludes to Picasso's Minotaur series. Picasso associated the minotaur with bullfighting, and many of his pictures show the minotaur goring horses, tormented by picadors, and so forth. In the famous etching *Minotauromachia*, reproduced in the Picasso number of *Cahiers d'art* (fig. 12), the minotaur—an image of the artist himself—threatens with a sword a female matador who is draped over a terrified horse in an attitude suggesting both death and desire. The sexually charged psychological complexity of this etching suggests why the minotaur was a figure dear to the Surrealists generally, as their famous periodical *Minotaure* (1933–39) attests. It is an image that combines rational with irrational forces, man with beast. Paradoxically, it is the beastlike half of the minotaur that was so immensely valued by the Surrealists, and this conception helps to explain, I think, parts of "The Man with the Blue Guitar." When Stevens speaks of wanting to "reduce the monster to / Myself" and defines the monster as "Nature" (L, 790), it is clear that he is entertaining the surrealist idea of gaining power over the irrational by *becoming* the irrational:

> That I may reduce the monster to
> Myself, and then may be myself
>
> In face of the monster, be more than part
> Of it, more than the monstrous player of

12. Pablo Picasso, *Minotauromachia* (1935). Etching, printed in black, on laid, ivory. Plate: 19 1/2 x 17 7/16 in. Collection, The Museum of Modern Art, New York.

One of its monstrous lutes, not be
Alone, but reduce the monster and be,

Two things, the two together as one
[xix]

In the same way, Stevens transforms the traditional body/soul dichotomy into the odd union of "person" and "animal":

The person has a mould. But not
Its animal. The angelic ones

Speak of the soul, the mind. It is
An animal. The blue guitar—

On that its claws propound, its fangs
Articulate its desert days.

[xvii]

As Stevens explains this unusual conception in a letter, "Anima = animal = soul. . . . The soul is the animal of the body."[36] So the Surrealists might have explained the image of the minotaur.

The reference to Picasso's Minotaur series also suggests another important relation between Stevens and the Surrealists: the imaginative use of violence. Breton epitomized the surrealist view of violence when he made his well-known statement, in the *Second Manifesto of Surrealism,* that the purest surrealist act would be to fire a revolver into the street at random. Christian Zervos, in "Social Fact and Cosmic Vision," defended the violence in Picasso's paintings as the heroic artistic response to the violence of modern life: "Is not his work the image of the cruelty that dominates the human condition in our day . . . ?"[37] Stevens would soon (in 1942) formulate a similar defense of the modern imagination: "It is a violence from within that protects us from a violence without" (NA, 36). Anticipating that formulation, in the third canto of "The Man with the Blue Guitar," he created a violent display that would have delighted a Surrealist:

Ah, but to play man number one,
To drive the dagger in his heart,

To lay his brain upon the board
And pick the acrid colors out,

To nail his thought across the door,
Its wings spread wide to rain and snow,

To strike his living hi and ho,
To tick it, tock it, turn it true,

To bang it from a savage blue
Jangling the metal of the strings . . . .
[iii]

There can be little doubt that Stevens would have associated the image of the nailed wing with surrealism. In the small pamphlet that accompanied the 1931 Surrealist exhibition in Hartford—an exhibition Stevens attended "not just once, but quite a number of times," according to James Thrall Soby[38]—there was printed one sample of surrealist prose. It was a brief excerpt from André Breton's collection of automatic pieces entitled *Soluble Fish*. One sentence in that short paragraph reads: "The prostitute begins her song in the country of the nailed Wing."[39]

Stevens also associated this image with a sight he himself had often seen, both in Pennsylvania and in Connecticut. He explained in a letter: "On farms in Pennsylvania a hawk is nailed up, I believe, to frighten off other hawks. Here in New England a bird is more likely to be nailed up merely as an extraordinary object to be exhibited; that is what I had in mind" (L, 359). This stanza therefore typifies one way Stevens sought to establish his "relation to contemporary ideas." The striking image of the nailed wing fixes clearly one point of contact between Stevens' own personal experience and surrealism.

By identifying with Picasso in "The Man with the Blue Guitar," Stevens was able to give full play to those elements of surrealism that most suited his poetic talent and, at the same time, to assert his own individuality as a poet. In hindsight, therefore, Stevens' summary comments on the Surrealists at the end of "The Irrational Element in Poetry" can be seen to be remarkably prophetic: "They are extraordinarily alive and that they make it possible for us to read poetry that seems filled with gaiety and youth, just when we were beginning to despair of gaiety and youth, is immensely to the good. . . . They, in time, will be absorbed, with the result that what is now so concentrated, so inconsequential in the restrictions of a technique, so provincial, will give and take and become part of the give and take of which the growth of poetry consists" (OP, 232). It is primarily the "gaiety and youth" of "The Man with the Blue Guitar" that makes it so striking an advance over "Owl's Clover." And that achievement was only possible because Stevens had finally "absorbed" surrealism as part of the growth of his own poetry.

Chapter 4

Parts of a World and the Abstraction/Surrealism Debate

. . . Imaginary poles whose intelligence
Streamed over chaos their civilities.
—CP, 479

Parts of a World is the poetic record
of Stevens' development from the re-
newed vitality of "The Man with the
Blue Guitar" (1937) to the confident mastery of "Notes toward a Supreme Fiction" (1942). It is a
transitional volume, and critical
opinion is divided concerning its in-
trinsic merit. Two judgments in particular interest me here. One critic
has regretted its closeness to "the
world of the art gallery."[1] Another
has praised its "more coherent sense
of intellectual purpose."[2] Taken together, these two comments sum-
marize what I take to be the most
characteristic quality of *Parts of a
World:* an increasingly theoretical
turn of mind expressed in more frequent references to painting. Encouraged by his success in writing
"The Man with the Blue Guitar,"
Stevens continued, during this cru-

cial period, to approach his poetic problems through conscious analogy with the contemporary art world.

Stevens had regained a certain ease and buoyancy in "The Man with the Blue Guitar," but that poem was not weighty enough to satisfy his poetic ambitions. Like the surrealist art to which it was related, its playfulness had a cost: too often it seemed to betray an essential lack of seriousness about the ideas it raised. For unsympathetic readers, "The Man with the Blue Guitar" simply confirmed Stevens' longstanding reputation as a frivolous aesthete. In order to correct that misconception, Stevens was determined that his next book would be more "important," as he wrote in a letter to Ronald Lane Latimer on January 21, 1938: "About a book: At the moment I am more or less drifting. I have one or two things in mind about which it would be possible to organize a book. But I am a little careful about committing myself to any of these ideas. . . . The force of a book is dependent on the force of the idea about which it is organized, and ideas of real force don't occur to one every day. Besides, I want my poetry to grow out of something more important than my inkwell" (L, 329). The organizing idea Stevens finally settled on for *Parts of a World* is suggested by that book's title and by the first poem in the book, "Parochial Theme," which treats the title idea in its concluding lines:

> There's no such thing as life; or if there is,
>
> It is faster than the weather, faster than
> Any character. It is more than any scene:
>
> Of the guillotine or of any glamorous hanging.
> Piece the world together, boys, but not with your hands.

In general, this notion of his poems as merely "parts" or "piece[s]" of a larger whole was a consistent motif throughout Stevens' career. In 1923, as an alternate title for *Harmonium,* he had proposed *The Grand Poem: Preliminary Minutiae* (L, 261), playing down (with some irony) the importance of individual poems in comparison to the grand scheme of which they are part. Similarly, in 1942, he would title his meditations on a grand theme "*Notes toward* a Supreme Fiction." The particular meaning of Stevens' title *Parts of a World* is suggested by a letter of 1940: "To most people poetry means certain specimens of it, but these specimens are merely parts of a great whole. . . . I am thinking of the poetic side of life, of the abstraction and the theory" (L, 383). He wished the poems of *Parts of a World* to be read not only as separate works but also as *examples* of this overarching "theory."

Stevens' development of this idea in *Parts of a World* depends to some extent on an unstated analogy drawn from the art world. The final lines of "Parochial Theme" introduce this analogy in an "outrageous pun," as Eleanor Cook has pointed out.[3] "It is more than any scene: / Of the guillotine or of any glamorous hanging." Stevens' "glamorous hanging" is both a public execution and an expensive painting.[4] This grotesque linking of two opposite aspects of experience—the realms of the social outcast and of the privileged connoisseur—exemplifies in a single phrase the power of poetry to create a coherent "world" from the most disparate "parts." And it does so by making reference to the art world. "Parochial Theme" is the first in a sequence of poems at the beginning of *Parts of a World* that are replete with allusions to painting. The twelve poems from "Parochial Theme" through "The Latest Freed Man"—originally published under the group title "Canonica"[5]—confirm Joseph Riddel's observation that *Parts of a World* reproduces "the world of the art gallery." In fact, I would take Riddel's phrase more literally than he intended. The particular analogy that best embodies the organizing principle of *Parts of a World* is, I think, that of an art exhibition.[6]

The most challenging aspect of an art exhibition, for the person who organizes it, is that it must be composed of a limited number of concrete works. Ideally, each of the art objects should have its own particular interest, but together they ought also to suggest a larger point of view that gives the exhibition point and coherence. This way of thinking characterizes, in several respects, Stevens' conception of his own poetry. His long poems are often organized spatially, as Michel Benamou observed of "Sunday Morning," as if the separate stanzas comprised "not a succession of ideas, but of pictures."[7] We might easily think of "Notes toward a Supreme Fiction" as a poem organized on the model of a portrait gallery, with individual cantos representing portrait-poems of the Canon Aspirin, Nanzia Nunzio, the Blue Woman, the Arabian, and so on.[8] Yet brilliant as these creations are, they are merely "notes" toward a far grander theme. Taken together, they are meant to illustrate the overarching concept of the Supreme Fiction, like carefully chosen pictures in a well-organized exhibition.

Stevens conceived of his entire poetic output in much the same way. For instance, he sometimes thought of his published poems as standing for countless other unwritten poems. In selecting a group of poems for an anthology in 1942, he remarked that "Domination of Black" was "only one of a projected series and it has, therefore, for its author, a value as referring to many poems never actually written" (OP, 242). The same habit of mind colors his summary of his entire poetic achievement in 1955: "It is not what I have written but what I should like to have written that constitutes my true poems" (OP, 289). In case after case, Stevens speaks of his poems as concrete fragments garnered from a larger, abstract whole, more or less representative parts of an otherwise inaccessible world. This way of thinking about poetry is unusual in a modern poet. But it seemed perfectly natural for Stevens, I think, because he was familiar with it from his experience in art galleries.

Putting together a book of poems, therefore, was closely analogous to putting together an exhibition of paintings. In each case, the selection and arrangement of the objects on view represent acts of imagination that are of interest in themselves. This was the aspect of gallery- and museum-going that most interested Stevens, as is clear from this letter to Henry Church: "Do you know the Fogg Museum? It is exactly what would make you happy. In addition to the discipline of choice, the presentation of things gives the sense of exact intelligence. I always come away from the Fogg feeling full of fresh recognitions" (L, 508). The kind of enjoyment

Stevens describes here depends upon an imaginative identification not so much with the artists who made the works on view as with the curator or museum director who decided which objects ought to be included and how they ought to be displayed. He clearly shared John Russell's fascination with the task of hanging paintings: "As it happens, hanging pictures is one of the most intense pleasures known to mankind."[9] It is this sort of activity that is the point of "Parochial Theme" and the organizing concept of *Parts of a World*: "Piece the world together, boys, but not with your hands."

The Painters of Still Life

                                . . . the poem of life,
Of the pans above the stove, the pots on the table, the tulips
    among them.
—CP, 423

Stevens uses the analogy of an art exhibition here to suggest an entire approach to life. Indeed, the analogy is so generalized that it hardly seems necessary to consider its source in any particular exhibition. However, as so often with Stevens, this poetic idea can be traced to a specific event in the contemporary art world. At the time he wrote the letter of January 21, 1938, quoted above (L, 329), Stevens still had not settled on an idea for his next book. But only eight days later, in a letter of January 29 he was able to write: "I am beginning to feel that I know what I want to do next" (L, 330). What occurred between these two letters was the opening of an exhibition entitled "The Painters of Still Life" at the Wadsworth Atheneum, on January 25, 1938.[10] This show was a historical survey of still-life painting from its "golden age" in the seventeenth century to the present. The conception of this exhibition, particularly the theoretical perspective of its catalogue, throws light on Stevens' development while he was writing *Parts of a World*.

The core of the "Canonica" sequence is a group of poems about painting: "The Poems of Our Climate," "Prelude to Objects," "Study of Two Pears," "The Glass of Water," "Add This to Rhetoric," and "Dry Loaf" (CP, 193–200). Still life is the dominant motif of these poems, and it epitomizes Stevens' point of view in "Canonica." Because that sequence is placed so prominently at the beginning of *Parts of a World,* serving as a kind of "program piece," the theme of still life sets the tone for the entire book.

Why would Stevens have chosen still-life painting as a useful analogy for his own poetry at this time? It seems odd that he should have moved so easily from his up-to-date engagement with surrealism in "The Man with the Blue Guitar" in 1936–37 to this seemingly *retardataire* interest in a historical survey of still-life painting in 1938. And it seems even odder that, having determined to write a more "important" book, he should have chosen as an analogy the traditionally *minor* genre of still life.

The key to Stevens' analogical way of thinking here, I think, is that the paradoxical relation of still life to modern painting closely parallels Stevens' own relation to modern poetry. First of all, Stevens' poetry shared with still-life painting the reputation of being minor. As late as 1948 the critic Clement Greenberg could remark, "Who is our greatest poet? If we leave T. S. Eliot to one side as a confirmed Englishman now, is it Wallace Stevens or Marianne Moore? Aren't both of them too minor really to be great?"[11] The same critical prejudice applies to still-life painting, which is seldom treated as worthy of serious critical attention. This is ironic because still life is the quintessentially modern subject, a fact which made it, from Stevens' point of view, an appropriately positive analogy for his own work. He knew perfectly well, as he wrote to Wilson E. Taylor on March 31, 1938, that "Cézanne has been the source of all painting of any interest during the last 20 years."[12] Many of Cézanne's greatest and most characteristic paintings are still lifes, and these were the inspiration for (in Stevens' phrase) "cubism and . . . everything that followed" (L, 822). The exhibition "The Painters of Still Life" made this point amply clear by including a large number of twentieth-century works.

The worsening political situation in Europe may help to explain the appeal of still-life painting for Stevens in 1938. In "Dry Loaf,"

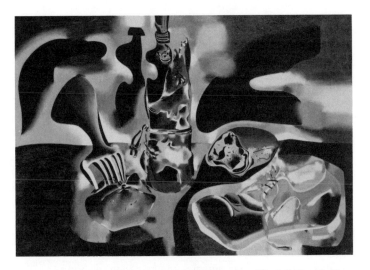

13. Joan Miró, *Still Life with Old Shoe* (1937). Oil on canvas, 32 x 46 in. Collection, The Museum of Modern Art, New York. Gift of James Thrall Soby.

the speaker is painting an ordinary still life with a loaf of bread; but behind it are "soldiers moving, / Marching and marching in a tragic time" (CP, 200). This poem was probably inspired by an article in *Partisan Review* entitled "Miró and the Spanish Civil War." It describes how the Spanish surrealist painter Joan Miró, exiled in France, "has been able to put on canvas . . . his reactions to the war. . . . It is eight months since Miró recommenced his work in Paris. . . . He must return to his natural beginnings if he is to stand securely, and so arranges into still-lives the household objects that dominated his first *dry* period [my italics]. He is back in the visual world and interprets it once more in the old tight style native to Catalonia, but this time more tortured and mature. For four months he works over a painting of his shoes."[13]

The painting *Still Life with Old Shoe* of 1937 (fig. 13) is reproduced in black and white in this issue. Its few objects include—in addition to the old shoe—a loaf of bread. It is painted with what

Morris calls "that *dry* [my italics] sharpness of vision which must haunt the air of Northern Spain." The abstract background is mottled with lurid, fitful patches of color, as if lit by lightning or by exploding shells. This still life marks a new phase for Miró, far removed from the buoyant fantasies he had been painting before the war. As the reviewer puts it, Miró's customarily "suave lyricism *dries up* [my italics] before the new staccato rhythms, the color withers into black and grey, the brush can no longer titillate and caress the canvass."[14] So in Stevens' "Dry Loaf" all is flat and bare, the landscape and loaf equally reduced to a monochrome brown.

> That was what I painted behind the loaf,
> The rocks not even touched by snow,
> The pines along the river and the dry men blown
> Brown as the bread, thinking of birds
> Flying from burning countries and brown sand shores . . .
> [CP, 200]

Both the style and the outlook of this poem are "dry." Like Miró's painting, Stevens' poetic still life becomes a personal statement on the war.

If Miró associated still life with the Spanish tradition in painting, Stevens had equally good reason to think of it as part of his Dutch heritage. For, as we have already noted, and as Stevens was well aware, the golden age of Dutch painting was also the golden age of still-life painting. It is common to remark that the spirit of still life pervades seventeenth-century Dutch art. We may think of it, in fact, as the defining characteristic of Dutch realism because it focuses on the most basic material aspects of existence—"low-plane reality," as Norman Bryson puts it: "No one can escape the conditions of creaturality, of eating and drinking and domestic life, with which still life is concerned."[15] This concept of low-plane reality is close to Stevens' idea of "the normal," and it is often what he means when he uses the term *reality*—not simply the grim reality of world events or of social injustice, but the "normal" reality that includes the ordinary pleasures of daily life. When

Stevens chose to emphasize the elements of everyday domestic life in the "Canonica" series—from its many images depicting "the culture of the table"[16] to the simply furnished bedroom in "The Latest Freed Man"—he was consciously indulging this Dutch aspect of his sensibility.

What this indulgence signified to Stevens in 1938 is suggested by the "Painters of Still Life" catalogue, which devotes special attention to the achievements of seventeenth-century Holland. The catalogue essay, signed "jrs,"[17] asserts that there is an important relation between Dutch painting and modern art, and that this "first great age of still-life" has particular relevance to the late 1930s: "The still-lifes of the Dutch school were neglected for more than a generation, by official taste, especially in America. But once more today they reward our attention. For now they seem to come to life again as the pendulum swings back from the abstract intellectualizations which dominated advanced art through the first third of the present century. Many who find little direct interest in Surrealism, find at least the courage to admire detailed painting again" (n.p.).

Representational painting had attracted increasing critical attention in Western art during the 1930s. In America, the conservative movements of regionalism and social realism most obviously embodied this trend. But for those interested in "advanced" art, it was surrealism that made the strongest case for figuration. As Piet Mondrian observed in 1936, surrealism was the "one tendency which cannot forego figuration without losing its descriptive character. . . . Born of a literary movement, its descriptive character demands figuration."[18] Stevens had always favored concrete imagery in his own poetry. In 1919, for example, he expressed his disappointment with a fairly abstract illustration for his poem "Earthy Anecdote": "Walter Pach's illustration is just the opposite of my idea. I intended something quite concrete: actual animals, not original chaos" (L, 209). This aspect of Stevens' imagination naturally drew him to surrealism in the 1930s.

The Atheneum catalogue finds a particular affinity between

Dutch still lifes and surrealism:[19] "[The Dutch still-lifes] are not at all like the still-lifes of the art schools, those *natures mortes* as the academic term so well has it. Rather these insects, these shells, these hams, seem to live with something of the mysterious double-life to which the Surrealists have called our attention." Stevens, who had contemplated André Breton's concept of "surrealist objects" while writing "The Man with the Blue Guitar," apparently found this observation suggestive. He soon composed his own version of a still life that reflects not only his interest in things Dutch but also the "mysterious double-life" of surrealist objects. His poem "The Glass of Water" begins:

> That the glass would melt in heat,
> That the water would freeze in cold,
> Shows that this object is merely a state,
> One of many, between two poles. So,
> In the metaphysical, there are these poles.
>
> Here in the centre stands the glass. Light
> Is the lion that comes down to drink. There
> And in that state, the glass is a pool.
> Ruddy are his eyes and ruddy are his claws
> When light comes down to wet his frothy jaws.
>
> [CP, 197]

Stevens' glass of water is an ordinary object, but he may well have selected it by analogy with the more interesting glass goblets so often depicted in Dutch still lifes. Two such goblets, labeled "Netherlandish, 17th century," were pictured in *Apollo* in 1937, where Stevens probably saw them (see fig. 14).[20] Each is engraved with a rampant lion whose open mouth, which represents roaring, might also have suggested to Stevens the unusual idea of light as a lion drinking the liquid in the glass. But if Stevens' inspiration came from seventeenth-century Holland, his "metaphysical" transformation of light sparkling in a glass of water into a lion with frothy jaws has all the modern strangeness of surrealist dream imagery.

14. Two goblets, Netherlandish, seventeenth century. Victoria and Albert Museum, London.
" . . . Light / Is the lion that comes down to drink" ("The Glass of Water," CP, 197).

The very quality of Stevens' imagination here is surreal, the surrealist beast imagery echoing other poems in the "Canonica" series (for example, the notion of poetry as a "lion . . . in his breast" from "Poetry is a Destructive Force," or the poet's sense of "being an ox" in "The Latest Freed Man"). Like the authors of the Atheneum's still-life catalogue, he seems to have been developing in his poetry of 1938 an analogy between Dutch painting and surrealism.

The intellectual framework which the Atheneum catalogue imposes on the history of modern art has important implications for Stevens' developing poetic theory. Not only does the catalogue assert that Surrealism is the most vital "advanced" art movement of the time; it also places surrealism in direct opposition to abstraction: "Surrealism, championing literary meaning and explicit sentiment, made its appearance just as the more advanced forms of abstract art were purging even the semi-object of the Cubists from painting. The object, in the startling guise of 'dream object,' rose, on the analogy of the Freudian parable, past the rationalist 'censor' of the theorists of abstraction."[21]

In pointing out the opposition between surrealism and abstraction, the authors of the catalogue were not simply making an academic distinction. The rivalry between these two art theories was a central fact of the art world of the 1930s. Stevens' awareness of this fact played an important part in his poetic development.

Surrealism rose to prominence in Paris in the late 1920s in explicit opposition to abstraction. As Julien Levy put it, "In the history of art surrealism is a revolution, first against the bondage of realism, secondly against the snob monopoly of *abstract painting*." [22] The Surrealists openly mocked the abstractionists. Miró asked rhetorically, "Have you ever heard of greater nonsense than the aims of the abstractionist group?" And Dalí, not to be outdone, railed against the "model mental debility called abstract art."[23] In response to this challenge, the partisans of abstract art joined forces against what they called "the Surrealist depravation."[24] Two groups devoted to the promotion of abstraction arose in Paris in 1930—Cercle et Carré and its factional offshoot, Art Concret; the following year these groups were subsumed by a larger and more effective coalition of abstract artists named Abstraction-Création (1931–36). The primary objective of all these abstractionist groups was to promote their own aesthetic ideals in opposition to those of the Surrealist movement, which by that time had captured the nearly exclusive attention of the press and the public.

The early history of modern art includes a welter of "isms"— cubism, futurism, suprematism, constructivism, synchromism, Orphism, purism, neoplasticism, and so forth. The number and variety of these competing theories of art can be bewildering. It is well to remember, therefore, that in the 1930s the theoretical opposition between surrealism and abstraction seemed to bring a certain order and clarity to the field of modern art. The American artist John Ferren, who worked in Paris during the 1930s, recalled that at that time "there were only two groups . . . the abstractionists and the Surrealists."[25] Because Paris was the center of Western art, the rivalry between these two camps soon polarized the entire art world. The intellectual climate of the 1930s was combative to begin with, and the public competition between these two claimants to the crown of modernism tended to make their theoretical positions more and more extreme, so that it became possible to consider them nearly absolute opposites. If surrealism stood for the irrational, for literary content, and for figuration, then abstraction came to stand for utter rationalism, pure formalism and nonobjectivity. By the mid-1930s, surrealism and abstraction seemed to define between them the spectrum of possibilities for modern art. Alfred Barr officially codified this dualistic way of interpreting the development of modernism when he presented the two landmark exhibitions of 1936 at the Museum of Modern Art: "Fantastic Art, Dada, Surrealism" and "Cubism and Abstract Art." The great impact of these two shows, together with their authoritative catalogues, helped establish "abstraction" and "surrealism" as the two standard intellectual categories for future discourse about modern art.

The artificiality of this dualism is immediately apparent when we recognize its omission of expressionism as a major, separate current in modernism. The truth seems to be that abstraction and surrealism held the day exclusively because they were the dominant movements in Paris. The center of expressionism, on the other hand, was Germany. The Museum of Modern Art's virtual exclusion of expressionism (along with American abstraction) was a sore point with the American artists later known as Abstract Expressionists.[26]

Stevens was well aware of this theoretical opposition between surrealism and abstraction. He owned the 1933 edition of Herbert Read's *Art Now,* whose last two chapters were devoted to the two most vital contemporary movements he called "abstraction" and "superrealism." The epilogue to the 1936 edition of *Art Now* made explicit what was implicit in the earlier edition: "In general the specifically modern field is left to two movements which tend more and more to diverge, and which may provisionally be labelled 'abstract' and 'superrealist.' Though at their extremes—a Mondrian against a Dali—these two movements have nothing in common, yet the space between them is occupied by an unbroken series, in the middle of which we find artists like Picasso and Henry Moore whom we cannot assign confidently to either school."[27] Stevens clearly would have included himself "in the middle" with Picasso and Moore. We have seen that he was familiar with surrealist art theory by the time he came to write *Parts of a World.* He was also well informed about abstract art theory at that time, for he was following the course of the abstract movement in America in what may seem at first an unlikely source: *Partisan Review.*

Stevens and Abstraction

Although Stevens himself was politically conservative, he was proud to acknowledge his association with *Partisan Review,* a frankly radical publication, from the very beginning of its famous rebirth under a new editorial staff in December 1937. His poem "The Dwarf" appeared in that first issue, and his name was featured prominently on its cover. Asked to recommend magazines by a friend in Ceylon in 1938, Stevens wrote, "*The Partisan Review* is the most intelligent thing that I know of" (L, 332). When a young reviewer asked him in 1942 whether he had read an article in that magazine, Stevens responded: "In *Partisan Review?* Well, then, I must have read it. I always read it, all of it. An excellent magazine, isn't it? The only exception to the dreary scene."[28] The extraordinary attention he devoted to this magazine is suggested in a letter to Henry Church in 1943: "This last weekend I had meant to read with more care the last number of *The Partisan Review,* which I have gone through once, but without quite making everything in it my own" (L, 441).[29]

The art editor of *Partisan Review* from 1937 through 1943 was George L. K. Morris, an abstract painter who also helped finance the magazine. Under his leadership, *Partisan Review* "was to become one of the principal exponents of 'abstract' painting in the United States."[30] Morris's writings were generally recognized as representing not simply his own private views but the official "platform" of the organization known as the American Abstract Artists (AAA), which he had helped to found in 1936 in outraged protest against the exclusion of American artists from the Museum of Modern Art's survey "Cubism and Abstract Art."[31] Morris's regular column "Art Chronicle" naturally reported the AAA's activities and expounded the virtues of abstraction. Wallace Stevens read there, during the late 1930s and early 1940s, a continuing demonstration of the historical necessity of abstract art.

Paradoxically, Morris, the unofficial spokesman for the liberal and heterogeneous AAA, was an advocate of pure geometric abstraction, the most dogmatic branch of the abstract movement. His writings in *Partisan Review* promoted strict adherence to the logical consequences of the cubist tradition, a rationalist reduction of forms to their most basic structural elements.[32] For an exponent of abstraction, this extreme theoretical position had several strategic advantages: it was coherent, it focused squarely on the most basic issues, and it was easy to explain. Although his radical formalism did not reflect the majority opinion of the AAA membership, the group acquiesced in Morris's de facto representation "because of his unified critical position and the visibility of his writings."[33] His enthusiastic and tireless promotion of abstract art theory helped to create a climate of opinion in which a broad range of abstract art could flourish.

Perhaps with the example of Morris's relation to the AAA in mind, Stevens thought of geometric abstraction as a metaphor for *all* abstract art in the late 1930s. His poem "The Common Life" (1938), for instance, uses the radical reduction of form to straight lines and flat planes as a figure for an overly intellectual approach to life and art:

> That's the down-town frieze,
> Principally the church steeple,
> A black line beside a white line;
> And the stack of the electric plant,
> A black line drawn on flat air.
>
> . . . In this light a man is a result,
> A demonstration, and a woman,
> Without rose and without violet,
> The shadows that are absent from Euclid,
> Is not a woman for a man.
>
> . . . The men have no shadows
> And the women have only one side.
>
> [CP, 221]

Here the imagery of geometric abstraction epitomizes Stevens' chief complaint (in the 1930s) about abstract art in general—that it is too rational, that it ignores the emotional and spiritual aspects of life. This was the main fault he found with Picasso, for example, in a note copied into his commonplace book in 1938: "He is an over-intellectual designer who moves one to thought, but not to feeling."[34] Even if we disagree with this judgment of Picasso, we may concede Stevens' point about overly intellectual art: However "modern" it may be, such art cannot ever fully satisfy the human imagination. "The Poems of Our Climate" (1938) makes a similar point:

> Say even that this complete simplicity
> Stripped one of all one's torments, concealed
> The evilly compounded, vital I
> And made it fresh in a world of white,
> A world of clear water, brilliant-edged,

Still one would want more, one would need more,
More than a world of white and snowy scents.

[CP, 193–94]

As Robert Motherwell recognized in 1944, these lines call into question the "rigid self-imposed limitations" of geometric abstract art, which achieves purity only by becoming an "art of negation."[35] Thus, when Stevens concludes "The Poems of Our Climate" by praising "the imperfect," he is distancing himself from abstract art, which he associates with the strict rationalism of the geometric-abstract tradition.

Given these circumstances, it is not surprising that Stevens was especially careful during the 1930s to avoid using the term *abstraction* in reference to his own work. (When he proclaimed confidently in 1942, "it must be abstract," it was a remarkable about-face. This is the subject of chapter 5.) In 1935, he asserted that "my real danger is . . . abstraction" (L,302), reflecting the orthodox preference for concrete particulars that had characterized poetry in English since Ezra Pound defined Imagism in the 1910s, and that would be perpetuated by the dominance of the New Criticism in English letters from the 1930s through the 1950s.[36] That Stevens associated literary with visual abstraction—and saw both as dangerous—seems clear from another letter of 1937, in which he carefully discounts any suggestion of abstraction in the cantos of "The Man with the Blue Guitar:" "Actually, they are not abstractions, even though what I have just said about them suggests that. Perhaps it would be better to say that what they really deal with is the painter's problem of realization" (L, 316).

Both of these instances show Stevens anxiously avoiding the word *abstraction,* at least as it applies to his own verse. This anxiety reflects his ambivalent attitude toward abstraction at the time. He avoided it all the more carefully because he was naturally *drawn* to it. As he wrote in 1935, "It is difficult for me to think and not to think abstractly. Consequently, in order to avoid abstractness in writing, I search out instinctively things that express the abstraction and yet are not in themselves abstractions" (L, 290). Stevens was sensitive to the common critical complaint that his verse was too cerebral, and he consciously kept his distance from abstract art in order not to call further attention to this problematic aspect of his poetry.

Inherent Opposites

Thus, Stevens' feelings about abstract art throughout the 1930s were similar to the feelings he had about surrealism in 1936: profoundly ambivalent. He had worked out his relation to surrealism in writing "The Man with the Blue Guitar." But his ambivalence about abstraction remained unresolved, partly because there seemed—at the time—to be less need to come to terms with abstract art. Although abstract art theory was central to understanding modern art, the abstract movement itself seemed, in the late 1930s, to have run its course. In 1939 it was possible to argue, as the art critic of the *New Yorker* observed, "that the movement's main purpose was the 'revolutionary' one of upsetting the neat little applecart of nineteenth-century academicism; that there are vivid social problems confronting the painter now which demand a more direct treatment than abstraction allows; and that the usefulness of the method is at an end."[37] Thus the preface to *The Painters of Still Life* speaks of abstraction in the past tense: "The pendulum swings back from the abstract intellectualizations which dominated advanced art through the first third of the present century." In this common view, the only "advanced" art worthy of notice in 1938 was surrealism, which continued to attract widespread attention. This situation probably encouraged Stevens to continue to think of imaginative activity as essentially irrational and opposed to the conscious intellect.

But the chief reason Stevens was out of sympathy with the abstractionists, and consequently felt himself drawn into the surrealist camp, had to do with the problem of *form*. The aesthetic program of George L. K. Morris was purely formalist, reflecting the main trend in modern art criticism from Roger Fry and Clive Bell through Clement Greenberg (who later replaced Morris as critic at *Partisan Review*). Such art criticism stresses the formal properties of works of art; it analyzes them without regard to biographical or social context, often ignoring content entirely as "literary" and therefore irrelevant to visual art. Stevens had little interest in this notion of form for its own sake. He was "inclined to disregard form so long as I am free and can express myself freely," as he wrote in 1938. "I don't know of anything, respecting form, that makes much difference" (OP, 240). In this respect, abstract art theory seemed fundamentally at odds with his own poetic aims, and surrealism offered a much more congenial alternative. His view of contemporary art theory in the late 1930s must have been similar to that of Julien Levy, who wrote in the preface to his *Surrealism* (1936) that "[while] the formalism of the cubist school was approaching the dead *purism* of Mondrian," surrealism was evolving and changing. "Unlike so many other *'isms'* surrealism is evidently not a dead end, it is not static, but is a dynamic and expansive point of view."[38]

This helps to explain the obviously surreal imagery that appears in certain of Stevens' poems of 1938–39. "Arcades of Philadelphia the Past," for instance, begins with the monstrous image of a "Philadelphia that the spiders ate" and makes typically surrealist use of dismembered body parts in its central image of people who "sit, holding their eyes in their hands" (CP, 225–26). Similarly, "Cuisine Bourgeoise" depicts a surreal feast of cannibalism:

These days of disinheritance, we feast
On human heads . . .
. . . brought in on leaves,
Crowned with the first, cold buds. On these we live,
No longer on the ancient cake of seed,
The almond and deep fruit. This bitter meat
Sustains us . . . Who, then, are they, seated here?

Is the table a mirror in which they sit and look?
Are they men eating reflections of themselves?

[CP, 227–28]

This grotesque imagery is a figure for the spiritual poverty of modern life. To the extent that it derives from "the culture of the table," it fits neatly into the surreal tradition of still life as interpreted by the Atheneum's exhibition "The Painters of Still Life." But as poetry, it falls rather flat. The imagery is too self-consciously weird, the point too obvious. The poem simply draws out the surrealist aspects of canto xv of "The Man with the Blue Guitar":

Is this picture of Picasso's, this "hoard
Of destructions," a picture of ourselves,

Now, an image of our society? . . .

. . . Am I a man that is dead

At a table on which the food is cold?
Is my thought a memory, not alive?

[CP, 173]

"Cuisine Bourgeoise" is an obvious extension of this passage. As Stevens had been concerned with Picasso and surrealism in "The Man with the Blue Guitar," so "Cuisine Bourgeoise" derives from the one canto of that poem that explicitly mentions Picasso, and it repeats the same theme in the same surrealist mode. This is repetition rather than development. It reflects, I think, a certain imaginative inertia on Stevens' part that can be traced to his involvement with contemporary art theory. He seems to have reached an impasse, unable to advance beyond a recognition of his own closeness to the theory of surrealism and his opposition to the theory of abstraction. This is at the root of the "uncertainty of purpose" that Helen Vendler finds in *Parts of a World,* a wavering between "two poles—a methodical recording and an eccentric fancy—[which] are mutually exclusive."[39] Viewed in this light, the cannibal imagery of "Cuisine Bourgeoise" takes on an unintended irony: Stevens' poetry is cannibalizing itself, recycling ideas and images without a clear sense of direction.

Such lapses, however, should not overshadow the positive importance of the surrealism/abstraction dichotomy to Stevens' development in *Parts of a World*. His ambivalence toward both movements contributed to his growing awareness of his own theoretical problems, and helped to shape some of his best poems. In this respect, the career of the British sculptor Henry Moore provides a suggestive parallel. Hilton Kramer has traced Moore's artistic success in the 1930s specifically to his ambivalence about abstraction and surrealism:

> What gave Moore's work of the Thirties its special emotional charge, I think, was precisely the tension which resulted from the artist's divided and unresolved feelings about both abstraction *and* Surrealism, which were then locked in a doctrinaire conflict with each other. Both exerted an immense and fecund pressure on Moore's imagination at this time, but their appeal also met with a certain resistance. He drew upon their ideas, but he was unwilling to surrender completely to the absolutism of either camp. To be at the crossroads of abstraction and Surrealism at that historical moment, to be at once an insider and an outsider in relation to both these movements, proved to be a huge creative advantage for Moore.[40]

The same is true, to some extent, of Stevens. He was aware of abstract and surrealist art theories as the twin sources of vitality in the contemporary art world. His engagement with these opposing theories was one aspect of his effort to establish his "relation to contemporary ideas" (L, 340), and its traces can be found in Stevens' increasingly theoretical poetry.

Stevens had always tended to think in terms of polarities, and from the start his poetry had been built on oppositions such as north and south, winter and summer, day and night, sun and moon. In his poems of 1938-39, especially, the abstract/surreal dichotomy productively encouraged this tendency. But like Moore, Stevens avoided "the absolutism of either camp," preferring to go his own way. The "Canonica" series, which includes poems related to both surrealism and abstraction, ends with two poems stressing Stevens' freedom from any doctrine. "On the Road Home" describes the exhilaration following the realization that "there is no such thing as the truth." And the title character of "The Latest Freed Man" awakes refreshed and invigorated because he has "just / Escaped from the truth." For the time being, Stevens was content to allow surrealism and abstraction to coexist in fruitful conflict. "Connoisseur of Chaos" even suggests that such "opposites" are simply different aspects of the same reality, that they are part of an "essential unity":

> . . . a law of inherent opposites,
> Of essential unity, is as pleasant as port,
> As pleasant as the brush-strokes of a bough,
> An upper, particular bough in, say, Marchand.[41]
>
> [CP, 215]

Examination of the Hero

A distinct shift of tone occurs in Stevens' poetry in 1940. The poet's sense that he had reached a watershed in his poetic development is clear from the opening of "Asides on the Oboe":

> The prologues are over. It is a question, now,
> Of final belief. So, say that belief
> Must be in a fiction. It is time to choose.
>
> [CP, 250]

These plain-spoken lines express a new seriousness, amounting almost to urgency, about poetry and poetic theory. The cause of this change was the beginning of World War II. War was a major theme of Stevens' poetry throughout his career, as A. Walton Litz has remarked.[42] His early series "Phases" and "Lettres d'un Soldat" were inspired by World War I, for example; and "The Men

That Are Falling" (1936) was written in response to the Spanish Civil War. But it was in 1940 that the idea of war became an essential part of his poetic theory. Stevens recorded this new development explicitly in two poems of that year, originally published together under the appropriate title "Two Theoretic Poems": "It has to persuade that war is part of itself" ("Man and Bottle"); and "It has to think about war" ("Of Modern Poetry").

This new attitude dominates the poems of 1940–42, which comprise the latter half of *Parts of a World*—from "Man and Bottle" through "Examination of the Hero in a Time of War."[43] There is a corresponding movement, in Stevens' poetry of these years, away from poems about painting and toward poems about the concept of the hero.[44] One effect of this movement is that the book falls uneasily into two separate halves, a fact that perhaps explains why many readers have found *Parts of a World* so unsatisfying. This disjunction is more keenly felt because the subjects that dominate the two halves of the book—still life in the first half, the hero in the second—invoke different and seemingly contradictory aspects of human experience.

As we have seen, Stevens associated still-life painting with what he called "the normal"—the common comforts of food, drink, shelter, company. The ordinary pleasures of this "low-plane reality" have little to do with the concept of the hero, who is by definition *extra*ordinary and whose existence is on the *highest* plane of reality. In the final poem of *Parts of a World,* "Examination of the Hero in Time of War," Stevens contrasts these two opposing ideals:

The hero is not a person. The marbles
Of Xenophon, his epitaphs, should
Exhibit Xenophon, what he was, since
Neither his head nor horse nor knife nor
Legend were part of what he was, forms
Of a still-life, symbols, brown things to think of
In brown books.

Here the poet discards the still-life forms with which *Parts of a World* began, choosing instead the white "marbles" of a heroic statue to represent his poetic ideal. Yet he finds even this heroic image unsatisfactory to the extent that it is *abstract:*

> The marbles of what he was stand
> Like a white abstraction only, a feeling
> In a feeling mass, a blank emotion,
> An anti-pathos, until we call it
> Xenophon, its implement and actor.
> [CP, 276–77]

The attitude toward abstraction in this passage is consistent with Stevens' view throughout the 1930s: it stands for a coldly intellectual approach to life and art. Given the state of contemporary art theory, however, the only viable alternative seems to be the vital, irrational energy of surrealism. So Stevens concludes the canto with an invocation of the primitive and demonic powers so dear to the Surrealists:

> Obscure Satanas, make a model
> Of this element, this force. Transfer it
> Into a barbarism as its image.

In this canto Stevens seems to be proposing some combination of abstract and surreal elements—perhaps a kind of "impure" abstraction or abstract surrealism—though it is unclear exactly what such a synthesis might entail. What is clear is that, in seeking to bring some theoretical coherence to the disparate "parts" of *Parts of a World,* he has in mind the intellectual categories of abstraction and surrealism. His efforts in this direction would soon achieve far better results in "Notes toward a Supreme Fiction," and the inspiration for that poem would come, once again, from the art world.

Chapter 5
"Notes toward a Supreme Fiction" and Abstract Art

When Stevens affixed the subtitle "It Must Be Abstract" to the first section of his poetic manifesto "Notes toward a Supreme Fiction" (hereafter referred to as "Notes"), he was recording a significant new development in his career. After avoiding the term *abstraction* so carefully throughout the 1930s, he straightforwardly endorsed the aesthetic use of abstraction in 1942. But exactly what he meant by the term has been one crux of Stevens criticism over the years. The varying definitions proposed have recently been well summarized by B. J. Leggett, who sorts them into "two conflicting notions of abstraction, depending in part on whether [Stevens] is viewed as the Poet of Imagination or the Poet of Reality."[1] In all of this discussion, no one has connected Stevens' use of the term to his interest in the visual arts.

Stevens' changed attitude coincides with a similar shift of taste in the New York art world. It is a curious fact of American cultural history that in the early 1940s, when Stevens wrote "Notes," abstract painting was rapidly emerging as the dominant strain in American art. After years of neglect, while regionalism and social realism held the stage during the 1930s, American abstraction took the lead in the 1940s and "triumphed" after World War II in the movement known as Abstract Expressionism.[2] It is not merely coincidence that Stevens chose the term *abstract* to describe his own poetic aims at this particular historical moment.[3] There is a significant relationship between these parallel developments in American painting and poetry.

An intellectual climate more hospitable to abstraction was already evident in the New York art season of 1940–41. In February 1941, *Art News* reported an "Abstraction Fest Uptown & Down." *Art Digest* ran a similar headline in March 1941: "Abstract Shows Flood 57th Street."[4] By the next year, the art critic of the *New York Times* perceived a general movement toward abstraction in the visual arts. Under the heading "Abstraction Lays Siege to Us Anew," he observed, "Abstraction has been sneaking up on us of late, coming to represent a more and more major phase of our exhibition schedule."[5]

George L. K. Morris, writing in *Partisan Review,* suggested a causal connection between the two world wars and the rise of abstract art. Cubism, in his view, was a reaction against the violence and disorder of World War I: "It may be that an enveloping chaos imposes upon the artist a new demand for order."[6] In the same way, he was convinced that World War II would bring about a renewal of interest in abstraction: "Abstract art can offer . . . something particularly pertinent for our time . . . . An era of convulsion evidently requires of artists that they restrict their horizons and close in upon a consciously ordered world where every facet is completely understood."[7]

Although Stevens did not share Morris's view of abstract art, he did trace the parallel change in his own poetry and poetic theory to the world wars. As he saw it, the Second World War was simply a prolongation of the First. He called it in 1941 "a renewal of what, if it was not the greatest war, became such by this continuation" (NA, 20). This slight modulation of the phrase "the Great War" to "the *greatest* war" marks a profound development in Stevens' poetic career. From this point onward he was to conceive of life in the twentieth century as "life in a state of violence" (NA, 26). Under the pressure of constant war and of the "war-like whole" (NA, 21), the chief measure of a modern poet becomes his ability to "press back against the pressure of reality" (NA, 36). In a significant choice of terms, Stevens describes this ability as the "power to abstract himself, and to withdraw with him into his abstraction the reality on which the lovers of truth insist. He must be able to abstract himself and also to abstract reality, which he does by placing it in his imagination" (NA, 23). In the violent context of modern life, the rational faculty of abstraction grows dramatically in value, acquiring in this passage a power second only to that of the imagination itself.

Along with a revitalized interest in abstraction, World War II also inspired in some critics a corresponding reaction against surrealism. As violence became an everyday occurrence, it became commonplace to observe that "it is no longer possible to distinguish between the surreal and the real."[8] As Jerome Mellquist wrote in the *New Republic,* "It is hard to see how the contemporary exponents of disorder [the surrealists] have anything further to say, now that the world itself is the very image of what they painted."[9]

"Notes" was partly inspired by a similar reaction, on Stevens' part, away from an emphasis on "the irrational element in poetry" and toward a greater emphasis on rationalism. Both elements had always been present in Stevens' poetry, of course, but "Notes" defines a new balance between them. The subtitle "It Must Be Abstract," and the precise form of "Notes" as a whole, are concessions to rationalism made under the pressure of war. Stevens originally conceived his subtitle as a strictly rationalist proposition. Very early in the course of writing, however, the term *abstract* lost

its strictly rational meaning, acquired greater breadth and flex-
ibility, and became in its transformation a central part of Stevens'
poetic theory.

That a strong rationalistic impulse inspired "Notes" is confirmed by Stevens' memory of his experience writing the poem. He
originally conceived of "Notes" as a much more rigidly organized
poem than the final version. As he explained in a letter to Henry
Church: "At first I attempted to follow a scheme, and the first
poem bore the caption REFACIMENTO. . . . But I very soon found
that, if I stuck closely to a development, I should lose all of the
qualities that I really wanted to get into the thing, and that I was
likely to produce something that did not come off in any sense, not
even as poetry" (L, 431). It seems clear from this description that
Stevens' first conception of "Notes" included not only a numerical
neatness of form reminiscent of Dante's *Divine Comedy*, but also
a systematically developed argument reminiscent of Descartes'
Regulae—with section headings, captions summarizing the point
of each canto, and a logical progression from point to point.[10] The
remnants of this scheme can be seen most clearly in the first four
cantos of "It Must Be Abstract," which develop the concept of "the
first idea" with marked regularity:

1. "Begin by perceiving the idea / Of this invention";
2. "It is the celestial ennui of apartments / That sends us
   back to the first idea";
3. "The poem refreshes life so that we share, / For a moment,
   the first idea";
4. "The first idea was not our own."

As we shall see, Stevens associated this original scheme with the
tradition of geometric-abstract art.[11]

That Stevens had the analogy of painting in mind when he began
"Notes" is evident in the passage from his *Letters* just quoted. The
Italian word *refacimento* (more commonly spelled *rifacimento*) is
drawn from the vocabulary of art criticism and denotes the restora-
tion of a work of art to its original condition.[12] This curatorial

origin of the "first idea" is confirmed in another letter: "Someone here wrote to me the other day and wanted to know what I meant by a thinker of the first idea. If you take the varnish and dirt of generations off a picture, you see it in its first idea. If you think about the world without its varnish and dirt, you are a thinker of the first idea" (L, 426–27). Stevens repeats this conception in "It Must Be Abstract" when he claims that even Adam and Eve were "the inhabitants of a very varnished green" (I.iv).[13]

The poet is not referring to an abstract picture in these passages. But the sort of painting he was thinking of was closely associated, in his mind, with abstraction. Stevens' one direct reference to a painter in "Notes" suggests that he had in mind the Dutch masters when he began the poem:

> Weather by Franz Hals,
>
> Brushed up by brushy winds in brushy clouds,
> Wetted by blue, colder for white.
> [I.vi]

Seventeenth-century Dutch painting may seem a far cry from geometric abstraction, especially the art of Hals, whose painterly ("brushy") style is the very opposite of linearity. But Stevens thought of Dutch painting and geometry together, as in this passage from a letter of 1935: "I remember reading an essay of Dr. [Wilhelm Reinhold] Valentiner's on squareness in Dutch painting, which he attributed to the flatness of the country and its linear effect. This sounds like nonsense, but after all, it can be demonstrated that Dutch painting is based on squares and that Italian painting is based on circles, or, at least, on something else than squares. Dr. Valentiner has not spent his life thinking about such things without having got rid of a good deal of nonsense" (L, 300). Stevens is recalling the essay "Linear Composition in Dutch Art" in Valentiner's *The Art of the Low Countries* (1914), which argues that a basic rectangular composition pervades the landscape, architecture, and art of Holland: "This tendency has marked the art of every period from the earliest to the latest—from Geertgen van Haarlem's to Lucas van Leyden's and Rembrandt's and down to the modern work of Jongkind and Van Gogh. As in Italy the triangle, so in Holland the rectangle, is used by preference to turn a fragment of nature into a composition complete in itself."[14]

The notion that the quality of the imagination varies from country to country, and that national traits correspond to favored abstract shapes, influenced Stevens deeply. He repeated it in his lecture of 1948, "Imagination as Value," once again associating Dutch art with the square: "The commonest idea of an imaginative object is something large. But apparently with the Japanese it is the other way round and with them the commonest idea of an imaginative object is something small. With the Hindu it appears to be something vermicular, with the Chinese, something round and with the Dutch, something square" (NA, 143). It seems likely that Stevens had in mind the orderly geometry he associated with Dutch art when he began writing "Notes."[15]

Stevens had a particular interest in things Dutch in 1942. He had always considered his own character fundamentally Dutch and in early 1942, at the very time he was beginning "Notes," he was actively tracing his Dutch ancestry (L, 405). Two other major poems of this year reflect this preoccupation with his Dutch heritage: "Examination of the Hero in Time of War," whose opening lines invoke the Dutch city of Leyden; and "Dutch Graves in Bucks County," in which the poet repeatedly addresses the spirits of his Dutch forebears as "my semblables" (CP, 273, 290–93). If the tendency toward rational order represented by geometric abstraction was a "national characteristic" of Dutchmen, as Valentiner argued, then to give free rein to this impulse was not, for Stevens, to be overly intellectual, but to express truly his own deepest character. This native rage for order was surely heightened by the prevailing chaos and irrationality of World War II, and perhaps especially by the German occupation of Holland.[16]

As Stevens was well aware, the chief "Dutch contribution to modern art" was the geometric abstract movement known as De

Stijl.[17] During the 1930s, the Wadsworth Atheneum in Hartford was one of the foremost champions of De Stijl principles in the United States. Amid great publicity in 1930, the director, A. Everett Austin, remodeled his office as "a free composition in colored planes," reflecting the principles "not only of the Bauhaus . . . but also of the Dutch *De Stijl* group."[18] And when its new Avery Memorial wing opened in 1934, the Atheneum became the "museum with the most modern interior in the world," in which "all ornamentation and detail have been dispensed with completely."[19] The Dutch contribution to modern architecture and design was stressed in the landmark exhibition "Modern Architecture" (organized by the Museum of Modern Art) that appeared at the Atheneum in 1932. One of the four founders of the "International Style" featured in that show (along with Gropius, Le Corbusier, and Mies van der Rohe) was the De Stijl architect J. J. P. Oud.[20] A scale model of one of Oud's buildings was included in that exhibit, and was displayed again three years later in the Atheneum's "Abstract Art" exhibit (1935), which also gave prominent attention to two other members of the De Stijl group: Cesar Domela and Piet Mondrian. As a member of the Atheneum, Stevens was likely to have been well versed in Dutch modernism.

So it is not surprising that, in 1942, Stevens was able to indulge his longing for Dutch tradition, and at the same time to establish his "relation to contemporary ideas" (L, 340), by conceiving "Notes" with the analogy of twentieth-century Dutch art in mind. The most famous living Dutch artist in 1942 was Mondrian (1872–1944), who, as a wartime refugee, was residing and working in New York City. Stevens had surely known of Mondrian for years, from his reading of European and American art publications, as well as from viewing Mondrian's paintings at the Wadsworth Atheneum and the Museum of Modern Art.[21] In any case, he could hardly have avoided encountering Mondrian in 1942. In that year Mondrian appeared in a virtual avalanche of group shows in New York.[22] He also had his first one-man show anywhere, the exhibition that "established his rapidly growing influence in America."[23] It opened at the Valentine Gallery in New York in January 1942, just at the time when Stevens conceived the idea of writing "Notes."[24] Although there is no evidence that Stevens attended this show, it seems likely that he knew of it and drew inspiration from it.

Mondrian was already a legendary figure in the art world of the 1940s, and certain aspects of his reputation suggest why Stevens would have been particularly drawn to him in 1942. He was, first of all, an utterly "pure" artist, who had systematically eliminated every trace of natural representation from his canvases. As a *New Yorker* profile put it in January 1942, his art represented "the absolute quintessence of abstract enjoyment."[25] This aspect of Mondrian surely appealed to Stevens, whose chief concern of the 1930s had been to "construct an aesthetic of 'pure poetry' "[26] and who gave to the third section of "Notes" the subtitle "It Must Give Pleasure."

"Pure" and detached as his art was, however, Mondrian's ideas had also given rise to artistic movements that changed the face of the modern world. "Piet Mondrian has had a widespread influence on the practical arts," proclaimed *Fortune* magazine in December 1941. "You can see the impact of Mondrian and the men of his school in books, magazines, posters, trademarks, linoleum, offices—even the table tops at Childs."[27] Robert M. Coates of the *New Yorker* made even greater claims for Mondrian's influence: "I suppose there is no other painter alive today whose effect on our daily lives has been as concrete and immediate as that of Piet Mondrian. The leader of the De Styl group of purist painters in Holland, which in turn inspired most of the new school of architectural design, he has influenced everything, from the shape of our modernist buildings down to furniture and posters."[28]

Mondrian was perhaps the chief living exemplar in 1942 of the Shelleyan artist who actually creates the world in which we live. His career could be cited as proof that, in Mondrian's own words, "pure art, even though it appear abstract, can be of direct utility for life."[29] This concept of the artist was particularly important to

Stevens' thinking at the time he was writing "Notes." As he put it in his essay "The Noble Rider and the Sound of Words" (1941), in a passage that obviously presages "Notes": "What makes the poet the potent figure that he is, or was, or ought to be, is that he creates the world to which we turn incessantly and without knowing it and that he gives to life the supreme fictions without which we are unable to conceive of it" (NA, 31). He might have had Mondrian in mind when he concluded, in a later essay, that the closest relation between poetry and painting is their common role as "sources of our present conception of reality" (NA, 176).

Mondrian's reputation as the virtual personification of the abstract movement may lie behind one of the most memorable images of "It Must Be Abstract." Mondrian was famous in the early 1940s for being "a spectacular devotee of solitary life," a "gentle hermit of almost seventy," living in a New York apartment that had an "almost monastic air of strict minimums."[30] It seems possible that this aspect of Mondrian's character inspired "Notes" I.ii:

> It is the celestial ennui of apartments
> That sends us back to the first idea, the quick
> Of this invention; and yet so poisonous
>
> Are the ravishments of truth, so fatal to
> The truth itself, the first idea becomes
> The hermit in a poet's metaphors,
>
> Who comes and goes and comes and goes all day
> . . . .
> The monastic man is an artist.

Here the abstract "first idea" is suddenly personified as "the hermit" or "monastic man" who inspires the poet's metaphors. (He reappears as the "vagabond in metaphor" in II.x.) This figure might well be a poetic record of suddenly finding the legendary Mondrian not only still alive and working in 1942, but living virtually next door.

Mondrian's reputation as the man who "has carried abstract art further than anyone else" points to a further affinity with "Notes."[31] For Stevens, Mondrian's radical aesthetics were a sign of his "integrity" and his status as a major artist, as we can see from this letter of 1949 in which he contrasts Jean Arp with Mondrian: "[Arp] knew Mondrian. . . . But he does not go along with Mondrian. It is nonsense to speak of his integrity as an abstractionist in the same breath with which one speaks of Mondrian. Arp is a minor stylist, however agreeable. But for Mondrian the abstract was the abstract" (L, 628). Stevens' tendency to think in radical terms in "Notes" is evident in both the stylistic idiosyncracy of this poem and the aesthetic program it proposes. I would argue that the most characteristic trope of "Notes" is its use of superlatives to indicate extremes of experience. A few characteristic examples should recall the frequency and importance of such tropes in "Notes": "The extremest book of the wisest man" (Prologue), "the grossest iridescence of ocean" (I.iii), "the loftiest antagonist" (II.ii), and "the difficultest rigor" (III.v). I would also include as "superlatives" in this sense such absolute phrases as "the final elegance" (I.x), "his zero green" (II.v), and of course the ubiquitous "first idea." Stevens had used such superlatives occasionally even in *Harmonium,* and with increasing frequency in the 1930s, but never so insistently and systematically as in "Notes." Here they are not simply stylistic elements but the most direct expression of the poem's leading point: like the concept of the "first idea," all these superlatives express the need to confront psychologically the extremest imaginable "test case" in order to establish the validity of a moral or aesthetic proposition. Stevens considered this way of thinking essentially poetic, and it was closely associated in his mind with the kind of abstraction for which Mondrian stood.

Thinking in terms of an extreme "test case" is one standard method of reasoning in moral philosophy. In particular, it is fundamental to existentialism whose focus on the extremes of experience is one modern answer to the desire for a lost absolute. Similarly, for Stevens the final test of value, in the absence of a God, was

"EXTRAORDINARY ACTUALITY" (L, 411), and his commonest example was the extraordinary actuality of war. As he summarized this concept at about the time he was writing "Notes": "In the presence of the violent reality of war, consciousness takes the place of the imagination" (OP, 206). It is at such times of existential insight, when the poet conceives the "first idea" without any coloring of imagination, or when the soldier acts in full awareness of the imminent possibility of death, that man is best able to judge true value in both art and life. Hence the close relationship between poet and soldier in the Epilogue to "Notes." Both fulfill their roles best in an atmosphere of war because it enforces the virtues of intensity and concentration: "The role of the writer in war remains the fundamental role of the writer intensified and concentrated" (OP, 310). It was just this sort of mind-clearing perception of concrete reality that Mondrian hoped to bring about through his minimalist art.

Critics have been puzzled by Stevens' use of the word *abstract* to denote such a process. B. J. Leggett summarizes the controversy surrounding this issue: "For readers who have placed Stevens' poetry on the reality side of the imagination-reality conflict, the title of the opening section of *Notes toward a Supreme Fiction* and Stevens' other references to the necessity of abstraction present an obstacle which can be surmounted only through a revision of the conception itself. Curiously, the definitions which result from this revision posit a meaning which is closer to *concrete* or *real* than to any accepted usage."[32] Among such critics Leggett includes Harold Bloom, J. Hillis Miller, Louis Martz, Frank Kermode, and Roy Harvey Pearce. My point here is not that these readers are wrong in interpreting the meaning Stevens assigns to *abstract,* but that Leggett is wrong to consider it so peculiar. Its oddness disappears in the context of the art world, where the use of "abstract" to mean "concrete" or "real" *is* accepted usage. As Alfred Barr explained in 1936, "An 'abstract' painting is really a most positively concrete painting since it confines the attention to its immediate, sensuous, physical surface far more than does the canvas of a sunset or a portrait."[33] So the magazine devoted to geometric abstraction that Theo van Doesburg founded in 1930 was called *Art concret,* and so Mondrian could write in 1942: "Some prefer the name 'Concrete' Art. Certainly, Abstract Art is concrete because of its determined means of expression, and even more than Naturalistic Art."[34] The further equation of abstraction with reality may be seen in the titles of two of Mondrian's essays: "Toward a True Vision of Reality" and "A New Realism." Stevens was familiar enough with this commonplace usage of the word *abstract* in the art world that it was a simple matter for him to adopt an analogous usage in "It Must Be Abstract."

In weighing the significance of such parallels between Stevens and Mondrian, we should not lose sight of the real differences that separate these two artists. It would be impossible, I think, to draw a convincing comparison between a Stevens poem and a classic Mondrian canvas. The rhetorical and metaphorical opulence of Stevens' poetry has no counterpart in the Dutch painter's starkly minimal style (fig. 15). Even Stevens' barest lyrics rely on traditional poetic figures in a way that Mondrian's nonrepresentational paintings strictly avoid. And Stevens' formal conservatism (his use of conventional metrics, his lack of interest in formal experimentation) has little to do with the utterly radical form of Mondrian's abstractions. How two artists, starting from similar premises about the nature of art, could arrive at such different forms of expression is a very interesting problem that is too complex to address here. Yet it is precisely these obvious differences in form and style that have kept us from seeing the more fundamental similarities in the realm of art theory that we are tracing here.

To realize that Stevens would have known Mondrian's reputation in the art world of 1942 contributes something to our understanding of "It Must Be Abstract." But there may also be a deeper and more direct connection between Mondrian's aesthetic theory and Stevens' achievement in "Notes" as a whole. Charles Altieri has called attention to certain parallels between "Notes" and Mondrian's essay "Plastic Art and Pure Plastic Art," published in

15. Piet Mondrian, *Composition in Blue and White* (1935). Oil on canvas, 41 x 38 in. Wadsworth Atheneum, Hartford, Conn.

Circle in 1937. This is the only essay of Mondrian's that was available in English prior to 1942, and it seems likely that Stevens read it.[35]

Certain general similarities between "Notes" and "Plastic Art and Pure Plastic Art" are evident from the very beginning of Mondrian's essay: "Although art is fundamentally everywhere and always the same, nevertheless two main human inclinations, diametrically opposed to each other, appear in the many and varied expressions. One aims at the *direct creation of universal beauty*, the other at the *aesthetic expression of oneself*, in other words, of that which one thinks and experiences. The first aims at representing reality objectively, the second subjectively. . . . Both the two opposing elements (universal-individual) are indispensable if the work is to arouse emotion."[36] Mondrian's didactic tone and aphoristic phrasing bear some resemblance to the opening of "Notes," which is conceived as a lecture to an "ephebe" and which tends to epigrammatic formulations such as "The first idea was not our own" (I.iv). But what is most striking, though we have read no further than this first paragraph, is that Mondrian's theory of abstract art is obviously neither purely formalist nor purely rationalist (like Stevens' generalized complaint against all abstraction). On the contrary, he states unequivocally that art has at least partly to do with self-expression and subjectivity, and that it must arouse emotion. The view of art summarized in this opening paragraph (and elaborated in the rest of Mondrian's essay) is not far removed from Stevens' three precepts for the creation of a supreme fiction. A basic dualism prevails in both cases: art is seen as the product of two opposing elements—the universal or objective ("It Must Be Abstract") and the individual or subjective ("It Must Change")—whose interaction arouses emotion ("It Must Give Pleasure.")

As Mondrian elaborates his theory, the points of comparison with "Notes" multiply. Although Mondrian aims to eliminate every reference to nature from his art, he nevertheless insists, like Stevens, on the fundamental relation between art and life: "In removing completely from the work all objects 'the world is not separated from the spirit,' but is on the contrary *put into a balanced opposition* with the spirit. . . . This creates a perfect unity between the two opposites. . . . Precisely on account of its profound love for things, non-figurative art does not aim at rendering them in their particular appearance" (60). The same dualistic way of thinking informs Stevens' famous declaration that poetry expresses "a violence from within that protects us from a violence without. It is the imagination pressing back against the pressure of reality" (NA, 36). For both men, the imagination is a force opposed to the pressure of external reality, and the artist's primary goal is to find the proper balance between these two forces.

Mondrian insists on believing that the balanced relations he perceives in life and attempts to express in his art are not simply "made" or "discovered" but are really "inherent in things": "For there are 'made' laws, 'discovered' laws, but also laws—a truth for all time. These are more or less hidden in the reality which surrounds us and do not change. Not only science, but art also, shows us that reality, at first incomprehensible, gradually reveals itself, by the mutual relations that are inherent in things" (52). In the same way, Stevens asserts in "Notes":

Perhaps there are times of inherent excellence,

As when the cock crows on the left and all
Is well, incalculable balances,
At which a kind of Swiss perfection comes

　　. . . not balances
That we achieve but balances that happen.

[I.vii]

Stevens' seemingly paradoxical demand that his supreme fiction (the artistic equivalent of these "times of inherent excellence") must not only "be abstract" but also "change" corresponds to Mondrian's conception of an art that must have "universal" significance yet not be "static": "First and foremost there is the fundamental law of *dynamic equilibrium* which is opposed to the static equilibrium necessitated by particular form. . . .The important task then of all art is to destroy the static equilibrium by establishing a dynamic one" (54, 57). To achieve "dynamic equilibrium" involves a two-part process: "Non-figurative art demands an attempt of what is a consequence of this task, the *destruction* of particular form and the *construction* of a rhythm of mutual relations. . . . It is of the greatest importance to note the destructive-constructive quality of dynamic equilibrium" (57). Stevens outlines a similar two-part creative process in "It Must Be Abstract": First the poet must destroy all preconceived ideas in order to get back to the "first idea"; then he must construct a new "idea of man" that will satisfy the requirements of his supreme fiction.

For Mondrian, the artist must adopt the role of "exponent of denaturalized nature, of civilization" because modern man has lost the ability to grasp unaided the abstract meaning in figurative art, and has not yet developed the ability to understand pure abstraction: "In past times when one lived in contact with nature and when man himself was more natural than he is today, abstraction from figuration in thought was easy; it was done unconsciously. But in our more or less denaturalized period, such abstraction becomes an effort" (58). Stevens analyzes exactly this problem in I.vi, which takes its starting point from Mondrian's italicized demand that *"the fixed laws of the plastic arts must be realized"* (52):

> Not to be realized because not to
> Be seen, not to be loved nor hated because
> Not to be realized. Weather by Franz Hals,
>
> Brushed up by brushy winds in brushy clouds,
> Wetted by blue, colder for white. Not to
> Be spoken to, . . . etc.[37]

This poem describes the poet's struggle to "realize" the fictive abstraction in exactly Mondrian's visual sense. As Stevens explains it in a letter: "The poem is a struggle with the inaccessibility of the abstract. First I make the effort; then I turn to the weather because that is not inaccessible and not abstract. . . . There is a constant reference from the abstract to the real, to and fro" (L, 434).

We may think of the constant shifting between subjective thought and objective weather in this poem as representing a dialogue between abstract and figurative art. It is also, in effect, a dialogue between Hals and Mondrian. For if the weather is represented by a Hals painting, then a Mondrian abstraction may well be the unstated analogy Stevens has in mind for "the inaccessibility of the abstract." Stevens knew the popular conception of Hals as an earthy realist, at home in a society of his fellows: "An insatiable drinker in a society of guzzlers, he painted, drunk or sober, with enormous vigor. . . . Hals portrayed people of all degrees and kinds, but was most successful with fishwives and tavern heroes."[38] Hals represented the "peasant" vitality that Stevens came increasingly to value in his later years. Mondrian, on the other hand, represented the opposite (and equally valuable) extreme of his Dutch heritage—the austere spirituality of Calvinist theology, the abstract tendencies of philosophical rationalism. In this canto the poet struggles to create a poem that is as thoroughly modern as a Mondrian abstraction, but without sacrificing the vitality of Hals' realism. He does this by maintaining a "constant reference from the abstract to the real, to and fro." He is attempting to "abstract reality, which he does by placing it in his imagination" (NA, 23).

"Plastic Art and Pure Plastic Art" describes the dynamics of art in ways which closely parallel "Notes." But the most striking aspect of that essay, and the point of its deepest affinity with "Notes," is its spiritual dimension. Mondrian's art springs directly from a desire to achieve a spiritual significance comparable to that of religion in previous centuries: "Today one is tired of the dogmas of the past, and of truths once accepted but successively jettisoned. One realizes more and more the relativity of everything, and therefore one tends to reject the idea of fixed laws, or a single truth. This is very understandable, but does not lead to profound vision" (52). Unable to accept the "dogmas of the past," Mondrian nevertheless refuses to give up what Stevens calls "the fiction of an absolute" (III.vii), making it in fact the central goal of his art, as he makes clear in "Plastic Art and Pure Plastic Art": "To love things in reality is to love them profoundly; it is to see them as a microcosmos. *Only in this way can one achieve a universal expression of reality.* Precisely on account of its profound love for things, non-figurative art does not aim at rendering them in their particular appearance" (60).[39] Similarly, Stevens at this time conceived of the artist as a "spiritual figure" (L, 378): "My own way out toward the future involves a confidence in the spiritual role of the poet, who will somehow have to assist the painter . . . in restoring to the imagination what it is losing at such a catastrophic pace, and in supporting what it has gained" (L, 340). He conceived of his supreme fiction as a "substitute for religion" (L, 348) and of his poetic task as "trying to create something as valid as the idea of God has been" (L, 435).[40] Abstraction was a means to this goal rather than an end in itself, just as it was for Mondrian.

This shared belief in the spiritual significance of art is an emphasis on the primacy of *content,* a fact that contradicts the popular view of Mondrian as an advocate of pure formalism. Mondrian's purpose in writing "Plastic Art and Pure Plastic Art" was to "clarify a little the *content* of art" [my italics].[41] He refers to that content variously as "universal beauty" or "objective reality," but it is always "abstract": "We repeat that its content cannot be described, and that it is only through pure plastics and through the execution of the work that it can be made apparent. Through this indeterminable content, the non-figurative work is 'fully human'" (61). When Stevens chose as his central subject a supreme fiction which also "cannot be described," he was setting himself an aesthetic objective directly analogous to Mondrian's abstract content.[42] Ironically, he was embracing abstract art theory for the same reason he had avoided it throughout the 1930s: because of its place in the contemporary argument over the relative importance of form and content. He had kept his distance from abstraction because he associated it with the purely formalist aesthetics of George L. K. Morris; now he was able to acknowledge his sympathy with the spiritual content of Mondrian's aesthetics, and therefore to come to terms with the abstract tendencies of his own art.

Stevens was well aware that his emphasis on content as the chief concern of modern poetry set him in opposition to most other contemporary poets in English: "Let me divide modern poetry into two classes, one that is modern in respect to what it says, the other that is modern in respect to form. The first kind is not interested primarily in form. The second is" (NA, 167–68). Stevens obviously included his own poetry in the first category, since he often declared himself "indifferent" to poetic form: "I have never felt that form matters enough to be controlled by it" (L, 817). The second category would include the poetry of William Carlos Williams, Ezra Pound, and virtually every experimental movement in modern poetry which conceived of innovation primarily in terms of form. It is significant that this aspect of Stevens' poetry, which sets him at the furthest remove from his poetic contemporaries, also represents his closest affinity with the aesthetic theory of Mondrian. In this respect, Stevens aligns himself with the abstract painters generally, who thought of Mondrian as the orthodox theorist of the movement. As James Thrall Soby wrote in 1941, in a book Stevens owned: "[The abstract movement] continues to thrive, nourished on Picasso's boundless energy, Mondrian's dogma, and Miro's inventiveness."[43] Mondrian's "dogma" seems to have nourished Stevens' poetic development as well, and this is surely part of what Stevens meant in declaring, "It Must Be Abstract."

Chapter 6

Rival Doctrines Harmonized

. . . it is not the reason
That makes us happy or unhappy.
—OP, 141

Stevens' engagement with Mondrian
in 1941–42 appears to have been
the chief catalyst that made possible
his achievement in "Notes." Identifying with his fellow Dutchman was
so inspiring to Stevens, I think,
largely because it enabled him to
come to terms with the highly intellectual quality of his own poetry. We
have seen that he thought of abstraction as his chief "danger" in the
1930s, that he thought of geometric
abstraction as a metaphor for *all* abstraction, and that he associated
geometric abstraction with rationalism. Therefore, when he declared
that "it must be abstract," he was
asserting, for one thing, that the
powers of the rational mind were an
essential aspect of the kind of poetry
he was now committed to writing.
So "major man"—spokesman ("exponent") for the "idea of man"—
"comes from *reason*." What Stevens

called "the cognitive element in poetry" (L, 500) had always been present in his work, from the depiction of cold rationality in poems like "The Snow Man" to the intellectual gamesmanship that links his poetry with the cerebral art of Marcel Duchamp. But from now on he embraced this aspect of his imagination confidently, without apology: "Supreme poetry can be produced only on the highest level of the cognitive," he declared in 1945 (L, 500). He made the same point in a letter of 1946: "If people are to become dependent on poetry for any of the fundamental satisfactions, poetry must have an increasingly intellectual scope and power. This is a time for the highest poetry" (L, 526).

So Stevens in later years became more comfortable explicating his own poems and, as Frank Doggett observes, "The later style has an air of explicit theorizing . . . the element of thought is brought more to the fore."[1] However, in asserting that poetry must have an abstract, rational component, Stevens was by no means abandoning his commitment to "the irrational element in poetry." On the contrary, the final section of "Notes"—"It Must Give Pleasure"—stresses the equal importance of the irrational. In this respect, it provides both a formal and a theoretical balance for the first section of "Notes," thereby harmonizing the rival doctrines of surrealism and abstraction.[2]

Mondrian's "dogma" accounts for the strict form and theoretical clarity that help make "Notes" Stevens' most successful long poem. But "Notes" itself is essentially undogmatic. The reader's chief impression, even in the beginning cantos of "It Must Be Abstract" which most clearly bear the traces of Stevens' original abstract scheme, is *not* of a carefully reasoned argument but of an exuberant imaginative energy. Stevens' choice of a rigid format seems, paradoxically, to have freed his imagination. The third canto, for instance, begins with the abstract, intellectual assertion that "The poem refreshes life so that we share, / For the moment, the first idea." But then, by way of example, the poet introduces the fantastic figure of the Arabian:

We say: At night an Arabian in my room,
With his damned hoobla-hoobla-hoobla-how,
Inscribes a primitive astronomy

Across the unscrawled fores the future casts,
And throws his stars around the floor . . . .

The shift from scholarly consideration of the "first idea" to the rhythmic nonsense-sounds of "hoobla-hoobla-hoobla-how," the combination of abstract discourse and earthy illustration, typifies the poetry of "Notes"—and much of Stevens' best poetry. The strength of this particular canto is that after four stanzas describing poetry in the loftiest terms ("An elixir, an excitation, a pure power"), Stevens takes up the challenge and creates a vividly original poetic figure that embodies (for the sympathetic reader) the very qualities he has just described. And he does this so casually that we share the exhilaration he must have felt in his own seemingly limitless creativity, as if his imagination could improvise countless other illustrations for our delight, all equally effective. "Notes" provides a series of such illustrations—Nanzia Nunzio, the Captain and Bawda, the Canon Aspirin, and so on—and I have already noted that their function in the poem is similar to that of pictures in an art exhibition. The point I want to make here is that our chief response to these inventions is not intellectual but emotional. We experience them with simple pleasure, and the source of that pleasure is purely irrational.

The third section of "Notes," "It Must Give Pleasure," stresses the role of the irrational in the creation of a supreme fiction, thereby balancing the initial emphasis on rationality in "It Must Be Abstract." And as Stevens had in mind the analogy of geometric abstract art at the beginning of "Notes," so he has in mind the analogy of surrealism in this concluding section. He begins "It Must Give Pleasure" by recalling the concept of the "first idea" from the beginning of "Notes," but shifting his focus from an objective, intellectual apprehension of the first idea to the poet's subjective, emotional response to it:

... the difficultest rigor is forthwith,
On the image of what we see, to catch from that

Irrational moment its unreasoning,
As when the sun comes rising, when the sea
Clears deeply, when the moon hangs on the wall

Of heaven-haven. These are not things transformed.
Yet we are shaken by them as if they were.
We reason about them with a later reason.

[CP, 398–99]

The poet's emotional reaction to these objective, external events turns out to be strangely close to his response to poetry: "These are not things transformed. / Yet we are shaken by them as if they were." This paradoxical notion fascinated Stevens, for he repeated it in "The Figure of the Youth as Virile Poet" when he referred to "things that seem to be poetry without any intervention on our part, as, for example, the blue sky" (NA, 59); and again in the same essay: "The world is a compact of real things so like the unreal things of the imagination that they are indistinguishable from one another" (NA, 65). When we perceive something in the external world that is utterly distinct from us (that is, perceive it in its first idea) and that, at the same time, seems invested with deep emotional significance, we are witnessing a momentary agreement between our subjective desires and objective fact: "Few people realize on that occasion, which comes to all of us, when we look at the blue sky for the first time, that is to say: not merely see it, but look at it and experience it . . . —few people realize that they are looking at the world of their own thoughts and the world of their own feelings" (NA, 65–66). The pleasure we experience at such moments is an eruption of unconscious emotion associated with the thing perceived. We are confronting, in Stevens' words, "a particular of life that we have thought of often, *even though unconsciously,* and that we have felt intensely in those crystallizations of freshness that we no more remember than we remember this or that gust of

wind in spring or autumn" (NA, 65–66; my italics). In such irrational moments the real and the imagined, the conscious and the
unconscious, are suddenly, effortlessly joined together. The troubling contradictions of our experience seem to be resolved, and we
feel ourselves in harmony with the world around us.

Stevens had long been fascinated by such irrational moments,
though he had not called them that, and he had not thought of
them as harmonious. In "Sombre Figuration" (1936)—Stevens'
poem about the subconscious, in which he consciously skirted the
boundaries of surrealism (L, 375)—such moments were sources of
disorder:

> Summer night,
> Night gold, and winter night, night silver, these
> Were the fluid, the cat-eyed atmosphere, in which
> The man and the man below were reconciled,
> The east wind in the west, order destroyed,
> The cycle of the solid having turned.
>
> [OP, 98]

Stevens glossed these lines for Hi Simons: "There are realities so
closely resembling the things of the imagination (summer night)
that in their presence, the realist and the man of imagination are
indistinguishable. This destroys the order of things" (L, 373). Here
the poet's experience of summer night—one example of what he
later called "irrational moments"—is threatening: it reconciles the
conscious and the unconscious, but only by destroying "the order
of things." In composing this passage, Stevens probably had in
mind the surrealists' reputation as "exponents of disorder."[3] By
the time he came to write "Notes," on the other hand, such "irrational moments" represented to him not chaos but the possibility
of a higher order. What seemed a problem in 1936 had become a
possible solution in 1942.

By focusing on the spontaneous harmony of such irrational
moments in "Notes," Stevens hoped to reduce the opposition between imagination and reality in his own poetic theory. And, as he
surely knew, he was also embracing one of the basic tenets of

surrealism. André Breton considered this point so fundamental to surrealist art theory, and so pertinent to the world situation in 1942, that he called special attention to it in a lecture at Yale, in December of that year, entitled "The Situation of Surrealism between the Wars":

> What I said in 1929, I believe now more than ever: "It is necessary to feel by all means, and to make known at all costs, the *artificial character of the old antinomies* . . . . Everything leads us to believe that there exists a certain point of the mind from which life and death, the real and the imaginary, past and future, the communicable and the incommunicable, high and low, cease to be perceived as contradictory." . . . For Surrealism—and I think this will be its glory someday—anything will have been considered good that could reduce these oppositions which have been presented as insurmountable.[4]

In "It Must Give Pleasure" Stevens sets himself the task of reducing precisely such oppositions, and this surrealist strategy climaxes in the Canon Aspirin's resolution in canto vi:

> He had to choose. But it was not a choice
> Between excluding things. It was not a choice
>
> Between, but of. He chose to include the things
> That in each other are included, the whole,
> The complicate, the amassing harmony.
>
> [CP, 403]

The trouble with such harmonious visions is that they can easily degenerate into merely "mystical rhetoric," something Stevens could not abide (OP, 228). This is the point of the next canto, where Stevens also seeks to establish his own distance from surrealism:

> But to impose is not
> To discover. To discover an order as of
> A season, to discover summer and know it,

To discover winter and know it well, to find,
Not to impose, not to have reasoned at all,
Out of nothing to have come on major weather,

It is possible, possible, possible. It must
Be possible.

[CP, 403–04]

In making this crucial distinction, "to impose is not / To discover," Stevens was defining his central poetic aims in opposition to what he considered "the essential fault of surrealism." This is clear from a notebook entry of 1940, which was published as part of Stevens' "Materia Poetica" in the Surrealist magazine *View* in 1942: "The essential fault of surrealism is that it invents without discovering. To make a clam play an accordion is to invent not to discover. The observation of the unconscious, so far as it can be observed, should reveal things of which we have previously been unconscious, not the familiar things of which we have been conscious plus imagination" (OP, 203).[5] Here Stevens is voicing a common complaint against surrealism—that despite its veneration of chance and the irrational, surrealist art is too often willful and calculating.[6]

Ironically, in recording his apparent lack of sympathy with surrealist art, Stevens was at the same time revealing his closeness to surrealist art *theory*. He shares the surrealist belief that the irrational is central to artistic creation. Compare another entry in "Materia Poetica": "Poetry must be irrational" (OP, 188). His only complaint is that surrealism is not irrational *enough*. This criticism applies not so much to Breton's theory as to the mechanical application of that theory by his less talented or less scrupulous disciples—like the publicity-mad Salvador Dalí—who tended to mistake any bizarre juxtaposition for a revelation of the unconscious. In contrast to such deliberate contrivance, Stevens' own "irrational moments," like Breton's surreal conjunctions, are by definition utterly spontaneous. They cannot be imposed, they must be discovered.

"Automatic" was the adjective the Surrealists applied to such spontaneous manifestations of the unconscious, and automatism was the chief technique that both the poets and the painters used to generate surreal imagery. "Pure psychic automatism" had been Breton's short definition of surrealism, and the Surrealists were largely responsible for popularizing the technique in art circles. Stevens, too, often used the word *automatic* in precisely this sense.[7] In focusing on this concept in "It Must Give Pleasure," Stevens was perhaps unwittingly putting his finger on the fundamental difference between two distinct branches of the Surrealist movement: veristic and absolute surrealism, to use Werner Haftmann's terminology.[8] Veristic surrealism is illusionistic; it distorts or oddly juxtaposes recognizable objects in order to create a kind of dream image or hallucinatory vision. The most extreme practitioner of veristic surrealism is Salvador Dalí. In such work automatism is secondary, as Stevens recognized when he observed, "To make a clam play an accordion is to invent not to discover." Absolute surrealism, on the other hand, is closer to Breton's notion of "pure psychic automatism." The chief exemplar of this mode is Joan Miró, whose basic procedure was to use chance occurrences or spontaneous gestures as a way of starting a painting and gaining access to the unconscious.[9]

The distinction between Dalí and Miró—the two Catalan surrealists—was a topic of great interest in the American art world of the early 1940s. In 1941, the Museum of Modern Art presented, simultaneously, exhibitions of both these artists. According to the art historian Barbara Rose, "The art magazines ran features on Miró vs. Dalí, as if it were the artistic competition of the century."[10] One effect of this dramatic juxtaposition of the two artists was that it helped "to clear up some misconceptions about the surrealist movement in general," as Robert M. Coates put it in the *New Yorker*. He spoke for Stevens as much as for himself when he observed that: "We tend too much, I'm afraid, to think of surrealism as a private manifestation of Dali's, a personal dream book to which he alone has the key, and hence to praise or blame it according to our feelings about Dali himself." The mistake of equating surrealism with Dalí is still prevalent in the popular mind even today. Stevens himself had made this mistake in his dismissive comments about the Museum of Modern Art's "Fantastic Art" exhibition in 1936: "Better fifty minutes of the Morgan Library than a cycle in the Surrealist Exhibition. The metaphysics of Aristotle embellished by a miniaturist who knew the meaning of the word embellishment knocks the metaphysics of Dali cold" (L, 315). He could not have held so narrow a view of surrealism in 1941. The dual exhibition at MOMA made it clear to everyone who followed the art world that surrealism was something larger and more important than the antics of Dalí. As Coates remarked, "The possibilities of the method are wide; how wide one has only to turn to this show to discover, for it would be hard to think of any other school large enough in its scope to include two such oddly dissimilar men as the pair who are featured in this show." [11]

It was largely because of this Miró/Dalí exhibition that the young American painters who would later become known as the Abstract Expressionists became interested in surrealism. As a group, these painters unanimously disdained Dalí. But they revered Miró, and when they began experimenting with surrealist automatism in the early 1940s, Miró was their chief model. [12] Here is one of them, Robert Motherwell, describing his own "automatic" painting technique, consciously adapted from Miró: "I begin a painting with a series of mistakes. The painting comes out of a correction of mistakes by feeling. I begin with shapes and colors which are not related internally nor to the external world; I work without images. Ultimate unifications come about through modulation of the surface through innumerable trials and errors. The final picture is the process arrested at the moment when what I was looking for flashes into view." [13]

If we imagine Motherwell's automatic process translated from the visual to the aural realm, it is very similar to Stevens' own "automatic" method of finding a poetic subject as he describes it in "The Irrational Element in Poetry":

I awoke once several hours before daylight and as I lay in bed I heard the steps of a cat running over the snow under my window almost inaudibly. The faintness and strangeness of the sound made on me one of those impressions which one so often seizes as pretexts for poetry. . . . [The poet] hears the cat on the snow. The running feet set the rhythm. There is no subject beyond the cat running on the snow in the moonlight. He grows completely tired of the thing, wants a subject, thought, feeling, his whole manner changes. All these things enter into the choice of subject. . . . All this is irrational.

(OP, 224, 227)

The artistic process is the same in both cases: The artist manipulates the artistic medium—colors and forms in the case of Motherwell; sounds and images in the case of Stevens—intently scrutinizing his own emotional responses, until suddenly, automatically, the desired subject manifests itself. We do not know what poem, if any, resulted from the above process, but we can be almost certain that it mentions neither a cat nor the snow.[14] Like Motherwell's method of painting, Stevens' poetic process is close in spirit to the automatism of the absolute surrealist Miró.[15]

The same automatic process is essential to Stevens' concept of the supreme fiction. Its creator will be a poet of exceptional intellectual power and emotional sensitivity, who both excels in abstract thought and delights in concrete pleasure. His experience of the harmonious "irrational moments" that are the focus of "It Must Give Pleasure" will provide the emotional analogy by which this greatest poet may ultimately recognize the supreme fiction.

The climax of this spiritual quest in "It Must Give Pleasure" occurs in canto viii, which begins with the question, "What am I to believe?"[16] Stevens' answer seems to be that the real experience of "irrational moments" is sufficient grounds for asserting the ultimate reality of human fulfillment:

Is it I then that keep saying there is an hour
Filled with expressible bliss, in which I have

> No need, am happy, forget need's golden hand,
> Am satisfied without solacing majesty,
> And if there is an hour there is a day,
>
> There is as month, a year, there is a time
> In which majesty is a mirror of the self:
> I have not but I am and as I am, I am.

We do not need "majesty" as solace because majesty is not beyond ourselves but *in* ourselves. The realization of our deepest desires—in the form of the hero, for instance, or of the supreme fiction itself—follows simply from the same union of the imagined and the real that we experience in seeing the blue sky.

From this proposition follows the resolution of the dichotomy that troubled Stevens in *Parts of a World:* the opposition between "the normal" (which he associated with still life) and the sublime (the concept of the hero). Canto ix recalls the monotonous birdsong which in II.vi created the desire for change. Here Stevens no longer chafes at the monotony of "mere repetitions," but takes pleasure in them:

> These things at least comprise
> An occupation, an exercise, a work,
>
> A thing final in itself and, therefore, good:
> One of the vast repetitions final in
> Themselves and, therefore, good, the going round
> And round and round, the merely going round,
> Until merely going round is a final good,
> The way wine comes at a table in a wood.

The wine in a wood—here representing a "final good"—is also shorthand for Stevens' vision of "the normal": "a lot of fat men and women in the woods, drinking beer and singing Hi-li, Hi-lo" (L, 352). Its occurrence at this point in "It Must Give Pleasure" signals the development of what Eleanor Cook calls the concept of "the normal sublime."[17] It means seeing the sublime *in* the normal. As Stevens put it, "To be able to see the portal of literature, that is to say: the portal of the imagination, as a scene of normal love and normal beauty is, of itself, a feat of great imagination" (NA, 155). He does this in "A Primitive Like an Orb," for example, describing the ideal life at "the center" as follows:

> What milk there is in such captivity,
> What wheaten bread and oaten cake and kind,
> Green guests and table in the woods and songs
> At heart . . . .
>
> [CP, 440]

Here the woodland celebration of "the normal" provides the spiritual satisfaction associated with the sublime. "The American Sublime" (1935) had ended with the questions "What wine does one drink? / What bread does one eat?" The frequent references to wine in "It Must Give Pleasure" provide the answer.[18] The mixture of the sacramental and the everyday in these occurrences is precisely the point. It is *pleasure* that unites the normal and the sublime, as Stevens makes clear in the ending of canto ix:

> And we enjoy like men, the way a leaf
> Above the table spins its constant spin,
> So that we look at it with pleasure, look
>
> At it spinning its eccentric measure. Perhaps,
> The man-hero is not the exceptional monster,
> But he that of repetition is most master.

Here the estranging distance between the elevated concept of the hero and the low-plane reality of still life, between the sublime and the normal, is easily and pleasantly bridged. The sense of nobility we long for to enrich our lives is available in the ordinary routine of daily life. The secret is a way of feeling: to "enjoy like men" is to experience a unity of imagination and reality equivalent to the harmonious vision of "irrational moments."

There is one danger in placing such emphasis on irrational mo-

ments as a possible solution to the conflict between imagination
and reality, or between the sublime and the normal: because it is
based on subjective feeling, it may lead only to an empty solipsism.
At the end of canto vii, Stevens seeks to counteract this possibility
by insisting on a goal of absolute realism:

> It must
> Be possible. It must be that in time
> The real will from its crude compoundings come,
>
> Seeming, at first, a beast disgorged, unlike,
> Warmed by a desperate milk. To find the real,
> To be stripped of every fiction except one,
>
> The fiction of an absolute . . . .
> [CP, 404]

The image of reality as a "beast disgorged" is typically surrealist,
and the seemingly paradoxical equation of "the real" with "an
absolute" is not far removed from Breton's basic definition of sur-
reality in the *First Manifesto of Surrealism:* "I believe in the future
resolution of these two states, dream and reality, which are
seemingly so contradictory, into a kind of *absolute reality*, a sur-
reality, if one may so speak" (my italics).[19]

This common search for an absolute led both Breton and Stevens to view aesthetic activity as equivalent to a mystical quest for
the divine. Stevens conceived of his supreme fiction as a substitute
for God, and Breton's attitude is clear from the following passage:
"[Surrealism] alone is the dispenser, albeit at intervals well spaced
out one from the other, of transfiguring rays of a grace I persist in
comparing in all respects to divine grace."[20]

Stevens' "irrational moments" at the beginning of "It Must Give
Pleasure" are precisely equivalent to these surreal "transfiguring
rays of grace." Both are moments of subjective experience so profoundly moving that we are shaken by them as if by a manifestation
of the divine.

Bearing in mind these parallels, we can see that Stevens' harmonious resolution of "Notes," in the beautiful concluding canto of "It Must Give Pleasure," also relates closely to surrealism. When the poet addresses the whole earth ("Fat girl, terrestrial") in intimate terms as "my summer, my night," we should recall that summer night was, for Stevens, one of those "realities so closely resembling the things of the imagination (summer night) that in their presence, the realist and the man of imagination are one" (L, 373). Canto x illustrates the transforming power of the "irrational moment[s]" with which "It Must Give Pleasure" began. Here the poet is suddenly able to experience a direct, personal relation between himself and the entire world, simply by means of "the more than rational distortion, / The fiction that results from feeling." The harmonious vision that ensues is appropriately surrealist in spirit:

> They will get it straight one day at the Sorbonne.
> We shall return at twilight from the lecture
> Pleased that the irrational is rational,
>
> Until flicked by feeling, in a gildered street,
> I call you by name, my green, my fluent mundo.
> You will have stopped revolving except in crystal.
>
> [CP, 406–07]

All of André Breton's surrealist theorizing—at the Sorbonne and elsewhere—was an attempt to demonstrate that "the irrational is rational," to systematize the workings of the unconscious. But like Stevens, Breton was a poet, and he therefore recognized the necessity of communicating not only intellectual ideas but also emotional pleasure. He would have been gratified to leave an audience not simply persuaded but "*pleased* that the irrational is rational," for that heightened emotional state is a necessary precondition for any genuine revelation.

Stevens' own prose description of his "mundo" represents a similar attempt to explain rationally an experience that is beyond the power of reason to conceive: "It is the mundo of the imagination in which the imaginative man delights and not the gaunt world of the reason. The pleasure is the pleasure of powers that create a truth that cannot be arrived at by the reason alone, a truth that the poet recognizes by sensation" (NA, 58).

By opposing the "mundo of the imagination" to the "gaunt world of the reason," Stevens aligns his "mundo" with the irrational. In this respect, the supreme fiction itself is essentially irrational, and therefore, in Stevens' experience, closely related to surrealism.

Stevens' harmonious vision in "Notes" parallels the changed mood of the New York art world during the early 1940s. World War II had brought to America many of the leading figures of *both* the abstract and the Surrealist groups. Herschel B. Chipp describes the effect of this European "invasion" on American artists: "The influx into New York of European artists . . . at the outbreak of war in Europe in 1939 ranks in importance second only to the Armory Show itself in the history of American art."[21]

Stevens' first mature poems had been written in New York during World War I, when he was able to draw inspiration from the exiled European artists and writers of the Arensberg salon. Now, during World War II, Europe's cultural loss was once again America's—and Stevens'—boon. As *Fortune* magazine reported in December 1941: "The migration that is coming to the United States today . . . may prove to be one of the most significant mass movements in history. . . . This is a transplantation of a whole culture from one continent to another."[22] The leaders of the German Bauhaus had already fled to America in the 1930s: László Moholy-Nagy, Walter Gropius, Josef Albers, Mies van der Rohe, Marcel Breuer, and others. Now virtually the whole European avant-garde came to join them in exile. Among these expatriates were André Breton, Max Ernst, André Masson, Yves Tanguy, Kurt Seligmann, Matta, Fernand Léger, Piet Mondrian, Marc Chagall, Lyonel Feininger, Naum Gabo, Amédée Ozenfant, Pavel Tchelitchew, and Jacques Lipchitz. "Though we may end this war rich in nothing else, it begins to look as if we'll at least be rich in artists" observed the *New Yorker* in 1941.[23] In an article that same year entitled "School of Paris Comes to U.S.," Sidney Janis announced that "New York is supplanting Paris as the art center of the world."[24] And the *Kenyon Review* was equally sure on this point: "The actual center of western culture is no longer in Europe. It is here."[25] Stevens' remarkable productivity in 1941–42 is almost certainly related to this fortunate state of affairs.

The effect of this new situation on the abstraction/surrealism debate was a movement toward harmony rather than opposition. In the context of World War II, the partisan squabbles of the 1930s came to seem less urgent. Civilization itself was now at stake, and former antagonists found themselves united against a common enemy. This development can be clearly seen in Peggy Guggenheim's famous Art of This Century, which opened in New York in October 1942. The gallery's interior space was divided equally into two specially designed exhibition areas, one devoted to surrealism and the other to abstraction. To express her "balanced impartiality between the two movements," Guggenheim wore to the opening "one abstract earring (a wire and metal mobile by Alexander Calder) and one surrealist earring (a tiny oval painting of a bone-strewn pink desert by Tanguy)."[26] Perhaps the most strikingly symbolic indication that the mood of the art world had changed utterly since the 1930s was the fact that Mondrian and Breton—the living embodiments of abstraction and surrealism, and presumed enemies during the 1930s in Paris—had several cordial and mutually respectful meetings in New York during the 1940s.[27] A group photo entitled *Artists in Exile,* probably taken in 1942 in Guggenheim's New York home, shows Breton and Mondrian posing together amid an amicable company of abstractionists and Surrealists (fig. 16).[28]

The shifting relations between abstraction and surrealism during the 1930s and early 1940s correspond in some ways to the dynamics of what Stevens called his "imagination-reality complex" (L, 792). In the troubled 1930s, when the intellectual climate was highly combative and "advanced" artists were on the defensive, they turned with relief to the bulwark of theory. The opposing

16. *Artists in Exile.* Photographer unknown. First row, 1. to r.: Stanley William Hayter, Leonora Carrington, Frederick Kiesler, Kurt Seligmann. Second row: Max Ernst, Amédée Ozenfant, André Breton, Fernand Léger, Berenice Abbott. Third row: Jimmy Ernst, Peggy Guggenheim, John Ferren, Marcel Duchamp, Piet Mondrian. Private collection.

theories of surrealism and of geometric-abstract art, each possessing the calm certainty of dogma, served as "Imaginary poles whose intelligence / Streamed over chaos their civilities" (CP, 479). The artists knew and appreciated how great a role theory played in promoting their welfare.

However, when the climate of the art world changed in the 1940s, the opposition between abstraction and surrealism, which only recently had represented a welcome sense of order, now

seemed a source of fruitless conflict. As the polarity lost its usefulness, the falseness of the two categories became more apparent.
Neither the dogmatic tenets of geometric abstract theory nor the
strict pronouncements of the Surrealist manifestoes had ever accurately described the broad range of artists and art works they
purported to represent. In fact, the two categories had always
overlapped, so that important artists like Miró, Picasso, and
Duchamp had been claimed by both camps. In this new situation,
artists and critics delighted in confusing the categories and flouting
all systematic theory. A good example is found in Sidney Janis'
influential *Abstract and Surrealist Art in America* (1944): "Although abstraction and Surrealism are considered counter-
movements in twentieth century painting, especially by the
painters themselves, tendencies in both often parallel each other
and at times overlap so that there is a fusion of elements from
each. . . . As a matter of fact, juxtaposing the abstract with the
Surrealist—pictures that purportedly spring from diametrically
opposed intentions—we find that these apparently antipodal
works resolve themselves into a group of contrasts and harmonies
that make a homogeneous ensemble."[29]

This pattern in the art world—an alternation between a passionate appreciation of theory and an equally passionate disregard
for it, accompanied in each case by the "exhilaration of changes"
(CP, 288)—is also the typical pattern of Stevens' imagination-
reality complex. "Sometimes I believe most in the imagination for
a long time and then, without reasoning about it, turn to reality
and believe in that and that alone. But both of these things project
themselves endlessly and I want them to do just that" (L, 747). So
Stevens delights in making dogmatic theoretical statements without being bound by them.[30] He asserts that artists should have "a
theory that validates what they do" (L, 763), but also insists that
"the last thing in the world that I should want to do would be to
formulate a system" (L, 864). He can entertain opposite ideas with
equal enthusiasm, depending on his mood, entitling one poem
"The Pure Good of Theory," for instance, and another "Not Ideas

about the Thing, but the Thing Itself." Confronted with such apparent inconsistencies, critics looking for a systematic philosophy in Stevens' writing may well conclude that he was not a serious thinker.

These seeming contradictions disappear, however, if we bear in mind the analogy of the art world. We have traced the shifting attitudes of "advanced" artists from the 1930s to the 1940s, from an emphasis on systematic theory to a reaction against it, from antagonism to cooperation. These changes were not simply a matter of superficial "taste." Nor did they occur in a vacuum. They were profound responses to a changed *reality*. So Stevens consistently stressed the "pressure of reality" as "the determining factor in the artistic character of an era and, as well, the determining factor in the artistic character of an individual" (NA, 22–23).

Stevens' habit of thinking in terms of "the pressure of reality" seems idiosyncratic in the realm of modern literature. But it expresses perfectly the common experience of modern painters, particularly the Abstract Expressionists who came to artistic maturity during the 1930s and early 1940s. When two of these artists, Robert Motherwell and Ad Reinhardt, edited *Modern Artists in America* (1951), they quoted Stevens in order to explain the recent ascendancy of abstract art: "This is where the 'pressure of reality,' in Wallace Stevens' phrase, has led the majority of our most imaginative and fertile artists: 'It is not that there is a new imagination but that there is a new reality.' To this might be added his preceding remarks: 'It is one of the peculiarities of the imagination that it is always at the end of an era. What happens is that it is always attaching itself to a new reality, and adhering to it.' It is this new reality, as it appears, that we want to document."[31]

Stevens' way of thinking—his "imagination-reality complex"— bears the lineaments of the art world, and it is especially compatible with the Abstract Expressionist movement. Because these artists shared with Stevens a common background in the rival theories of surrealism and abstraction, there are also other significant relations between their art and Stevens' poetry. But that is the subject of another chapter.

Part **Three**
Abstract Expressionism

Chapter 7

Stevens and the Abstract Expressionists

The American artists known as the Abstract Expressionists are notoriously difficult to discuss as a coherent group. They do not share a common style or method of painting, and critics disagree about which artists ought to be included in the movement. In attempting to define Stevens' relation to Abstract Expressionism, therefore—as I propose to do in these final chapters—it must first be acknowledged that this relation is many-sided, and that it is not possible to explore in depth each aspect of it. What I hope to do, in this chapter, is to provide a general outline of how Stevens' aesthetics intersect with those of the Abstract Expressionists. Chapter 8 will concentrate on a detailed analysis of the relation between Stevens' late poetry and the painting of one representative Abstract Expressionist, Jackson Pollock.

I have not attempted to present a full history of Abstract Expressionism, but have chosen to focus only on parallels that are central to Stevens' poetry and aesthetic theory. To an art historian, therefore, my discussion of Abstract Expressionism will seem in some respects highly selective and idiosyncratic. The advantage of this approach is that it will afford readers who are familiar with Stevens, but not with art history, a secure foothold where they most need it. I have tried to answer the question, What did these artists think of Wallace Stevens? Whenever possible, I have sought to include documentary evidence of Stevens' reputation among the painters and critics of the New York School. In this respect, my focus in this chapter is the *reverse* of my focus in chapters 1 through 6. Instead of tracing what Stevens thought of the art world, I am tracing what the art world thought of *him*. What I hope will emerge from the wide-ranging set of parallels in this chapter is a sense of Stevens' unusually close affinity with the Abstract Expressionists' ways of thinking about art, and of his important place in their cultural milieu.

The Abstract Expressionists came to artistic maturity during the 1930s and 1940s; and they did so, like Stevens, in the context of abstraction and surrealism. One of the first critics to note that a distinctively American movement was emerging out of this Parisian polarity was Robert Coates, who wrote in the *New Yorker* in 1944: "There is a style of painting gaining ground in this country which is neither Abstract nor Surrealist, though it has suggestions of both. . . . I feel that some new name will have to be coined for it, but at the moment I can't think of any."[1] It has since become a critical commonplace that Abstract Expressionism developed out of a synthesis of abstract and surrealist elements. The artists themselves were aware of their debt to these rival European movements, and their attitude toward this heritage was ambivalent. During the 1930s, American abstract artists had been labeled "derivative" because they aligned themselves with the European modernists rather than with the American realist tradition. Therefore, when Abstract Expressionism finally achieved recognition as a significant movement in its own right, many of these artists were more concerned to stress its originality than to point out its European roots. George McNeil, for example, although stressing the role of the unconscious in his own painting, nevertheless firmly denies the importance of surrealism in the development of Abstract Expressionism.[2] And Barnett Newman, whose most characteristic canvases seem on first viewing very close to the geometric-abstract tradition, actually conceived his series *Who's Afraid of Red, Yellow, and Blue* (which uses only rectangular shapes and primary colors) as a deliberate challenge to Mondrian's purist dogma.

Other painters cheerfully acknowledged their relation to surrealism and abstraction. Here, for example, is Adolph Gottlieb writing about Arshile Gorky—one abstract expressionist describing another: "As for a few others, the vital task was a wedding of abstraction and surrealism. Out of these opposites something new could emerge. . . . These are the opposite poles in his work. Logic and irrationality; violence and gentleness; happiness and sadness; surrealism and abstraction. Out of these elements I think Gorky evolved his style."[3] In the same way, Robert Motherwell's description in 1944 of his own *Spanish Prison (Window)* shows that he consciously thought of his own artistic development in terms of the abstraction/surrealism dichotomy: "[This picture represents] a dialectic between the conscious (straight lines, designed shapes, weighed color, abstract language) and the unconscious (soft lines, obscured shapes, *automatism*) resolved into a synthesis which differs as a whole from either."[4] The Abstract Expressionist movement is so diverse that no simple scheme can accurately describe it. But many, if not most, of the artists would probably have agreed with Mark Rothko's judicious summing up of their relation to abstraction and surrealism: "I quarrel with surrealist and abstract art only as one quarrels with his father and mother; recognizing the inevitability and function of my roots, but insistent upon my dissension: I, being both they, and an integral completely independent of them."[5]

It is in their theoretical statements about their art that the relation between these artists and Stevens is clearest. This fact alone is significant. Prior to the 1930s, as Dore Ashton has remarked, American artists were "not theorists at all, not even artistically." Given this antitheoretical tradition, it is remarkable that the Abstract Expressionists were able to articulate an aesthetic theory at all: "Europeans such as Courbet or Manet had a general cultural and political foundation which equipped them to separate out the issues and to formulate a fairly coherent artistic position. Americans had no comparable culture and were slow to enunciate even a rudimentary aesthetic."[6] When, in the 1930s, the pressure of reality (to use Stevens' term) at last provoked these artists into a theoretical response, it was chiefly the Surrealist movement that served them as a model. André Breton's widely disseminated manifestoes, with their persuasive rhetoric and impressive intellectuality, were a constant reminder of the vital role that art theory could play in creating an art movement. When the famous Surrealist journal *Minotaure* ceased publication in 1939, most of its contributors soon found themselves at home in its successor, *View,* which began publication in America in 1940. Stevens was associated with *View* from the start: its very first issue featured an interview with him on its front page, and also included (on page 3) a collection of epigrams from Stevens' notebooks entitled "Materia Poetica."[7] Those artists who were drawn to the surrealist end of the artistic spectrum were also likely to be drawn to Stevens because of his "unflagging faith in the romantic imagination," as Dore Ashton puts it.[8] But like Stevens, these artists also rejected certain aspects of surrealism. What the Americans found objectionable in surrealism is typified by this passage from a letter by Gorky, who was deeply influenced by surrealism early in his career: "Surrealism is an academic art under disguise and anti-aesthetic and suspicious of excellence and largely restrictive because of its narrow rigidity. . . . Really [the Surrealists] are not as earnest about painting as I should like artists to be."[9] Similarly, George McNeil observes that "there never was a style that was more contrived than surrealism."[10] This is essentially the same fault Stevens found with surrealism when he called it "so inconsequential in the restrictions of a technique, so provincial" (OP, 232) and when he complained that "it invents without discovering" (OP, 203). We have seen that this fault does not apply to the absolute surrealism of Miró. The important point, however, is that Stevens' judgment is not simply ignorant or idiosyncratic. On the contrary, it corresponds to one widely held view among the avant-garde artists of the time.

Ultimately, the Surrealist movement was not serious enough to satisfy the American painters. It lacked *earnestness:* "The modification [in surrealism] which eventuated in an identifiable point of view called abstract expressionism, was wrought by artists who, like Gorky, could not finally accept the element of play in surrealist life. Earnestness was essential to the abstract expressionist project, and although it certainly was subtly present in the European surrealists, it could not be discerned by their more sober American acolytes."[11] The abstract expressionist painter Lee Krasner confirmed this observation when she told Francis V. O'Connor that she and Jackson Pollock were annoyed by the silliness of the Surrealists, detesting such antics as "playing games about dressing their wives."[12] Stevens surely also would have found such behavior tiresome and frivolous. His earnestness about the role of art in life is one of the most striking characteristics of *The Necessary Angel* (1952).

If the Abstract Expressionists missed earnestness in surrealism, they, like Stevens, found it in the figure of Piet Mondrian. Mondrian is now so generally considered a towering figure in the history of modern art that it is important to recall that this was not always so. Stevens' interest in the Dutch artist was shared by only a few avant-garde artists in 1942. Thomas Hess points out that while Mondrian was held in high regard by such American painters as de Kooning, Pollock, Rothko, Kline, and Guston, he was "all but ignored by their colleagues in Paris, London, and Rome . . . . When I first visited the Musée d'Art Moderne in Paris in 1949, I was amazed that Mondrian was not represented in its collection—after all, the artist had spent the greater part of his maturity in Paris. In New York's Museum of Modern Art, where my generation learned its chronology of vanguards, Mondrian was always allocated a key spot. Jean Cassou, the brilliant novelist, poet, friend of artists, and director of the Paris museum, did not seem in the least disturbed by this gap when I mentioned it. 'Oh, we knew Mondrian well,' he said. 'I used to see him regularly— around Montparnasse.' About ten years later, a commercial gallery exhibited a series of Mondrian's tree and harbor pictures, very few of which had ever been seen in Paris. The exhibition met with a resounding silence. Meanwhile, in New York in the 1940s and 1950s, Mondrian was on everyone's lips."[13]

If the Europeans tended to ignore Mondrian, the American artists venerated him. George McNeil's attitude is typical: "I love the purity, the exaltation in his work. In Mondrian's finished work, nothing could be added, nothing could be taken away. Looking at his paintings in that room at the Museum of Modern Art is like going to a chapel."[14] The Abstract Expressionists emulated Mondrian's seriousness of purpose and personal integrity.[15] They did not imitate his art, but rather his attitude toward art. We might say that the example of Mondrian served the same purpose for Stevens, who aspired in poetry to the kind of spiritual purity that Mondrian represented. We have seen how important Mondrian's presence in New York was to Stevens' development during the war years. In this respect, too, his career closely parallels that of the American artists.

Against Isolationism

Since Stevens and the Abstract Expressionists shared an intellectual climate in which the same basic categories of thought prevailed, it is not surprising to find that certain of the artists felt a particular kinship with Stevens. One thing they obviously had in common with him was their internationalist bias, which put them in direct conflict with the dominant trends in American art. During the 1930s, regionalism or "American Scene" painting held the field; the Museum of Modern Art ignored the American modernists, showing instead the work of Thomas Hart Benton, John Stuart Curry, and Grant Wood alongside the latest examples of European surrealism and abstraction. Regionalism still seemed the dominant American mode in 1942, when the future Abstract Expressionist Barnett Newman composed a polemical essay entitled "What about Isolationist Art?" Newman's argument was that, although Pearl Harbor had effectively ended American isolationism in the political sphere, the isolationist attitude still prevailed in the art world: "Art in America is an isolationist monopoly."[16] Opposed to this monopoly was at least one prominent figure who had remained aloof from the cultural chauvinism between the wars: Wallace Stevens. With the outbreak of World War II and America's forced entry into international affairs, Stevens' fundamentally consistent aestheticism—which had caused him to feel so isolated and embattled during much of the 1930s—now seemed a positive guarantee of his artistic integrity. Newman certainly thought of Stevens as a kindred spirit in the artists' fight against American isolationism, as this unpublished letter shows:

February 22, 1943

Mr. Wallace Stevens
222 East 57 Street
New York, N.Y.

Dear Mr. Stevens:

We are organizing to fight isolationist "art."

We believe that isolationism is more than a political clique. It is a cultural movement that is crushing American art and literature with its "American Scene" aesthetique. No victory against isolationism is possible unless this false art movement with its regionalisms, journalisms, and cheap nationalism is exposed.

We feel that the time is now. We are anxious to enlist your leadership to rally the creative writers so that we may clear the cultural atmosphere of America in order that young artists will have a free atmosphere in which to create.

May we call on you to discuss this matter in detail?
>Sincerely,
>Barnett Newman, Chairman
>COMMITTEE AGAINST ISOLATIONIST "ART"
>343 East 19 Street
>New York, N.Y.[17]

This letter is an important document in the history of American art and literature. It substantiates Dore Ashton's observation that American culture—traditionally marked by "the total isolation of the different arts"—achieved a new cohesiveness sometime during the 1940s that was partly the result of, partly a necessary precondition for, the rise of Abstract Expressionism.[18] One of the distinguishing characteristics of the New York School in its full flowering would be the ease with which its poets and painters intermingled. In this changing situation Stevens played a central role: "Wallace Stevens [was] the one American poet with whom the artists could identify . . . largely because he was the only poet who could identify with them. Unlike most of his contemporaries, Stevens had accepted the French traditions that made the poet the natural ally of the painter. Throughout his poetry and criticism, he alluded to the art of the painter as equal to his own and—more important— as springing from the same imaginative sources. Painters, who often saw themselves somewhat as their society saw them—as useless and craft-ridden supernumeraries to real culture—were given a measure of self-esteem in the deference paid them by this poet."[19]

Newman's letter is historically significant as one of the earliest direct gestures of solidarity between this group of artists and their literary counterparts. Yet, even as it illustrates the painters' feeling of kinship with Stevens, it also reveals the great distance that separated American artists and intellectuals at this time. For although Newman wrote out of a genuine desire for community, in practical terms his letter was entirely ineffective. There is no indication that Stevens ever received it, which is not surprising since it was sent to the wrong address. (Apparently Newman had consulted the

New York telephone directory for 1943, which lists a "Stevens, Wallace"—presumably someone else with the same name—at the above address.) Newman obviously knew little about Stevens the man at this time, however much he admired him as a poet, or he would not have asked so private a person to take a leading role in his proposed movement. But the clearest evidence that Newman's confident tone in this letter was largely wishful thinking is supplied by his widow, who remarks that the Committee against Isolationist "Art" probably never existed! Newman would quickly have drafted members if Stevens had responded positively to his call, but his committee had no more existence as a real movement than did the Abstract Expressionists themselves in 1943.[20]

The Myth Makers

A mythological form, festival sphere,
A great bosom, beard and being, alive with age.
—CP, 466

The issue of America's cultural chauvinism concerned all advanced artists in the early 1940s. Witness the formation, in 1940, of the American Federation of Modern Painters and Sculptors, which declared: "We condemn artistic nationalism which negates the world tradition of art at the base of modern art movements."[21] In connection with its Third Annual Exhibition in June 1943— four months after Newman had composed his letter to Stevens— the federation stressed again its internationalist position: "As a nation we are now being forced to outgrow our narrow political isolationism. Now that America is recognized as the center where artists of all the world meet, it is time for us to accept cultural values on a truly global plane."[22] The historical significance of this exhibition is that it provoked an open confrontation between these artists and the backward American critical establishment. The *Times* reviewer's bewildered response to the art on display finally goaded Adolph Gottlieb and Mark Rothko into composing one of the first public statements explaining the theoretical basis of Abstract Expressionism. Their letter to the *Times* illustrates how close their artistic concerns were to those of Stevens.

The *Times* reviewer had written, "You will have to make of Marcus Rothko's 'The Syrian Bull' what you can; nor is this department prepared to shed the slightest enlightenment when it comes to Adolph Gottlieb's 'Rape of Persephone.'"[23] The two artists responded in a letter to the editor that sets forth their aims during this early stage in the development of Abstract Expressionism: "It is an easy matter to explain to the befuddled that 'The Rape of Persephone' is a poetic expression of the essence of the myth; the presentation of the concept of seed and its earth with all its brutal implications: the impact of elemental truth. . . . It is just as easy to explain 'The Syrian Bull' as a new interpretation of an archaic image, involving unprecedented distortions."[24] The titles alone of Gottlieb's and Rothko's paintings express their preoccupation with mythology, an interest they shared with Newman, who helped them compose this letter. (Newman would soon be painting similar works—for example, his *The Slaying of Osiris* and *The Song of Orpheus,* both of 1944.) We may take these three painters to represent a number of the Abstract Expressionists— including Robert Motherwell, Jackson Pollock, Richard Pousette-Dart, William Baziotes, Theodore Stamos, and Clyfford Still— who, during the mid-1940s, referred to ancient myths in their art, often giving their paintings mythic titles. These "Myth Makers" (to use the term Mark Rothko coined for them in 1946) were consciously extending into new territory—the realm of pure abstraction—the Surrealists' interest in a "New Mythology." André Breton called for a "new myth" in the two American surrealist publications *View* and *VVV* in 1942.[25] At the same time, Stevens was outlining his own plan for a new myth—"Notes toward a Supreme Fiction"—whose purpose was, quite simply, "to create something as valid as the idea of God has been" (L, 435). This highly romantic aspect of Stevens' poetry has always seemed stubbornly idiosyncratic when considered in the context of his poetic contemporaries. But it corresponds perfectly to the chief purpose of the Abstract Expressionists, which was to restore a sense of spiritual grandeur to a contemporary world impoverished by the failure of the old mythologies.

Part of the Abstract Expressionists' desire for a new mythology involved reference to older myths, as in the painting titles quoted above, or as in Stevens' reference to his muse as the "sister of the Minotaur" in "The Figure of the Youth as Virile Poet" (NA, 39–67). The point of such allusions was not to revive the old myths, as Mark Rothko explained: "If our titles recall the known myths of antiquity, we have used them again because they are eternal symbols. . . . They are the symbols of man's primitive fears and motivations, no matter in what land, at what time, changing only in detail but never in substance."[26] This archetypal view of mythology, which attributes universal significance to certain human tales, reflects Jung's theory of the collective unconscious, a topic current in the art world of the 1940s. "Jung was available in the air," recalls the Abstract Expressionist Fritz Bultman, "there was general talk [about his theories] among the painters."[27] Stevens, too, often entertains ideas very close to the Jungian concepts of archetypes and the collective unconscious, as various critics have shown.[28]

Most recently, Joseph Carroll has noted that the figure of the "subman" in "Owl's Clover" (1935–36) must be understood in terms of Jung's theories rather than Freud's. "[The subman is] a personification of the subconscious as a source of archetypal images . . . [and] an important stage in the development of Stevens' theory of pure poetry as a poetry of mythic vision."[29] The very notion of a supreme fiction in which all men could believe depends fundamentally on this way of thinking.

The archetypal view of mythology became more important to the Abstract Expressionists the more purely abstract their art became. As the artists began searching their unconscious minds for imagery that would be both intensely personal and utterly without reference to the external world, their underlying faith was that such imagery—if genuine—would communicate profound emotion to the viewer because it derived from some primal, universal experience. This intensely inward focus of Abstract Expressionism corresponds to Stevens' increasing poetic interest in the experience of consciousness itself. The painters' interior explorations were not solipsistic but were aimed at recapturing the essential power of myth. As Newman put it, "The self, terrible and constant, is for me the subject of painting."[30] The apt subtitle of Milton Bates' study of Wallace Stevens—*A Mythology of Self*—might be used equally well to describe the central goal of the Abstract Expressionists.

As their canvases became more abstract, the Abstract Expressionists' early references to myth became more generalized. Instead of alluding to particular ancient myths, Newman would title one enormous abstraction *Vir Heroicus Sublimis;* and both Jack Tworkov and Grace Hartigan did paintings titled simply *The Hero.* Similarly, in what Carroll calls "the visionary mythology" of *The Auroras of Autumn,* Stevens calls his archetypal characters simply "the father" and "the mother."[31] By presenting such mythic archetypes in abstract form, he was developing the approach to myth he had broached in the first canto of "Notes toward a Supreme Fiction":

> Phoebus is dead, ephebe. But Phoebus was
> A name for something that never could be named.

Barnett Newman echoed this idea when, in 1946, he labeled the painters' abstract symbols "Ideographs," citing a dictionary definition: "a character, symbol, or figure which suggests the idea of an object without expressing its name."[32] Harold Rosenberg, writing in *View* in 1943, quoted Stevens' lines about Phoebus with approval, praising the poet's attitude as something "rare in our time":

> Stevens will not accept a revived myth. No Orpheus, no angels.
>
> > How clean the sun when seen in its idea,
> > Washed in the remotest cleanliness of a heaven
> > That has expelled us and our images.
>
> > The death of one god is the death of all.

And he grasped how easily Stevens' aesthetic program might be related to the visual arts: "Stevens' Fiction has relatives by Picasso."[33]

The Subjects of the Artist

The Abstract Expressionists' interests in myth and automatism stemmed, ultimately, from their insistence on the vital importance of *subject matter,* a seemingly paradoxical demand from painters who also insisted on nonrepresentation. Rothko and Gottlieb made this point in their 1943 letter to the *New York Times*: "We assert that the subject is crucial and only that subject matter is valid which is tragic and timeless. That is why we profess kinship with primitives and archaic art."[34] When, in the fall of 1948, several of the painters—William Baziotes, David Hare, Robert Motherwell, Barnett Newman, and Mark Rothko—opened their own art school, they called it "Subjects of the Artist." The name was meant "to emphasize that abstract art, too, has a subject, and . . . the curriculum consisted of the subjects that interest advanced artists."[35] Precisely the same impulse inspired Stevens to suggest in 1940 that his wealthy friend Henry Church ought to endow a Chair of Poetry specifically to study the *subjects* of poetry: "What is intended is to study the theory of poetry in relation to what poetry has been and in relation to what it ought to be. . . . The subject matter of poetry is the thing to be ascertained" (L, 377).

We have seen Stevens' insistence on abstract content, a tenet he shared with Mondrian as well as with the Abstract Expressionists. The subjects that interested them were self-consciously heroic, as the highly serious tone of their pronouncements indicates. This marks their closest affinity to Stevens. If, as Milton Bates has observed, "Stevens has little company among modern poets in giving serious attention to the hero," he has plenty of company among these modern painters.[36] Most often they thought of the *tragic* hero as their ideal, as in Rothko's painting *Antigone* or Gottlieb's *Oedipus,* or in Rothko's more generalized description of his own *Omen of the Eagle* as representing "The Spirit of Myth . . . a single tragic idea."[37] Stevens also sought "tragic and timeless" subject matter in such major poems of the 1940s as "Esthétique du Mal" (1944), which views life from the perspective of tragedy; "The Owl in the Sarcophagus" (1947), which proposes a "mythology of modern death"; "The Auroras of Autumn" (1947), whose title image (the aurora borealis) was meant to convey a "tragic and desolate background" (L, 852); and "A Primitive Like an Orb" (1948), with its elevated conception of the "primitive."

In deliberately choosing to address traditionally lofty subject matter, these painters were reversing one of the major trends of modern art, the preference given to formerly "lowly" genres like landscape and still life. Their heroic view of art led them, instead, to revive the romantic concept of the *sublime*, which ranks grandeur of conception and nobility of spirit above beauty of form. The currency of this term in Abstract Expressionist circles is exemplified by the forum "What Is Sublime in Art?" published in the magazine *Tiger's Eye*.[38] Stevens, too, uses the term *sublime* in his poetry, sometimes ironically (as in "A High-Toned Old Christian Woman"), sometimes not (as in "Esthétique du Mal" and "The Sail of Ulysses"). His use of the word at all is unusual for a modern poet and, combined with his lofty conception of poetry as one of "the sanctions of life,"[39] it supports Harold Bloom's version of Stevens as the culmination of the romantic tradition. Stevens' heroic idea of the artist, and his preoccupation with the concept of nobility, link him more closely to contemporary painters than to contemporary poets. This kinship was commemorated at the Mark Rothko retrospective exhibition at the Guggenheim Museum in 1978, when Stevens' poem "The American Sublime" served as epigraph to the catalogue. Diane Waldman, curator of that exhibition, selected this poem because it raises issues central to Rothko and to the Abstract Expressionists in general, and because Stevens himself was so admired among the Abstract Expressionists she knew.[40]

THE AMERICAN SUBLIME

How does one stand
To behold the sublime,
To confront the mockers,
The mickey mockers
And plated pairs?

When General Jackson
Posed for his statue
He knew how one feels.
Shall a man go barefoot
Blinking and blank?

But how does one feel?
One grows used to the weather,
The landscape and that;
And the sublime comes down
To the spirit itself,

The spirit and space,
The empty spirit
In vacant space.
What wine does one drink?
What bread does one eat?

Longing to "behold the sublime," the poet is thwarted by the hostile or uncomprehending attitudes of his contemporaries. His situation is one with which the Abstract Expressionists were only too familiar. From this embattled position, Stevens poses the central question that preoccupied the American painters as well: What *subject* is possible for modern art? "The sublime" in Stevens' poem represents the desired subject that is both an abstraction and a feeling. As Ronald Sukenick remarks: "The ideal he pursues is a certain experience, and comes down to a way he sometimes feels."[41] How does a twentieth-century American artist invoke the sublime, the poem asks, without religious rituals or social traditions to buttress "the empty spirit / In vacant space"? Rothko's abstract canvases are one possible answer. Stevens' poetry is another.

Formalism: Clement Greenberg

By insisting on the primacy of subject matter, the Abstract Expressionists were also going against another main current in modern art: the ascendancy of formalism in art criticism. The English painter-critic Roger Fry laid the foundation for formalist criticism in the 1910s when, in trying to explain the innovations of the post-impressionists, he came to the conclusion that "the essential aesthetic quality has to do with pure form."[42] He soon developed (along with his disciple Clive Bell) a method of analyzing art solely according to its formal characteristics. In this view, subject matter was irrelevant to aesthetic considerations. Formalist art theory was attractive because it could be applied democratically to any work, from any period or culture, no matter what the subject and no matter how abstractly it was treated. The influence of formalism spread rapidly as modern art developed further and further away from the European tradition of representational art. By the time Rothko and Gottlieb wrote their letter to the *New York Times,* they were reacting against the new situation this development had created in the art world: "It is a widely accepted notion among painters that it does not matter what one paints as long as it is well painted. This is the essence of academicism. There is no such thing as a good painting about nothing."[43]

It is one of the ironies of modern art history that the most influential critic of the New York School—Clement Greenberg—was (and is) perhaps the most extreme formalist of them all. In his view, the painters' interest in subject matter—no matter how sincere—was entirely irrelevant to their artistic success. The only problems that concerned him were those of form. "The history of avant-garde painting is that of a progressive surrender to the resistance of its medium," wrote Greenberg in 1940, reducing the painters' concerns to the relations of paint to canvas and picture-plane, and ignoring their spiritual intentions. And his view of the history of abstract art soon became the orthodox version.

In the realm of modern literature, a similar tendency to emphasize form is evident in the ascendancy of the New Criticism from the 1930s through the 1950s, and in the formal experimentation that has characterized most avant-garde poetry in English since the 1910s. Although Stevens is in many ways the most modern of poets, he always felt at odds with literary formalism, even as the Abstract Expressionists were at odds with Greenberg's formalist approach to art. In his 1951 lecture "The Relations between Poetry and Painting," Stevens divided modern poetry into categories according to this distinction: "Let me divide modern poetry into two classes, one that is modern in respect to what it says, the other that is modern in respect to form. The first kind is not interested primarily in form. The second is. . . . The division between the two classes . . . is the same division into factions that we find everywhere in modern painting" (NA, 167–69). Stevens naturally included his own poetry in the first category. What is most striking about this passage, however, is that few other contemporary poets would have thought to divide poetry into these categories at all.[44] Stevens was using classifications that were current in the art world, not the world of poetry. The question of form versus subject was simply not an issue in literary circles in 1951. Virtually all the vital movements in poetry, from imagism onward, had been concerned primarily with formal innovations. "Modernism" in poetry had become virtually synonymous with formal experimentation. Stevens' way of thinking in this passage seems, from the point of view of modern poetry, at best quaintly old-fashioned, at worst complacently uninformed. If we consider this lecture in the context of the art world, on the other hand—recalling that it was delivered at the Museum of Modern Art—Stevens' remarks suddenly take on an immediacy and relevance appropriate to the occasion. His nonformalist views align him squarely with the Abstract Expressionist painters.[45]

It is possible to recognize parallels between Stevens' poetry and abstract expressionist painting even within the context of strict formalism. J. Hillis Miller long ago compared them in terms of a common use of shallow "space": "As in the paintings of abstract expressionism, [so in Stevens' poems] there is no 'beyond' to which the images refer, and they do not appear to exist against a background which exceeds them and goes backward into invisible distances."[46] Similarly, the critic Ruth Field, writing in the Abstract Expressionist magazine *trans/formation,* cited Stevens' poetry as the literary equivalent of the "flat landscape" in the art of Baziotes, Pollock, and Rothko.[47] For a fuller understanding of this relationship, however, we must look beyond the formalist bias of much existing art criticism.

Antiformalism: Fairfield Porter

The chief fault of Clement Greenberg's critical approach is his dogmatism. Very early he began pronouncing strict rules about what was and was not permissible in art at that historical moment. Since he was interested primarily in the continuing development of the *abstract* tradition, he was particularly hostile toward surrealism and the "impure" trends it represented. "Literary" became a term of disparagement in his art criticism. He titled one of his important early essays "Towards a Newer Laocoön," aligning himself with Lessing's classic argument against the romantic confusion of the arts, and with Irving Babbitt's more recent contribution to the same tradition, *The New Laocoön* (1910). According to Greenberg's essay, all the arts in the twentieth century "have been hunted back to their mediums and there have been isolated, concentrated and defined. It is by virtue of its medium that each art is unique and strictly itself. To restore the identity of an art the opacity of its medium must be emphasized."[48] In painting, this inevitable historical movement toward purity meant the exclusion of all "literary" qualities, including any traces of representation or subject matter.

The narrowness of Greenberg's vision naturally distanced him from many artists who did not share his rigid preconceptions of what modern art should be. A good example is the painter Fairfield Porter (1907–75), who deliberately developed his own art in opposition to Greenberg's dogmatism, as he recalled in an interview in 1968: "One reason I never became an abstract painter is that I used to see Clement Greenberg regularly and we always argued, we always disagreed. . . . I introduced him to De Kooning (Greenberg was publicizing Pollock at this time), and he said to De Kooning (who was painting the women), 'You can't paint this way nowadays.' And I thought: If that's what he says, I think I will do exactly what he says I can't do."[49] Although Porter was not an abstract painter, he was an active member of the inner circle of the Abstract Expressionists. For instance, he was a good friend and early champion of Willem de Kooning. Porter was also an art critic, and his critical principles—like his artistic ones—were formed in opposition to Greenberg's. He wrote for *Art News* from 1951 until 1959, the time when it was the most influential art magazine in America; and he wrote weekly reviews for the *Nation* for the next three years. Since Porter was a personal friend of many of the painters and poets of the New York School, and since he was sympathetic to such a broad range of art styles—including abstract expressionism— we may consider his critical writing representative of the antiformalist tendencies in art criticism during the 1950s. What is most interesting in this context is that, almost to the same extent that Porter opposed Greenberg's formalism, he consciously thought of Stevens as a kindred spirit.

One issue on which Porter and Greenberg disagreed utterly was that of the relations between the arts. An episode in 1955 reveals the importance Porter attached to such relations. Since he was both a painter and a writer, it is hardly surprising that Porter should have responded strongly to an article entitled "Artists/Writers: An Impure Excursion" by Thomas Hess, editor of *Art News*. Hess' article is a fairly lengthy consideration of the relation between literature and the visual arts, showing with a great many examples that when the two arts are combined—in a single work or in a single artist—the "impure" result is almost invariably detrimental to one art or the other. The article is written from a point of view implicitly sympathetic to Greenberg's call for "purity" in the arts. At one point in his argument, Hess specifically laments the faults inherent in literary descriptions of works of art, referring to Stevens as an example: "The Giottos in *Remembrance of Things Past,* Wallace Stevens' equestrian sculptures, Yeats' *bijouterie,* the Apocalyptic painting of Christ in Hollywood in Nathanael West's *Day of the Locust* are works of verbal art based upon inaccurate observation of the objects—in other words Pathetic Fallacies."[50]

Porter's respectful and friendly response (for Hess was his friend as well as his employer) begins, significantly, by questioning the reference to Stevens in particular. In a letter dated December 19, 1955, he wrote, "Dear Tom: I like your article on Artists/ Writers. . . . The only thing I disagree with is that Wallace Stevens' description of equestrian statues is "verbal art based on inaccurate observation of the objects"—at least not the description of Verrocchio's—I have not seen or do not remember the one of General Jackson, though I do not doubt that his dismissal of it is correct."[51] The main body of the letter points out that Hess' topical focus on the "impurity" of particular combinations of the two art forms overlooks the more interesting (in Porter's view) analogies between them:

> The question of purity vs. impurity for me is not just that the arts must be kept unmixed but one of knowing what each art is. And when I try to think about this I come to a relationship between the two arts; possibly I approach an aesthetic theory. . . . What interests me is . . . the analogy between painting and an expert use of words. . . . There are analogies between pure painting and pure writing, and . . . a criticism of an artist as a writer or of a writer as an artist can be considered by referring to these standards, if you think they exist, just as if he did not engage in two arts, or as if you could hold off consideration of this fact until later.

This letter is clearly a self-defense, a kind of *apologia pro vita sua.* It focuses precisely on an aspect of art that Greenberg strove to exclude from critical discourse. And, although Porter does not say so explicitly, his entire argument stands on the authority of Stevens. He mentions only one example, Stevens' description of the *Colleoni* in "The Noble Rider and the Sound of Words," but both the overall point of view and the specific language of his letter unmistakably recall *The Necessary Angel*. We need only remember the titles of two other essays in that book, "Effects of Analogy" and "The Relations between Poetry and Painting," to see how closely Porter has identified himself with Stevens in this theoretical exchange.

Porter's identification with Stevens here is not an isolated incident. As I have shown elsewhere, he consciously thought of Stevens as a kindred spirit, reading and quoting from his poetry throughout his long career.[52] He drew artistic inspiration from Stevens' poetry as early as 1936, when he based a linoleum cut on the title image of Stevens' "The Men That Are Falling"; and he included a copy of *Opus Posthumous* as a still-life element in his well-known painting *Lizzie at the Table* (1958). He cited Stevens as an authority when, near the end of his life, he sought to propound his own aesthetic theory. But perhaps most revealing of Porter's deep respect for Stevens is the fact that he thought of him as an exemplary art critic. Partly in response to Greenberg's domineering, prescriptive attitude toward art, Porter sought, in his own writing, to create a kind of art criticism that would be more responsive and *de*scriptive. In this effort, he consciously thought of Stevens as a model. The poet's description of Verrocchio's *Colleoni* in particular—the passage about which he had disagreed with Thomas Hess—became, for Porter, a touchstone of excellence in art criticism. He quoted it in a letter to his son early in 1956:

Dear Laurence:

I have just finished jury duty in New York. . . . Most of the time I spent reading Wallace Stevens' THE NECESSARY ANGEL, which contains a beautiful description of the statue of Bartollomeo Colleoni by Verrocchio, which he contrasts with the statue of Jackson in front of the White House. The former is a work of Imagination, the latter a work of fancy, and, says Stevens, a glance at it tells you it has no reality. It is a question of Nobility, which he says is a quality that we especially here are suspicious of, and it is finally indicated that nobility is not a quality, but a force—"a violence from within that protects us from a violence without." The statue is "like the form of an invincible man, who has come, slowly and boldly, through every warlike opposition of the past and who moves in our midst without dropping the bridle of the powerful horse from his hand, without taking off his helmet and without relaxing the attitude of a warrior of noble origin. What man on whose side the horseman fought could ever be anything but fearless, anything but indomitable?"

"I would not hesitate to say that Porter thought of [the Colleoni passage] as paradigmatic," comments Rackstraw Downes, editor of Porter's art criticism.[53] Stevens' description of the *Colleoni* embodies Porter's belief that "the best criticism is simply the best description,"[54] and that such criticism proceeds, like poetry, chiefly by analogies: "Criticism creates an analogy, and by examining the analogy you see what the art essentially is. Criticism should tell you what is there. A long criticism may have irrelevant observations, and almost surely lacks the intensity of say, Wallace Stevens' description of Verrocchio's Colleoni."[55]

The description that Porter so admires here does not limit itself to the superficial appearance of the statue. Rather, it attempts to identify the statue's essential quality (nobility) and to describe by analogy ("like the form of an invincible man") precisely what that quality conveys, emotionally and intellectually, to the responsive viewer. Stevens himself stressed the potential power of this type of description later in the essay: "A description of Verrocchio's statue could be the integration of an illusion equal to the statue itself" (NA, 32–33). Porter agreed, referring to the Colleoni passage again in 1972, in a letter to Rackstraw Downes, as an example of proper critical focus: "I think you do something here that all aestheticians I know about (precious few) do, (except Suzanne Langer) and that I think leads them away from the object of their analysis. (Perhaps only in criticisms of painting and sculpture.) You begin to depart into what the painting ostensibly refers to, that is expressed in the title. I do not think Wallace Stevens does this, though, in his discussion of the *Colleoni;* he talks about what the statue refers to almost in the artist's subconscious. I believe in doing this."[56]

Existentialism: Harold Rosenberg

As Porter's example suggests, it was primarily the publication of *The Necessary Angel* in 1951 that made it possible to think of Stevens as an art critic and an art theorist. In the 1940s, many cultivated people still tended to think of Stevens as a decadent hedonist content with minor art. Clement Greenberg, as we have already noted, could ask rhetorically in December 1948: "Who is our greatest poet? If we leave T. S. Eliot to one side as a confirmed Englishman by now, is it Wallace Stevens or Marianne Moore? Aren't both of them too minor really to be great?"[57] The magisterial tone and high-minded sentiments of Stevens' essays took such readers by surprise. "How different are these ideas from those we usually hear of Wallace Stevens," remarked one reviewer; and another noted now refreshingly "virile" the Stevens of *The Necessary Angel* seemed.[58] Above all, it was Stevens' unusual seriousness about art that impressed the critics. Winfield Townley Scott wrote: "Now that Eliot and Auden have made it fashionable to regard poetry as a sort of 'game,' it is heartening to hear from Wallace Stevens that poetry is 'one of the sanctions of life.'"[59] Hayden Carruth made a similar point: "Stevens is a poet who still believes that poetry is the supreme activity. Unlike many of his colleagues, who have turned to traditional dogmas or positivisms, Stevens refuses the opinion that art is a game, propaganda, or a ceremony. For him, poetry—he can say this unabashedly—is a means toward truth."[60]

The Necessary Angel appeared at a crucial moment in the development of the New York School. By 1950, the major figures in the movement had already achieved their "classic" styles: Pollock's poured paintings, Still's jagged, flamelike compositions, Rothko's floating clouds of color, Newman's "zips," Motherwell's *Elegies for the Spanish Republic,* and so forth. Now they were trying to work out—in discussions at the Club on Eighth Street and elsewhere—their aesthetic theory in order to explain the new painting they had developed in the 1940s. It was during this same time that Stevens was becoming known as perhaps the greatest living American poet, whose work owed its "major" status primarily to a coherent, overarching aesthetic theory. Naturally, the painters looked to Stevens' poetry and essays for help in expressing their own concerns. I have already cited one important instance of this tendency. In the fall of 1951, just when *The Necessary Angel* was published, Robert Motherwell and Ad Reinhardt completed editing *Modern Artists in America,* a volume intended to show the "scope and nature" of the "more radical innovations and variations of Modern American Art."[61] To explain the rise of abstract art, they quoted Wallace Stevens: "This is where the 'pressure of reality,' in Wallace Stevens' phrase, has led the majority of our most imaginative and fertile artists: 'It is not that there is a new imagination but that there is a new reality.' . . . It is this new reality . . . that we want to document."[62] Stevens' way of thinking about art was so compatible with that of the Abstract Expressionists that his essays were immediately put into the service of the new movement.

One reason the art world was so quick to appreciate Stevens' *The Necessary Angel* was that earlier that same year, in January 1951, Stevens had delivered his lecture "The Relations between Poetry and Painting" at the Museum of Modern Art. Soon afterwards the museum had published it as a pamphlet. Dore Ashton records that this lecture was "pondered and quoted for years afterward" by the New York painters.[63] One place where they did so was the famous Eighth Street Club, one of the chief gathering places for the Abstract Expressionists during the early 1950s.

Philip Pavia, who organized and "singlehandedly kept the Club going," remembers that Stevens was often discussed there.[64] One person who surely talked about Stevens at the Club was the art critic Harold Rosenberg, the first writer admitted as a charter member. He recalled that occasion for John Gruen in 1969: "As soon as I became a member they said, 'Let's have a meeting with the old-timers and talk about the relationship between art and poetry.' This was the first thing that occurred to them, which is fascinating. So we did just that. The members sat around a table, got a couple of bottles of booze, and we talked about Baudelaire and Cézanne and the relation between Cézanne and Mallarmé—which fascinated Bill [de Kooning]. This was the first meeting of the Club—that is, the first intellectual, organized discussion."[65] Rosenberg was a poet himself in his early career, and Stevens was one of the poets he most admired. He shared with Stevens—as with many of the painters—an interest in the relations between the arts. Unlike Clement Greenberg—with whom he dominated American art criticism in the 1950s and 1960s—Rosenberg was less interested in distinguishing between the arts than in examining their deeper, common roots. He was stimulated by Baudelaire's notion of a "fundamental aesthetic, or order, of which poetry and painting are manifestations," which Stevens quotes in *The Necessary Angel* (160). Rosenberg was naturally interested in Stevens' essays when they appeared in 1951, and his response to them is revealing.

In December 1952, Rosenberg published in *Art News* a piece entitled "American Action Painters." This was to be his "most widely discussed article," according to Irving Sandler;[66] it introduced the phrase "action painting" into the lexicon of modern art. Rosenberg prefaced this seminal article with two epigraphs, as follows:

"J'ai fait des gestes blancs parmis les solitudes."

—Apollinaire

"The American will is easily satisfied in its efforts to realize itself in knowing itself."

—Wallace Stevens

The quotation from Stevens is taken from "The Noble Rider and the Sound of Words," the first essay collected in *The Necessary Angel*. The passage from which this sentence is excerpted describes Clark Mills' statue of Andrew Jackson in Lafayette Square facing the White House. In contrast with Verrocchio's statue of Bartollomeo Colleoni (Stevens' "noble rider," the description of which so impressed Fairfield Porter), this statue of Jackson exhibits, in Stevens' words, "not the slightest trace of imagination." This observation leads him to a more general comment on the American character: "Treating this work as typical, it is obvious that the American will as a principle of the mind's being is easily satisfied in its efforts to realize itself in knowing itself" (NA, 11). This is a generous way of saying that the American public is generally reluctant to confront directly, without sentimentality, the nobler manifestations of the human spirit, such as military heroism or artistic sublimity. Rosenberg recognized how well this observation applied to the situation of the Abstract Expressionists in 1952. The article to which he affixed this sentence as epigraph called for "a new kind of criticism" that would be high-minded enough to comprehend the greatness of the new American painting: "So far, the silence of American literature on the new painting all but amounts to a scandal."[67]

The kind of criticism Rosenberg favored is best characterized as existentialist. Like many American intellectuals at this time, he was deeply influenced by the writings of Jean-Paul Sartre and Albert Camus, who were the leading figures in Paris during the postwar period. In what is probably the most famous passage of "The American Action Painters," he describes the new art as action, using language that calls to mind the literature of existentialism: "At a certain moment the canvas began to appear to one American painter after another as an arena in which to act—rather than as a space in which to reproduce, re-design, analyze or 'express' an object, actual or imagined. What was to go on the canvas was not a picture but an event."[68]

Rosenberg's existentialist point of view is obvious here and in the rest of this essay. He refers to the new painting as a secular religion, employing terms that include the "Myth Makers" in this existentialist adventure: "Based on the phenomenon of conversion the new movement is, with the majority of the painters, essentially a religious movement. In almost every case, however, the conversion has been experienced in secular terms. The result has been the creation of private myths.The tension of the private myth is the content of every painting of this vanguard. The act on the canvas springs from an attempt to resurrect the saving moment in his 'story' when the painter first felt himself released from Value— myth of past self-recognition. Or it attempts to initiate a new moment in which the painter will realize his total personality— myth of future self-recognition."[69]

In "action painting," the artistic act is charged with moral significance; with every gesture the artist is defining his self. Painting, in this view, becomes a desperate and exhilarating activity: "On the one hand, a desperate recognition of moral and intellectual exhaustion; on the other, the exhilaration of an adventure over depths in which he might find reflected the true image of his identity." When Rosenberg describes the canvas as "itself the 'mind' through which the painter thinks by changing a surface with paint," we may infer a close parallel with Stevens' conception of poetry as "The poem of the mind in the act of finding / What will suffice" (CP, 239)[70]. Rosenberg was well aware of this parallel, several times pointing out the similarity between Stevens' existential notion of the "first idea" in "Notes toward a Supreme Fiction" and the mature paintings of Barnett Newman.[71] Stevens' sayings about poetry are often cast in the existential mold, as in this aphorism from the "Adagia": "To read a poem should be an experience, like experiencing an act (OP, 164)."[72] The concepts of "action painting" and of "the poem of the act of the mind" (CP, 240) are clearly cut from the same cloth.

Such a view of art is a far cry from Greenberg's strict formalism. Not surprisingly, "The American Action Painters" attacks Greenberg's aesthetic principles as outdated and irrelevant: "The critic who goes on judging in terms of schools, styles, form—as if the painter were still concerned with producing a certain kind of object (the work of art), instead of living on the canvas—is bound to seem a stranger." Formalism misses the point, according to Rosenberg, because it focuses on elements that are inessential. "The new American painting is not 'pure' art. . . . Form, color, composition, drawing are auxiliaries, any one of which—or practically all, as has been attempted logically, with unpainted canvas—can be dispensed with." Chiefly what Greenberg overlooks is the *human* element in the new art: "Limited to the aesthetic, the taste bureaucracies of Modern Art cannot grasp the human experience involved in the new action paintings." Rosenberg emphasizes, instead, the importance of the artist's personality in creating the work of art: "A painting that is an act is inseparable from the biography of the artist." To support this view, he quotes Wallace Stevens: "As Stevens says of poetry, 'it is a process of the personality of the poet [NA, 45].'"[73]

As this quotation suggests, Stevens shared Rosenberg's opinion that the artist's personality was a central aspect of any art. He once copied into his commonplace book a passage from an article about Cézanne by Graham Bell because, he noted, "it adds to subject and manner the thing that is incessantly overlooked: the artist, the presence of the determining personality. Without that reality no amount of other things matters much."[74] Such a critical approach tends to blur the boundaries between art and life. Rosenberg embraced this notion with gusto: "The new painting has broken down every distinction between art and life."[75] Greenberg regarded this as Rosenberg's chief mistake, as Donald Kuspit remarks: "To misapply the spiritual standards of life to the realm of art is a serious error of criticism for him. It is the error of Rosenberg."[76] Stevens, too, might well have quarreled with the absolute phrasing of Rosenberg's claim that the artist should "[break] down *every* distinction between art and life." His own writing is more often characterized by careful qualifications and conditional phrasing. But Rosenberg's subtitle for the section in which this phrase appears does emphasize the conditional aspect of his subject: "Dramas of As If." And the goal of breaking down all distinctions between art and life is implicit in Stevens' idea of the supreme fiction, in which it would be possible to believe that "the theory / Of poetry is the theory of life" (CP, 486).

Whatever the philosophical implications of Rosenberg's view of art, it is certain that he spoke for many of the painters when he adopted his existentialist stance. Dore Ashton remarks that, although the painters were hostile toward some critics in the 1950s—Lionel Trilling, for instance—"they were certainly not hostile to Harold Rosenberg, who had long before established himself as 'one of the boys,' to use his own words, and whose respect for painters was boundless."[77] Irving Sandler confirms that "Rosenberg's conception of action painting reflected the thinking and rhetoric of the gesture painters, for they, too, valued existential action and reviled aesthetic performance."[78] Jackson Pollock's famous claim to be "literally *in* the painting" like an existential gladiator, and William Baziotes' idea that the artist is like a boxer stepping into the ring, illustrate how commonplace this existential view of art was in Abstract Expressionist circles.[79]

Essential to such a view is the artist's active, even violent bearing toward reality. Rothko and Gottlieb had broached the idea of imaginative violence in 1943 in their letter to the *New York Times:* "To us art is an adventure into an unknown world, which can be explored only by those willing to take risks. This world of the imagination is fancy-free and violently opposed to common sense."[80] The notions of risk and violence are also central to Stevens' famous description, in "The Noble Rider and the Sound of Words" (1941), of the imagination as "a violence from within that protects us from a violence without" (NA, 36). This parallel reflects a common assumption about the basic relation between modern art and modern life. For Stevens, the "violent" posture of the artist's imagination is the appropriate response to the violent reality of twentieth century life: "[We live our lives] in a state of violence, not physically violent, as yet, for us in America, but physically violent for millions of our friends and for still more millions of our enemies and spiritually violent, it may be said, for everyone alive" (NA, 26–27). This hostile climate demands an aggressive response, so that art becomes, for Stevens, "the imagination pressing back against the pressure of reality" (NA, 36). This idea so impressed Robert Motherwell and Ad Reinhardt that they used it, as we have seen, in *Modern Artists in America* (1951) to define the basis of Abstract Expressionism. Gottlieb and Rothko defended their own use of "primitive" methods with the same argument: "In times of violence, personal predilections for niceties of color and form seem irrelevant. All primitive expression reveals the constant awareness of powerful forces, the immediate presence of terror and fear, a recognition of the brutality of the natural world as well as the eternal insecurities of life. That these feelings are being experienced by many people throughout the world today is an unfortunate fact and to us an art that glosses over or evades these feelings is superficial and meaningless."[81]

The aggressive nature of modern politics—the "spiritual violence" of Stevens' essay—was also what Harold Rosenberg had in mind when, in the editorial statement he composed with Robert Motherwell for their 1947 journal *Possibilities,* he pointed to modern reality as the driving force of modern art: "If one is to continue to paint or to write as the political trap seems to close upon him he must have the extremest faith in sheer possibility."[82] In the rhetoric of this statement we can observe the existentialist stance of the 1940s emerging out of the social-activist stance of the 1930s, as Dore Ashton has remarked: "As a statement of their last remaining value—that of their individuality somehow mirrored forth in their work—[this editorial] represents both their despair and their wild hope. It definitely indicates that their earlier faith in the value of political action, symbolic social-content painting, group activity and programmatic movements had been eroded. All that remained was what Rosenberg later called their 'action' on the canvas, and the 'extremist faith in sheer possibility.' "A similar movement inward, accompanied by an interiorization of the rhetoric of social activism, accounts for Stevens' development from a direct engagement with social issues in "Owl's Clover" and other poems of the 1930s, to a confident faith, during the 1940s, in the solitary power of the imagination as "a violence from within that protects us from a violence without."

It was natural for Rosenberg to quote Stevens in support of his concept of "action painting" in 1952, for by that time he had long associated Stevens with this "existential" kind of art. Reviewing *Notes toward a Supreme Fiction* for *View* in 1943, Rosenberg had praised Stevens' poetry as an "experimental activity" applied "to finding the Real."[83] By 1949 he had come to think of Stevens as the American poet who best exemplified this existential mode. In his introduction to Marcel Raymond's *From Baudelaire to Surrealism*,[84] Rosenberg associates this mode with France, and its opposite (an emphasis on tradition) with England: "For American poetry, France meant experiment, risk, perception, conversion of the everyday; England means a poetry of comments that sound like poetry." In this view, all that is vital in American poetry comes from France: "The poets who spoke American best—Williams, Cummings, Stein, Pound, Moore, Eliot, Stevens—had all been enthusiastically frenchified." Significantly, to exemplify this French strain in American poetry, Rosenberg singles out Stevens. (Note that, like Stevens, Rosenberg judges a poem less by its form than by what it says.) " 'Call the roller of big cigars,' sang Stevens, the most conventional of them in form. With cigars and ice cream, billboards and wheelbarrows, American poetry became the poet's act of making his existence real to him, an act not 'assimilable' to any previous poetry." The opposite tendency in American poetry is represented by the adoptive Englishman T. S. Eliot: "With [Eliot's] famous formula of the supremacy of tradition over the individual talent, he succeeded in making poetry appear as a thing with a life of its own, to which a certain caste had given itself as to a minor trade or cult."[85]

In contrast with Eliot's rigid traditionalism, Stevens represents for Rosenberg the French ideal of poetry as "an adventure," a search for "the actuality which is always new," "a way of experiencing," a record of "acts of consciousness."[86] This vital strain in American art would find its strongest contemporary expression in "action painting." Rosenberg naturally thought of Stevens as the American poet closest in spirit to this new movement.

Chapter **8**

The Auroras of Autumn and Jackson Pollock

The true work of art, whatever it may be, is not the work of the individual artist. It is time and it is place, as these perfect themselves.—NA, 140

We have seen that Stevens' poetic development bears a significant relation to the Abstract Expressionist movement as a whole. Having established the existence and nature of this relation, we now have a solid basis for drawing a more detailed analogy between Stevens' late poetry and a comparable body of work by a representative Abstract Expressionist painter. The aim of such a comparison will be to determine in what sense we can consider Stevens' poetry the literary equivalent of abstract expressionist painting. Let us take the example of Jackson Pollock (1912–56), because he is perhaps the leading figure and certainly the best known of the group, and because his canvases may be said to define the movement in the popular imagination.[1] Although Pollock may never have read Stevens' poetry, and Stevens may never have seen Pollock's paintings, there are important parallels between their works.[2]

To my knowledge, no one has ever compared Stevens to Pollock. The reasons for this are not far to seek. The two artists had very different personalities—Stevens leading the life of a conventional businessman, Pollock that of the rebellious artist. Nor do Pollock's painting and Stevens' poetry seem at all similar according to the criteria usually applied in comparisons of modern poetry and painting. Although Pollock's thrown and spattered paint obviously parallels the contemporary verbal experiments of the Beats and the Black Mountain poets, his radical technique seems poles apart from Stevens' use of standard metrics, punctuation, stanza forms, and so forth. Equally unhelpful is the conventional iconographic approach to poetry-painting analogies, since Pollock's classic pourings are totally abstract, without any recognizable imagery.

But observe how natural the comparison between Stevens and Pollock seems as we approach it from the perspective we have achieved in the preceding chapters. We have already seen how much Stevens has in common with the Abstract Expressionist movement as a whole. He shared with Pollock a background of art theory; his poetry and Pollock's painting developed in the same intellectual and cultural context. This fundamental connection underlies the particular parallels I am about to draw between Stevens' late poetry and Pollock's abstract painting, giving them a significance that goes well beyond superficial matters of style and technique. They express a profound—and profoundly similar—response of two artists to the very spirit of their mutual time and place.

Pollock began as a figurative painter, studying with Thomas Hart Benton in the early 1930s.[3] Late in that decade he became interested in the Mexican muralists Orozco, Rivera, and Siqueiros, from whom he acquired a taste for epic scale that later inspired his abstract expressionist paintings. He also adopted their use of Indian motifs, to which he attributed archetypal significance, having begun Jungian psychotherapy in 1939. At the same time, during the late 1930s, Pollock began to be influenced by Parisian modernism, especially the wide-ranging artistic experiments of Picasso. By the time the European exiles arrived in New York in the early 1940s, Pollock was already well schooled in the discoveries of cubism and the pure geometric abstraction of Mondrian.[4] He was also convinced of the central role of the unconscious in artistic creation, so that he was well prepared to appreciate the presence of the Surrealists in exile, as is clear from this interview of 1944: "I accept the fact that the important painting of the last hundred years was done in France. . . . The fact that good European moderns are now here is very important, for they bring with them an understanding of the problems of modern painting. I am particularly impressed with their concept of the source of art being the unconscious."[5]

Under these combined influences, Pollock during the 1940s painted increasingly abstract works that invoked primitive myths and archetypal symbolism. Then, in 1947, he plunged into pure abstraction in his best-known works, the "poured" paintings done between 1947 and 1950. Pollock's purely abstract phase coincides exactly with the period (1947–50) during which nearly all the Abstract Expressionists arrived at their mature styles and discovered their most characteristic abstract imagery: Motherwell's *Elegies,* Newman's "zips," Still's jagged-edged areas of flat color, Rothko's hovering, soft-edged rectangles, and so on. Thus Pollock's career may be considered typical, in its outline, of the development of Abstract Expressionism generally.

It was during these same years that Stevens composed the poems collected in *The Auroras of Autumn* (1950), his most abstract book and the one most critics mean when they refer to "the late poetry." Such poems as "The Auroras of Autumn," "The Owl in the Sarcophagus," and "An Ordinary Evening in New Haven" represent a new kind of poetry that developed directly out of the theoretical clarity Stevens had achieved in "Notes."

The principal theme of *The Auroras of Autumn* is the constant change—the Heraclitean flux—that is the essence of our experience. This was not a new idea for Stevens. Metamorphosis had been one recurrent theme of *Harmonium,* and one requirement of his supreme fiction was that "it must change." He had ended "Notes" with an apostrophe to the world that stressed this idea:

> Fat girl, terrestrial, my summer, my night,
> How is it I find you in difference, see you there
> In a moving contour, a change not quite completed?
>
> [CP, 406]

In *The Auroras of Autumn,* he made this his central subject: life itself in its most characteristic mode, in the process of change.[6] This theme is embodied in the figure of the "necessary angel" of reality, who appears in "Angel Surrounded by Paysans," the last poem of the book:

> . . . Am I not,
> Myself, only half a figure of a sort,
>
> A figure half seen, or seen for a moment, a man
> Of the mind, an apparition apparelled in
>
> Apparels of such lightest look that a turn
> Of my shoulder and quickly, too quickly, I am gone?
>
> [CP, 497]

The speaker is the "angel" who has disappeared from view the instant before the poem begins. Since he represents reality, whose essence is constant metamorphosis, his self-description takes the form of a series of appositives that mimics his own protean character even to the extent that it never really concludes, because it ends as a question. This passage illustrates the sense of approximation, incompletion, and endless transition that defines Stevens' late vision and style. It is a poetry that seeks to capture in words the reality of the fleeting moment. J. Hillis Miller has fittingly labeled it Stevens' "poetry of being."[7]

17. Jackson Pollock, *One (Number 31, 1950)* (1950). Oil and enamel on unprimed canvas, 8 ft. 10 in. x 17 ft. 5 5/8 in. Collection, The Museum of Modern Art, New York. Sidney and Harriet Janis Collecton Fund, by exchange.

Pollock's abstract pourings are equally concerned with flux, metamorphosis, and the present moment. The utterly nonrepresentational *One (Number 31, 1950)* (1950; fig. 17), for instance, confronts the viewer as a thing in itself rather than as a representation of anything else. Its graceful network of arabesques and splatterings is a record of constant movement whose significance we can only fully appreciate if we know how it was made. Pollock himself described his pouring technique in a rare statement in 1947: "My painting does not come from the easel. I hardly ever stretch my canvas before painting. I prefer to tack the unstretched canvas to the hard wall or the floor. I need the resistance of a hard surface. On the floor I am more at ease. I feel nearer, more a part of the painting, since this way I can walk around it, work from the four sides and literally be *in* the painting. This is akin to the method of the Indian sand painters of the West."[8] Hans Namuth's famous photographs of Pollock at work confirm the details of this statement and make the artist's technique easier to visualize (fig. 18.) The canvas is laid out on the floor, and the artist moves around it in

18. Hans Namuth, photograph of Jackson Pollock painting *Autumn Rhythm* (1950). The painting *One* is hung on the wall behind the artist. "Am I not, / Myself, only half a figure of a sort, / A figure half seen, or seen for a moment, a man / Of the mind, an apparition apparelled in / Apparels of such lightest look that a turn / Of my shoulder and quickly, too quickly, I am gone?" ("Angel Surrounded by Paysans," CP, 497).

dancelike movements, flinging, dripping, or pouring paint from sticks or other implements. The finished painting is a record of this process, not a representation of any preconceived subject.

Pollock's method developed directly out of surrealist automatism. By his own admission, he painted in a trancelike state that brought into play his unconscious mind: "When I am *in* my painting, I'm not aware of what I'm doing. It is only after a sort of 'get acquainted' period that I see what I have been about. I have no fears about making changes, destroying the image, etc., because the painting has a life of its own. I try to let it come through. It is only when I lose contact with the painting that the result is a mess. Otherwise there is pure harmony, an easy give and take, and the painting comes out well."[9] Pollock thought of himself during the process of creation as the medium through which an irrational force—"the painting"—achieved expression: "I try to let it come through." This recalls the surrealist idea of becoming one with the irrational forces of nature that Stevens had considered in canto xix of "The Man with the Blue Guitar." Pollock's famous declaration, "I am Nature," makes this parallel even clearer.[10] But Pollock's pouring method made use of automatism in a more active, ongoing way than the Surrealists had done. His every gesture was an automatic response to an ever-changing pattern of previous gestures. His aim was to create a kind of painting that would flow continuously, as one critic has written, "straight from the unconscious."[11] This means that a painting like *One* represents, as another critic puts it, "Surrealist metamorphosis multiplied a thousandfold."[12] In William Rubin's words, "The 'classic' style of Pollock constituted a kind of apotheosis of automatism. It went beyond the wildest speculations of Surrealism in the extent of its automatism."[13]

Pollock invented the pouring technique not as an end in itself but in order to facilitate this primarily mental process of free association or continuous automatism. It permitted him to sustain long, continuous lines, and to use his entire arm rather than the wrist alone, in order to register directly every painterly impulse without breaking the flow of his concentration. The physical "gesture" that critics make so much of is only significant because it records the movement of the mind.[14] As the artist himself put it, "Technique is just a means of arriving at a statement."[15] What Stevens attempts in *The Auroras of Autumn,* especially in the long poems of that volume, is a comparable form of speeded-up, continuous automatism. "An Ordinary Evening in New Haven" is perhaps the best example. In this poem, Stevens set himself a difficult challenge: "Here my interest is to try to get as close to the ordinary, the commonplace and the ugly as it is possible for a poet to get. It is not a question of grim reality but of plain reality. The object is of course to purge oneself of anything false" (L, 636). To "get at" so apparently unpoetic a subject was a deliberate test of his own virtuosity. The poem that resulted "may seem diffuse and casual," as Stevens admitted (L, 719), and his critics have often agreed. He accepted this criticism as the price to be paid for the remarkable achievement of his late style.

It is helpful to think of Stevens' method in "An Ordinary Evening in New Haven" as a form of improvisation. He composed most of his poems while walking—to and from the office, at noontime, on weekends.[16] Walking was always one of his favorite activities, and his poetry is grounded in the pleasurable rhythm of the body in motion. His spontaneous poetic music needed that measured pace, just as a jazz musician improvises within a given time signature. Although painting is physical in a way that poetry is not, the analogy with Pollock's painting stands.

Stevens' kind of improvisation is different from that of William Carlos Williams in, for instance, *Kora in Hell: Improvisations* (1920). Paul Mariani describes that book as "a kind of automatic writing, Williams' attempt to 'loosen the attention' and descend deeper than ever into his poetic unconsciousness to tap energies so far left dormant."[17] But Williams' disconnected prose paragraphs deliberately confuse the reader and slow him down; the effect of reading them is primarily disjunctive. Stevens' late poetry, on the other hand, aims at a continuously flowing improvisation that is more closely comparable to Pollock's pourings. As the last canto of "An Ordinary Evening in New Haven" summarizes it:

These are the edgings and inchings of final form,
The swarming activities of the formulae
Of statement, directly and indirectly getting at . . . .

[CP, 488]

Stevens had first explored the possibilities of improvisation as an organizing principle of the long poem in "The Man with the Blue Guitar." There the guitarist's variations gave an appropriately casual shape to the poem's playful spirit. In "An Ordinary Evening in New Haven" the guitarist reappears in the same guise, but now playing a more serious and important role:

Life fixed him, wandering on the stair of glass,
With its attentive eyes. . . .

. . . This was
Who watched him, always, for unfaithful thought.

This sat beside his bed, with its guitar,
To keep him from forgetting, without a word,
A note or two describing what it was.

Nothing about him ever stayed the same,
Except this hidalgo and his eye and tune,
The shawl across one shoulder and the hat.

[CP, 483]

The guitarist is no longer simply a playful figure. He has come to represent not only "life" itself in its aspect of perpetual change, but also the very spirit of poetry whose "faith" sustains the hope of human happiness in the face of this ever-changing reality.

The central place of improvisation in Stevens' poetic *theory* is clearest in "Notes." There he uses poetic figures like the Arabian, Nanzia Nunzio, and the Canon Aspirin as illustrations of abstract ideas; their function in the poem is similar, as we have seen, to that of pictures in an exhibition. But since Stevens himself is the maker of these "pictures," we are also aware of their status as improvisations. We never lose sight of the fact that they are only sample tokens of the poet's imaginative power. That he can improvise such apt and vivid poetic figures with such apparent ease conveys the impression that he is capable of meeting any poetic challenge. The success of "Notes" depends, to a great extent, on precisely this impression. We understand Stevens' improvisational manner as a sign of inexhaustible creative power, so that the possibility of ultimate imaginative fulfillment—a supreme fiction—seems credible.

In "An Ordinary Evening in New Haven," Stevens' use of improvisation is both more concentrated and more sustained, like Pollock's development of surrealist automatism. Canto ii, for example, conjures a trancelike state in which the boundaries between subjective and objective experience, between imagination and reality, simply dissolve:

> Suppose these houses are composed of ourselves,
> So that they become an impalpable town, full of
> Impalpable bells, transparencies of sound,
>
> Sounding in transparent dwellings of the self,
> Impalpable habitations that seem to move
> In the movement of the colors of the mind,
>
> The far-fire flowing and the dim-coned bells
> Coming together in a sense in which we are poised,
> Without regard to time or where we are,
>
> In the perpetual reference, object
> Of the perpetual meditation, point
> Of the enduring, visionary love,
>
> Obscure, in colors whether of the sun
> Or mind, uncertain in the clearest bells,
> The spirit's speeches, the indefinite,
>
> Confused illuminations and sonorities,
> So much ourselves, we cannot tell apart
> The idea and the bearer-being of the idea.

[CP, 466]

The object of this single-sentence canto is to transport the reader to a timeless realm of "perpetual meditation" in which he can experience a sense of "enduring, visionary love." This harmonious vision is identical to that of the "irrational moments" that provided the resolution of "Notes." We have seen that the poet insisted, in "It Must Give Pleasure," that such moments are necessarily "automatic," and that the highest function of poetry is to communicate precisely the same kind of harmonious vision that such moments embody.

Following out the logical consequences of that position, in "An Ordinary Evening in New Haven" Stevens developed a style based on continuous improvisation or free association. If the poem sometimes seems, as he said, "diffuse and casual," that is because it deliberately follows chance associations of sound or imagery, allowing repetitions of words and slight variations of ideas to occur as they occur, letting the rhythm of language and thought flow freely without interruption, like the motion of the mind in sleep or meditation. The object of Stevens' late style is to create a state of mind receptive to the harmony of "irrational moments." It is a personal variant of surrealist automatism, like Pollock's pouring method.

Automatism in painting is generally a method of finding imagery. Part of Pollock's great innovation in the years 1947–50 was to use it without arriving at recognizable imagery. He transferred the Surrealists' central technique into the realm of pure abstraction. In doing so, he abandoned the imagery based on primitive myths that had characterized his work during the early 1940s. "Previously his work had symbolized and personified mythic powers and forces . . . now it manifested them directly."[18]

This movement from discarded myth to a purely abstract substitute for myth is the same two-part creative pattern that Stevens outlined in "Notes." The title poem of *The Auroras of Autumn* develops this pattern. The basic concept with which this poem begins is best summarized in a passage from Stevens' lecture "Two or Three Ideas": "To see the gods dispelled in mid-air and dissolve like clouds is one of the great human experiences. . . . It was their annihilation, not ours, and yet it left us feeling that in a measure we, too, had been annihilated. It left us feeling dispossessed and alone in a solitude, like children without parents, in a home that seemed deserted" (OP, 260). "The Auroras of Autumn" opens with a series of farewells, first to the deserted childhood home ("the cabin," canto ii), and then to its once comforting mythic presences ("the mother," iii, and "the father," iv). These valedictions are metaphors for the emotional experience of losing faith in God.[19] The resulting sense of being "dispossessed and alone in a solitude" climaxes in the fearful vision of the auroras that concludes canto vi:

> He opens the door of his house
>
> On flames. The scholar of one candle sees
> An Arctic effulgence flaring on the frame
> Of everything he is. And he feels afraid.

The poet has stripped reality bare of every illusion, reducing it to its first idea. But his imagination cannot endure such a cold, comfortless vision, so it proposes—in cantos vii through ix—abstract substitutes for the protecting and nurturing aspects of the lost parents. "The father," the personification of intellectual and imaginative power, is transformed into the abstract "enthroned imagination" (vii).[20] "The mother," the embodiment of physical and emotional satisfaction, is replaced by the abstract ideal of "innocence":

> So, then, these lights are not a spell of light,
> A saying out of a cloud, but innocence. . . .
>
> As if the innocent mother sang in the dark
> Of the room and on an accordion, half-heard,
> Created the time and place in which we breathed.
> [viii]

This is not the sentimental notion it might seem, since this "innocence of the earth" includes the inevitability of death (ix). Together these purely abstract paternal and maternal principles humanize the auroras, making their otherwise terrifying power accessible to the imagination. In the same way, Pollock's abstract pourings aim to confront the intimidating power of natural forces in works that affirm, by their own sublimity, the noblest aspirations of the human spirit. For both artists, abstraction serves as a substitute for myth.

This combination and development of surrealist and abstract elements led, in the work of both Stevens and Pollock, to a new kind of *kinetic* abstraction. Daniel Tompkins has shown that this development is evident even at the level of Stevens' poetic diction. Throughout Stevens' career, the tendency toward abstract language was linked to the desire to convey action. Tompkins' perceptive analysis of Stevens' use of abstract nouns is worth quoting at length:

> Almost half have what must be called a verbal basis—that is, they are used in the poems to emphasize the process and movement implied by their etymology: "aberration," "appeasement," "analysis," "apprehending," "compromise," "anatomy," "appearance," "Arrival," "disclosure," and "adulteries." These words represent the varieties of termination to be found in Stevens' "verbal" abstractions. They are nouns with origins in French, Greek, or Latin, all closely connected with action and process. Of them, by far the largest group is made up of gerunds: "ascending," babbling," "begetting," etc. (not simply verbal adjectives, the more usual function of words ending in -*ing*). Stevens often tries to make the words yet more general by using them as plurals, or attaching indefinite articles to them, to produce phrases like these:
>
> An impossible aberration with the moon (CP, 239)
>
> An appearance of Again, the diva-dame (CP, 353)
>
> . . . a savage assuagement . . . (CP, 467)

. . . in branchings after day . . . (CP, 468)

A skillful apprehension (OP, 35)

. . . an insolid billowing of the solid (OP, 111)

Abstractions of actions, often made more indefinite: these are the major category, nearly half, of Stevens' abstract terms. Even when he is standing back from the phenomena he describes, Stevens notices constant motion, the process that underlies reality—the river of being (CP, 533).[21]

Although Tompkins' conclusions are based on a sample set of entries in the Stevens *Concordance* (letters A through D),[22] and his examples therefore come from poems written throughout Stevens' career, he has nevertheless put his finger on the quality of language most characteristic of *The Auroras of Autumn*: the kind of kinetic abstraction—"abstractions of actions"—that is the chief link between Stevens' late poetry and the Abstract Expressionist movement in painting.[23]

What relates Stevens' *The Auroras of Autumn* most closely to Pollock's abstract pourings in particular is the nearly identical configuration of their central imagery. There is an obvious visual similarity between the flashing, ceaseless, wavelike movements of Stevens' title image—the aurora borealis—and Pollock's "signature" abstract imagery, the serpentine tracery of his "poured" paintings. Both images are composed of a flowing network of graceful, linear curves and arabesques suggesting constant motion. Stevens' description of the northern lights in canto vi of "The Auroras of Autumn" could easily serve as a poetic description of Pollock's *One:*

It is a theater floating through the clouds,
Itself a cloud, although of misted rock
And mountains running like water, wave on wave,

Through waves of light. It is of cloud transformed

To cloud transformed again, idly, the way
A season changes color to no end,

Except the lavishing of itself in change,
As light changes yellow into gold and gold
To its opal elements and fire's delight,

Splashed wide-wise because it likes magnificence
And the solemn pleasures of magnificent space.

[CP, 416]

Both poem and painting are organized around the same theme of ceaseless, wavelike motion; both convey an atmosphere of continual metamorphosis in which solid shapes dissolve and flow.

Stevens' description of the auroras as "Splashed wide-wise because it likes magnificence" applies particularly well to Pollock's *One,* capturing both the liquid quality of Pollock's thinned paint ("splashed") and his high seriousness of purpose ("magnificence"). The monumental size of *One*—it is nearly nine feet tall and more than seventeen feet wide—forbids any easy aesthetic response, any attempt to read Pollock's delicate tracery as merely pretty. In the presence of this painting at the Museum of Modern Art, one experiences without irony the exalted mood that Stevens attributes to the auroras: "the solemn pleasure of magnificent space."

The suggestion of *outer* space in the phrase "magnificent space" is also appropriate to both works. Stevens' auroras appear in the dark, starlit northern sky, so that he can describe them metaphorically as the dazzling vestments of the stars:

The stars are putting on their glittering belts.
They throw around their shoulders cloaks that flash . . . .

[CP, 419]

Pollock's pourings—like *One,* with its dense filigree of spattered dots and poured, curving lines—have suggested to many viewers a similar nocturnal vision of the heavens. His earliest poured paintings were sometimes even titled accordingly, for example, *Reflections of the Big Dipper, Galaxy, Comet,* and *Shooting Star* (all of 1947).

"The Auroras of Autumn" is a difficult poem. Joseph Riddel, more candid than most critics, calls it "bafflingly obscure in some of its parts," and the often contradictory readings of other commentators confirm his judgment.[24] Part of this difficulty stems from the fact that the poem's central visual image—the aurora borealis—is deliberately ambiguous in its meaning. The auroras represent not only the meaningless flux of life, the chaos of everyday reality, but also the ordering concept of the supreme fiction. This may seem at first glance impossibly contradictory, but a moment's reflection shows that it must be true. If the supreme fiction is to be credible at all, it must appear to be identical with reality. The auroras, therefore, as a visual symbol of the supreme fiction, must represent both imagination and reality at the point when they are indistinguishable from each other. They can do so easily because the endless flowing of life (reality), and the constant motion of the mind adjusting itself to this changing reality (imagination), are necessarily parallel; if we could graph them, they would form nearly identical patterns. Ultimately, the auroras represent a continuous version of the surreal "irrational moments" that resolved "Notes." They are a vision of sustained harmony between ourselves and the world, between our subjective desires and objective fact.

Pollock's pouring method is a closely parallel process of continuous, ideally maintained balance. The artist's chief concern during the painting process was to maintain "contact" with the painting in its ever-changing state of coming into being. As long as he maintained that contact, the result was "pure harmony": "It is only when I lose contact with the painting that the result is a mess. Otherwise there is pure harmony, an easy give and take, and the painting comes out well."[25] Because Pollock's pouring technique involves his whole being—both intense mental concentration and full bodily participation—it represents a continuously changing but always harmonious balance between imagination and reality that is comparable to Stevens' vision of the auroras.

The years 1947–50 define the "classic" phase of Abstract Expressionism. It was during this period that a new kind of pure abstraction came into being, and that its full potential was developed, in different ways, by the leading artists of the movement. Pollock perfected his pouring method at this time in such colorful, pure abstractions as *One*. But in 1951 he reacted against this style by reintroducing the human figure into his canvases and by reducing his palette to black on unprimed canvas. *Number 22, 1951* (fig. 19) shows a squatting, malevolent female figure that is related to similar "earth-mother" images in Pollock's earlier figurative work.[26] This dramatic change of direction in Pollock's painting coincides with Willem De Kooning's creation of his famous *Women,* the series of paintings that shocked art critics with its violence and disturbed the avant-garde painters because of its apparent regression to figuration.

This new trend in the art world in the early 1950s is matched, in Stevens' career, by a similar movement away from the abstract mode of *The Auroras of Autumn* and toward the greater clarity and simplicity of the poems collected in "The Rock" (the final section of the *Collected Poems*). And this new phase in Stevens' development is marked by the sudden appearance of menacing female imagery. It is remarkable that the one poem Stevens wrote in 1951—a year in which his literary energies were devoted mainly to lecturing and accepting awards—is "Madame La Fleurie," whose title figure is a "wicked," man-eating woman:

Weight him down, O side-stars, with the great
    weightings of the end.
Seal him there. He looked in a glass of the earth
    and thought he lived in it.
Now, he brings all that he saw into the earth,
    to the waiting parent.

19. Jackson Pollock, *Number 22, 1951* (1951). Oil on canvas, 29 x 23 in. Collection of Denise and Andrew Saul.

> His crisp knowledge is devoured by her,
>   beneath a dew. . . .
>
> The black fugatos are strumming the blacknesses
>   of black . . . .
> . . . His grief is that his mother should feed on him,
>   himself and what he saw,
> In that distant chamber, a bearded queen, wicked
>   in her dead light.
>
> [CP, 507]

This image of the devouring earth-mother exactly parallels the violent images of women in Pollock's and de Kooning's paintings of the same year.

Although this is certainly not a case of "influence" one way or the other, it should be clear at this point that such visual parallels are not merely coincidental. We may suppose that each artist had his own deeply personal psychological motives for suddenly focusing on such a mythic, emotionally charged image. But that it should appear so prominently, at the same moment, in all their work suggests that it is also the expression of some larger, shared experience. The obvious similarity between Stevens' central visual imagery and Pollock's in the late 1940s and early 1950s reflects a deep affinity that derives from their common background in art theory—particularly the combined influences of surrealism and abstraction—and from their common cultural experience—the intellectual climate of the American art world from the 1930s through the 1950s. These shared circumstances of time and place were part of what Stevens meant when he spoke of the "pressure of reality," and he recognized the central importance of such pressure not only in the formation of artistic movements but also in the development of the individual artist: "The pressure of reality is, I think, the determining factor in the artistic character of an era and, as well, the determining factor in the artistic character of an individual" (NA, 22–23). It is in this sense that Stevens could write, "The true work of art, whatever it may be, is not the work of the individual artist. It is time and it is place, as these perfect themselves" (NA, 140). If this is true of Wallace Stevens, it is just as true Jackson Pollock. It may stand as the basic principle underlying the many relations, direct and indirect, between Stevens and Abstract Expressionism, the most important American art movement of his time.

This book began as an attempt to explain Stevens' relation to the Abstract Expressionists. I am glad to end it with the above analysis of that relationship. But I would not want to leave the reader with the impression that Stevens' relevance to modern art is limited to, or ends with, that movement. Stevens' poetry reflects, in Hayden Carruth's words, "the whole movement of this century in art," from the Armory Show of 1913 through the "triumph" of Abstract Expressionism in the 1950s.[27] The foregoing chapters have traced what I take to be the central strand in that movement, from the point of view of Stevens' own poetic development. But both twentieth-century art and Stevens' poetry are far more various than I have been able to indicate, without blurring the clear focus I have thought necessary to the presentation of my argument. Perhaps one final example may serve to illustrate the true breadth of Stevens' relation to modern art.

Jasper Johns (b. 1930) is generally considered one of the greatest living American artists. He came to prominence in the 1960s as one of the leading figures of "Pop" art, a movement diametrically opposed to abstract expressionism. Johns's deadpan paintings of such impersonal images as targets and flags could not have been further removed from the high seriousness and deep psychic engagement of "action painting." They paved the way for the development of minimalism and conceptual art.

Johns' chosen mentor was none other than Marcel Duchamp (1887–1968), whose aloof intellectuality and ironic humor made him the hero of those artists in the 1960s and 1970s who were reacting against the emotional excesses of abstract expressionism. Recalling Stevens' closeness to Duchamp and his circle during the *Harmonium* years, we should not be surprised to discover Harold

Rosenberg quoting "Anecdote of the Jar" in 1967 to illuminate what he called "Environmental" art:

> Anything, naturally, put down in a given area changes that area. How an object transforms its environment and turns it into a work of art was thoroughly investigated by Wallace Stevens in his "Anecdote of the Jar":

> > I placed a jar in Tennessee,
> > And round it was, upon a hill.
> > It made the slovenly wilderness
> > Surround that hill.

> > The wilderness rose up to it,
> > And sprawled around, no longer wild.
> > The jar was round upon the ground,
> > And tall and of a port in air.

> > It took dominion everywhere.
> > The jar was gray and bare.[28]

Nor is it surprising that in more recent years Johns himself has been directly influenced by Stevens. In the late 1980s Johns executed a group of four paintings called *The Seasons*. They are his most autobiographical works, full of personal symbols and echoes of his earlier work, and each panel containing as part of the composition a rendering of his own shadow. The series also pays tribute to important influences on his artistic development. There are many references to Picasso, particularly to his paintings *Minotaur Moving His House* (1936) and *The Shadow* (1953), and to Marcel Duchamp, whose profile is included as an element in *Fall*. The *Winter* panel (fig. 20) includes an image of a snowman that refers to Stevens, whose poetry directly inspired this series. Barbara Rose describes this connection: "While Johns was painting 'Summer' he was asked to illustrate a special edition of the poems of Wallace Stevens. A lover of poetry and friend to many poets, Johns decided to make an etching based on this painting for the book. Although he had not initially conceived the entire sequence of the four *Sea-*

20. Jasper Johns, *Winter* (1986). Encaustic on canvas, 75 x 50 in. Copyright Jasper Johns/VAGA, New York, 1992.

sons, Stevens's poem "Snow Man" made him think of winter and he began rough sketches of the three other paintings."[29] Rose does not mention what several of the artist's acquaintances confirm, that Johns had been interested in Stevens' poetry long before this event occurred.[30]

Stevens' poetry could inspire such a personally and artistically important series of paintings because it addresses problems that concern a broad spectrum of modern artists. Stevens himself put it quite simply: "To a large extent, the problems of poets are the problems of painters" (OP, 187). His poetry is the record of one extraordinary sensibility's coming to terms with the shifting realities that concerned both painters and poets for more than forty years, from the Armory Show to Abstract Expressionism. It was a period of enormous variety and change, and it made Stevens constantly aware that the intellectual and aesthetic problems most relevant at any particular historical moment are always changing. This experience is the foundation of his personal "imagination-reality complex," a way of thinking he associated specifically with the field of painting: "We are speaking of a thing in continual flux. There is no field in which this is more apparent than painting. Again, there is no field in which it is more constantly and more intelligently the subject of discussion than painting. The permissible reality in painting wavers with an insistence which is itself a value. One might just as well say the permissible imagination. It is as if the painter carried on with himself a continual argument as to whether what delights us in the exercise of the mind is what we produce or whether it is the exercise of a power of the mind" (NA, 149–50).

The "continual argument" of modern art is still in progress, and beneath the sometimes bewildering noise of this ongoing adventure, we can often make out—if we know what to listen for—the clear, distinctive voice of Wallace Stevens.

Appendix

Wallace Stevens' Art Collection

This compilation is based on the list of thirty-six paintings included in the exhibition "Wallace Stevens' Collection of Paintings and Prints" at Trinity College, Hartford, Conn. (May–June 1963). Most of these works remain in the collection of Holly Stevens.

Anonymous	*Village Street* (brown wash or watercolor)
Anonymous	*Man in Red Robe* (Japanese print)
Bombois, Camille	*Le Loiret à Olivet* (oil)
Bouda, Cyril	*Strawberry Torte* (etching)
Bouda, Cyril	*Village Street* (black-and-white print)
Braque, Georges	*Nature morte III: Verre et fruit* (lithograph)
Brayer, Yves	*Venice—Grand Canal* (oil)
Brianchon, Maurice	*Still Life* (oil)
Cavailles, Jean Jules	*Interior with Still Life* (oil)
Cavailles, Jean Jules	*Port of Cannes (Sea Surface Full of Clouds)* (oil)
Céria, Edmond	*Harbor Scene* (oil)
Céria, Edmond	*La Trinité des Monts, Rome* (oil)
Clark, Roland	*Backwater of the Cooper, Black Duck* (watercolor)
Detthow, Eric	*Blue Bowl of Red Flowers* (oil)
Detthow, Eric	*Paysage du Midi* (oil)

Dodd, Francis	*Anchor Inn, Greenwich* (etching)
Dodd, Francis	*Piazzeta, Venice* (etching)
Dodd, Francis	*Reading Mrs. Carlisle's Letters* (etching)
Gromaire, Marcel	*Plaine hollandaise* (ink and watercolor)
Haley, John Chas.	*Portrait of Wallace Stevens* (photograph and crayon)
Hiroshige, Ando	*Fireworks at Ryojoku* (print)
Hiroshige, Ando	*Foxes Assembling under the Shozoku Enoki Tree at Ojion, New Year's Eve* (print)
Kienbusch, Wm.	*Dead Tree* (oil)
Labasque, Jean	*La Démolition* (oil)
Labasque, Jean	*Tableau [?]* (see A. Vidal to Stevens, March 26, 1938, Huntington Library)
Labasque, Jean	*Portrait of Vidal* (oil)
La Patellière	*Mexican Scene* (oil)
Lebasque, Henri	*Bathing* (oil)
Lebasque, Henri	*Landscape with Woman in Foreground* (oil)
Lebasque, Marthe	*Bridge with Angels* (pastel)
Marchand, Jean	*Les Oliviers* (oil)
Mariano [Rodríguez]	*Pineapple* (watercolor)
Mariano [Rodríguez]	*Woman in Chair*
Oudot, Roland	*Paysage* (oil)
Oudot, Roland	*The Bathers* (oil)
Pine [?]	*Mountain Lake* (watercolor)
Pissarro, Camille	untitled charcoal drawing
Pope, Arthur	title unknown (watercolor) (see SP, 13)
Rodin, Auguste	*Nude* (lithograph)
Smith, Alive [Alice?]	Ravenel Huger, *Morning Glory and Moonlight* (watercolor)
Strang, Ian Bond	*Street* (etching)
Strang, Ian Bond	*Dome of St. Paul's* (etching)
Strang, Ian Bond	*Fitzroy Street* (etching)
Strang, Ian Bond	*Shepherd Market, Mayfair* (etching)
Tal Coat, Pierre	*Still Life (Angel Surrounded by Paysans)* (oil)

Notes

Introduction

1 Michel Benamou, *Wallace Stevens and the Symbolist Imagination* (Princeton: Princeton University Press, 1972). The relevant chapters are 1, "Poetry and Painting," and 4, "Apollinaire," in which Benamou compares Stevens and Apollinaire as poets whose development stemmed directly from their confrontations with modern painting.

2 Robert Buttel, *Wallace Stevens: The Making of "Harmonium"* (Princeton: Princeton University Press, 1967); James Baird, *The Dome and the Rock: Structure in the Poetry of Wallace Stevens* (Baltimore: Johns Hopkins University Press, 1968). Buttel asserts that, although Stevens was "a follower of all the movements in modern painting," he learned most from the impressionists (168). See also Kathleen Petrisky Weiss, "The Fundamental Aesthetic: Wallace Stevens and the Painters," Ph.D. diss., University of Massachusetts, 1975. Weiss concludes that Stevens' aesthetics are basically impressionist.

3 Charles Altieri, *Painterly Abstraction in Modern American Poetry* (New York: Cambridge University Press, 1989). See also his "Why Stevens Must Be Abstract, or What a Poet Can Learn from Painting," in Albert Gelpi, ed., *Wallace Stevens: The Poetics of Modernism* (New York: Cambridge University Press, 1985), 86–118. Bonnie Costello's excellent analysis of how

painting served Stevens as an analogy for his own poetry ("Effects of an Analogy: Wallace Stevens and Painting," in Gelpi, *Stevens,* 65–85) also avoids the question of Stevens' relation to the contemporary art world.

4 Françoise Marin, "A Note on Stevens' Personal Art Collection," in Benamou, *Stevens,* 141–44.

5 Stevens began doing business with Vidal in 1931, and corresponded with him or his daughter regularly thereafter. See Peter Brazeau, *Parts of a World: Wallace Stevens Remembered* (New York: Random House, 1983), 27n.

6 In Stevens' library were Lionello Venturi's *Georges Rouault* (New York: E. Weyhe, 1940); James Thrall Soby's *Georges Rouault* (New York: Museum of Modern Art, 1945); Henry Church's *Les Clowns* (Paris: Deux Amis, 1922), illustrated by Rouault; and the catalogue from an exhibition of Rouault's *Le Miserere* (Paris: Louis Carré Gallery, 1952), sent "compliments of L.C." Stevens' friend Henry Church knew Rouault and collected his work.

7 TLS, Wallace Stevens to Charles Henri Ford, Aug. 15, 1938, Harry Ransom Humanities Research Center, Austin. It also seems possible, as William Burney once pointed out to me in conversation, that Stevens would have found such artists as Rouault and Miró overpowering—that having examples of their mastery in his home would have inhibited rather than inspired his own creativity.

8 James Thrall Soby, Samuel French Morse, and James Johnson Sweeney all testify to Stevens' love of Klee's painting in Brazeau, *Parts of a World,* 119, 157, and 227.

9 Ibid., 227.

10 Consider this statement of 1948, for example: "I think that all this abstract painting that is going on nowadays is just so much frustration and evasion" (L, 593). This seems to indicate that Stevens has no sympathy with "advanced" contemporary art. But his statements about art are generally difficult to interpret. How is one to reconcile this sentiment, for instance, with his recognition the next year of the need "to paint / In the present state of painting and not the state / Of thirty years ago" (CP, 478)?

11 See Milton J. Bates, "Stevens' Books at the Huntington: An Annotated Checklist," *Wallace Stevens Journal* 3, nos. 1 and 2 (Spring 1979): 16.

12 "The instinct of joy" seems to be a translation of "l'instinct du bonheur," a phrase Stevens copied into his commonplace book in 1934. See Milton J. Bates, ed., *Sur Plusieurs Beaux Sujects: Wallace Stevens' Commonplace*

Book (Stanford and San Marino: Stanford University Press and The Huntington Library, 1989), 37.

13 Milton W. Brown, *The Story of the Armory Show,* rev. ed. (New York: Abbeville, 1988), 222.

14 My information concerning the 1935 van Gogh exhibition at MOMA comes from Russell Lynes, *Good Old Modern: An Intimate Portrait of the Museum of Modern Art* (New York: Atheneum, 1973), 132–36.

15 Ibid., 135.

16 Alan Filreis discusses Stevens' interest in this exhibition in the context of the "war effort." See his *Wallace Stevens and the Actual World* (Princeton: Princeton University Press, 1991), 52–53.

17 Costello, "Effects of an Analogy," 66.

18 The following books focus on Williams and the visual arts: Bram Dijkstra, *The Hieroglyphics of a New Speech: Cubism, Stieglitz and the Early Poetry of William Carlos Williams* (Princeton: Princeton University Press, 1969); Dickran Tashjian, *William Carlos Williams and the American Scene, 1920–1940* (New York: Whitney Museum of American Art, 1978); William Marling, *William Carlos Williams and the Painters, 1909–1923* (Athens: Ohio University Press, 1982); Henry Sayre, *The Visual Text of William Carlos Williams* (Champaign: Illinois University Press, 1983); Christopher MacGowan, *William Carlos Williams' Early Poetry: The Visual Arts Background* (Ann Arbor: UMI Research Press, 1984); Peter Schmidt, *William Carlos Williams, the Arts, and Literary Tradition* (Baton Rouge: Louisiana State University Press, 1988); and Terence Diggory, *William Carlos Williams and the Ethics of Painting* (Princeton: Princeton University Press, 1991).

19 Dijkstra (*Hieroglyphics,* 173–76) asserts that Williams based his poem on Gris's *Roses;* however, MacGowan has shown that the painting Williams had in mind was more probably *The Open Window* (*Williams' Early Poetry,* 112–14).

20 Letter to me from Robert Motherwell, Jan. 19, 1988. Quoted by permission of the Dedalus Foundation, Inc.

21 Hayden Carruth, "Without the Inventions of Sorrow," *Poetry* 85, no. 5 (February 1955): 288–93; rpt. in Charles Doyle, ed., *Wallace Stevens: The Critical Heritage* (London: Routledge and Kegan Paul, 1985), 405–09.

22 For a more detailed analysis of Stevens' relation to the Arensberg circle, see my *Wallace Stevens and Company: The "Harmonium" Years, 1913–1923* (Ann Arbor: UMI Research Press, 1983), esp. chap. 2, "The Art Crowd."

23 Milton Bates uses Stevens' phrase—from "The Comedian as the Letter C" (CP, 28)—as the organizing concept of his *Wallace Stevens: A Mythology*

of Self (Berkeley: University of California Press, 1985). My debt to this book will be evident throughout.

Chapter 1. *Harmonium* and the Arensberg Circle

1   For further discussion of Stevens' relation to the Arensberg circle, see my *Wallace Stevens and Company: The "Harmonium" Years, 1913–1923* (Ann Arbor: UMI Research Press, 1983). On Stevens' *Harmonium* period, see Robert Buttel, *Wallace Stevens: The Making of "Harmonium"* (Princeton: Princeton University Press, 1967) and A. Walton Litz, *Introspective Voyager: The Poetic Development of Wallace Stevens* (New York: Oxford University Press, 1971).

2   For a biography, see Francis Naumann, "Walter Conrad Arensberg: Poet, Patron, and Participant in the New York Avant-Garde, 1914–1920," *Philadelphia Museum of Art Bulletin* 76, no. 328 (Spring 1980): 1–32.

3   The standard history of the Armory Show is Milton W. Brown, *The Story of the Armory Show,* rev. ed. (New York: Abbeville, 1988).

4   Katherine Kuh, *The Open Eye: In Pursuit of Art* (New York: Harper & Row, 1971), 60.

5   Brown, *Armory Show,* 72.

6   Sandra S. Phillips, "The Art Criticism of Walter Pach," *Art Bulletin* 65 (March 1983): 111, 112.

7   Brown, *Armory Show,* 178.

8   See Naumann, "Walter Conrad Arensberg," 7.

9   Francis Naumann discusses at length each of these European members of the Arensberg salon in his *New York Dada: In Advance of the Avant-Garde* (New York: Abrams, forthcoming).

10   *The Autobiography of William Carlos Williams* (New York: New Directions, 1951), 137.

11   Contrary to the implication of this letter of 1945, Stevens did own at least one print by Braque. It was found among his papers, unframed, after his death. He probably acquired this print through the agency of Charles Henri Ford. In a letter to Ford dated Aug. 15, 1938 (in the Harry Ransom Humanities Research Center, University of Texas, Austin), Stevens writes that he will be happy to look at one or two Braques that a friend of Ford's has for sale. Stevens owned a small oil painting by the French primitive Camille Bombois entitled *Le Loiret à Olivet.* Both works are now in the collection of Holly Stevens; see Appendix.

12 See Michel Benamou, *Wallace Stevens and the Symbolist Imagination* (Princeton: Princeton University Press, 1972), 1-24, 87–107; Buttel, 163–65; Wylie Sypher, *Rococo to Cubism in Art and Literature* (New York: Random House, 1960), 259, 315–21; Rajeev S. Patke, *The Long Poems of Wallace Stevens: An Interpretative Study* (New York: Cambridge University Press, 1985), 69–108; and Joan Richardson, *Wallace Stevens: The Early Years, 1879–1923* (New York: Morrow, 1986), 402–08. Jacqueline Vaught Brogan singles out "The Man with the Blue Guitar" as Stevens' "supreme synthetic cubist poem" in her *Part of the Climate: American Cubist Poetry* (Berkeley: University of California Press, 1991), 234.

    The best short study I know of cubism as "the dominant aesthetic (and perhaps intellectual) ideology of our day" is in Wendy Steiner, *The Colors of Rhetoric: Problems in the Relation between Modern Literature and Painting* (Chicago: University of Chicago Press, 1982), 177–97.

13 The *Nude Descending a Staircase* in Arensberg's collection during the 1910s was not the original painting, which was then owned by another collector (though Arensberg acquired it later). The *Nude* in Sheeler's photograph is a full-color reproduction of the original, hand-colored by Duchamp.

14 Anne d'Harnoncourt and Kynaston McShine, eds., *Marcel Duchamp* (Museum of Modern Art and Philadelphia Museum of Art, 1973), 258.

15 Man Ray and Arturo Schwartz, "An Interview with Man Ray: 'This Is Not for America,'" *Arts Magazine* 51, no. 9 (May 1977): 119.

16 d'Harnoncourt and McShine, *Duchamp*, 249.

17 Two of Stevens' lists of possible titles, *Schemata* and *From Pieces of Paper*, are reproduced in George S. Lensing, *Wallace Stevens: A Poet's Growth* (Baton Rouge: Louisiana State University Press, 1986), 158–200.

18 d'Harnoncourt and McShine, *Duchamp*, 260.

19 Benamou, *Wallace Stevens*, 14.

20 Milton J. Bates, *Wallace Stevens: A Mythology of Self* (Berkeley: University of California Press, 1985), 152.

21 d'Harnoncourt and McShine, *Duchamp*, 263.

22 Ibid., 272.

23 For a full account of the *Fountain* episode, see William A. Camfield, "Marcel Duchamp's *Fountain*: Its History and Aesthetics in the Context of 1917," in Rudolf E. Kuenzli and Francis M. Naumann, eds., *Marcel Duchamp: Artist of the Century* (Cambridge: MIT Press, 1989), 64–94.

24 TLS, Pitts Sanborn to Wallace Stevens, May 23, 1917, in the Huntington Library, San Marino, Calif.: "I am sending you a copy of the Blind Man for May in case you have not seen it. It is not for sale. Carl V. V. [Van

Vechten] got me several copies and tells me Mrs. Harry Payne Whitney paid for the publication of this number—the second—provided it should not be offered for sale. The contents are variously interesting."

25 Dickran Tashjian, *Skyscraper Primitives: Dada and the American Avant-Garde, 1910–1925* (Middletown, Conn.: Wesleyan University Press, 1975), 54.

26 Arturo Schwartz, *Marcel Duchamp* (New York: Abrams, 1975), quoted from the introduction, which is unpaginated.

27 *The Blind Man,* no. 2 (May 1917): 6. This statement was written by Beatrice Wood and approved by Marcel Duchamp.

28 d'Harnoncourt and McShine, *Duchamp,* 275–76.

29 Milton Bates suggests (*Wallace Stevens,* p. 129) that Stevens borrowed the phrase "the act of the mind" from John Sparrow's *Sense and Poetry: Essays on the Place of Meaning in Contemporary Verse* (New Haven: Yale University Press, 1934) where it denotes a behaviorist conception of consciousness. If so, then Stevens revised its meaning in a manner compatible with "choice."

30 Robert Motherwell, ed., *The Dada Painters and Poets: An Anthology* (New York: Wittenborn, Schultz, 1951), xvii.

31 Letter from Wallace Stevens to R. P. Blackmur, Nov. 16, 1931, published in Holly Stevens, "Flux-2," *Southern Review* 15, no. 4 (October 1979): 773–74.

32 Roy Harvey Pearce, *Gesta Humanorum: Studies in the Historicist Mode* (Columbia: University of Missouri Press, 1987), 128–30.

33 Rudolf E. Kuenzli, ed., *New York Dada* (New York: Willis Locker and Owens, 1986), 1.

34 William Innes Homer and Louise Hassett Lincoln, "New York Dada and the Arensberg Circle," in William Innes Homer, *Alfred Stieglitz and the American Avant-Garde* (Boston: New York Graphic Society, 1977), 184.

Chapter 2. Stevens in the 1930s

1 Numerous theories have been offered to explain Stevens' silent years. Recently, David R. Jarraway has traced his inactivity to psychological contradictions that were unresolved in *Harmonium.* See his "Crispin's Dependent 'Airs': Psychic Crisis in the Early Stevens," *Wallace Stevens Journal* 14, no. 1 (Spring 1990): 21–32. James Longenbach's *Wallace Stevens: The Plain Sense of Things* (New York: Oxford University Press, 1991) devotes two chapters to this "silent" period (pp. 105–32).

2   For my understanding of Stevens' development in the 1930s, I am particularly indebted to Milton Bates' excellent analysis in his *Wallace Stevens: A Mythology of Self* (Berkeley: University of California Press, 1985), chap. 5.

3   Letter from Stevens to Charles Henri Ford, Oct. 4, 1940, Harry Ransom Humanities Research Center, University of Texas, Austin. The collector referred to is James Thrall Soby.

4   John Russell, "A Fine Scottish Hand," *New York Times Magazine,* July 22, 1990: 45.

5   Peter Brazeau, *Parts of a World: Wallace Stevens Remembered* (New York: Random House, 1983), 220.

6   Milton Bates, ed., *Sur Plusieurs Beaux Sujects: Wallace Stevens' Commonplace Book* (Stanford and San Marino: Stanford University Press and The Huntington Library, 1989), 71.

7   Frederick Lewis Allen, *The Great Pierpont Morgan* (1949; rpt. New York: Dorset Press, 1989), 137–38.

8   "From a European palace to an American multi-millionaire's castle to a public foundation—this is the way of art collections in the United States, and usually in one generation. . . . This kind of thing happens nowhere else in the world. . . . In Europe accumulations of paintings and art objects at all comparable in value to American collections 'in the grand style' belong only to monarchs or very powerful nobles and are not subject to the kind of hard-boiled bookkeeping imposed by Uncle Sam." This passage is excerpted from an article about the Widener gift to the National Gallery entitled "The Public Inherits Princely Art," *New York Times Magazine,* March 9, 1941: 9.

9   Morid Spalding, in a review of *Masterpieces of European Painting in America,* ed. H. Tietze (London: Allen & Unwin, 1940), in *Life and Letters Today* 24, no. 32 (April 1940): 99.

10 Allen, *Morgan,* 138.

11 *Dictionary of American Biography* (New York: Scribners, 1934), 13:179; Aline B. Saarinen, *The Proud Possessors: The Lives, Times and Tastes of Some Adventurous American Art Collectors* (New York: Random House, 1958), 57; Francis Henry Taylor, *Pierpont Morgan as Collector and Patron* (New York: Pierpont Morgan Library, 1957, 1970), 39.

12 Metropolitan Museum of Art, *Guide to the Loan Exhibition of the J. Pierpont Morgan Collection* (1914), viii.

13 Howard Hibbard, *The Metropolitan Museum of Art* (New York: Harper & Row, 1980), 208. Among such negative views, Roger Fry's famous verdict is the most damning, coming from a great critic and a champion of

modern art. In his tenure as European adviser of paintings at the Metropolitan Museum of Art from 1906 through 1910, Fry concluded of President Morgan that "a crude historical imagination was the only flaw in his otherwise perfect insensibility" (quoted in Virginia Woolf, *Roger Fry: A Biography* [1940; rpt. New York: Harcourt Brace Jovanovich, 1976], 141). Fry's harsh judgment of Morgan's abilities reflects his strong personal aversion to his employer. His upper-class British manners were offended by Morgan's rough-and-ready style; he believed that the aggressive businessman and the sensitive connoisseur were fundamentally incompatible types.

14   Randall Jarrell, *Poetry and the Age* (1953; rpt. New York: Noonday, 1972), 135.

15   Stevens' specially bound copies of all his books of poetry, except *Harmonium* and the *Collected Poems,* are in the Huntington Library. See Milton Bates, "Stevens' Books at the Huntington: An Annotated Checklist," *Wallace Stevens Journal* 3, nos. 1 and 2 (Spring 1979): 23–25.

16   Walter Pach, *Queer Thing, Painting: Forty Years in the World of Art* (New York: Harper, 1938), 71–72.

17   Stevens' letter reads "the National Academy of Art," but this seems clearly to be an error for the National Academy of Design.

18   Alan Filreis, "Still Life without Substance: Wallace Stevens and the Language of Agency," *Poetics Today* 10, no. 2 (Summer 1989): 352.

19   William Carlos Williams, *Imaginations* (New York: New Directions, 1970), 14.

20   Letter to Wilson Taylor, Nov. 18, 1942, in Frank Doggett and Robert Buttel, eds., *Wallace Stevens: A Celebration* (Princeton: Princeton University Press, 1980), 81.

21   Compare Emerson, "Money . . . is, in its effects and laws, as beautiful as roses" (from *Nominalist and Realist*). Also: "[Money] is the romance, the poetry of our age. It's the thing that chiefly strikes the imagination" (spoken by the character Bromfield Corey in William Dean Howells' *The Rise of Silas Lapham,* ed. Walter J. Meserve and David J. Nordloh [Bloomington: Indiana University Press, 1971], 64). My thanks to Clare Eby for calling this to my attention.

22   Letter to Lila James Roney, Aug. 25, 1944, The Huntington Library. Quoted in Brazeau, *Parts of a World,* 271.

23   On Stevens' genealogical studies, see Bates, *Wallace Stevens,* 279–85; and his "To Realize the Past: Wallace Stevens' Genealogical Study," *American Literature* 52 (1984): 607–27. Also Brazeau, *Parts of a World,* 265–88.

24   Thomas Craven, *Treasury of Art Masterpieces* (New York: Simon &

Schuster, 1939), 282. This book is the source of Stevens' quotation in "The Noble Rider and the Sound of Words" (1941) from a note on Reginald Marsh's painting *Wooden Horses* (NA, 11). The passage quoted here begins Craven's essay on Frans Hals, and it helps to explain Stevens' reference to Hals in "Notes toward a Supreme Fiction" (see chap. 5). I wish to thank Diana Menkes for identifying the Marsh painting, the clue that led me to the Craven book.

25 Madlyn Millner Kahr, *Dutch Painting in the Seventeenth Century* (New York: Harper & Row, 1978), 7. As I have pointed out in the Introduction, Panofskian iconography finds many suggestions of evil in these paintings. Stevens either did not know Panofsky's method of interpretation or was not interested in it.

26 Max J. Friedlaender, *Landscape, Portrait, Still-Life* (New York: Schocken, 1963), 281.

27 This example demonstrates that Stevens' taste in painting was still unformed at this time (at age 27). Four decades later, in a letter to Thomas McGreevy, he expressed a settled lack of sympathy for Rembrandt's painting: "Rembrandt, I must confess, has never stimulated me a great deal. I bow to him. But he leaves me, somehow or other, indifferent. The sense of his greatness is something I have to read about: I do not feel it" (L, 668).

28 Stevens' love of epigrams is another trait he shared with seventeenth-century Dutchmen. Emblem books of illustrated proverbs were enormously popular, as were paintings in the same manner, such as Jan Steen's *Easy Come, Easy Go* (see Svetlana Alpers, *The Art of Describing: Dutch Art in the Seventeenth Century* [Chicago: University of Chicago Press, 1983], 76). The proverbs of the poet Jacob Cats were said to be "in every Dutch house" (Kahr, *Dutch Painting*, 8; Alpers, *Art of Describing*, 230). For the importance of aphorism in Stevens' poetry, see Beverly Coyle, *A Thought to Be Rehearsed: Aphorism in Wallace Stevens' Poetry* (Ann Arbor: UMI Research Press, 1983).

29 Quoted in Adriaan J. Barnouw, *The Dutch: A Portrait Study of the People of Holland* (New York: Columbia University Press, 1940), 29.

30 Stevens' detailed knowledge of flowers is evident throughout his poetry. In this respect he is like the Dutch painters who composed elaborate, impossible still lifes of flowers gathered from around the world that bloomed in different climates and at different times of the year. Their buyers knew and appreciated such careful distinctions between types of flowers (Kahr, *Dutch Painting*, 191).

Stevens recorded his systematic study of flowers in his journal. He made it his business to learn their names and characteristics, and found it a "monstrous pleasure to be able to be specific" about them (L, 28–29). He wrote for an audience that would appreciate such careful discrimination. He expects his readers to share his pleasure in being able to include a long, accurate, poetic list of early-spring flowers in "The Man on the Dump" (CP, 202), merely in order to define the time of year by throwing them away. The conception of "Anecdote of Canna" (CP, 55) is clearer when one knows that canna are indeed "huge." And the reader can fully appreciate the ironic juxtaposition of "a fuchsia in a can" (CP, 478) only if he is able to picture the gaudy voluptuousness of that particular flower. "Next to the passion flower, I love fuchsias, and no kidding," wrote Stevens (L, 565). There are countless such examples.

31 Kenneth Clark, *Landscape into Art* (1949; rpt. London: Pelican, 1961), 106.

32 Stevens' taste for fine wines, expensive imported foods, and exotic items from around the world may not seem to exemplify the love of "simple" pleasures. The point, however, is the pleasure one gets from the simple, direct gratification of the senses. Moreover, a delight in exotic things is typical of seventeenth-century Holland. As a nation of international traders, the Dutch were in an ideal position to sample the bounty of faraway places. Exotic foods and flowers were readily available in their markets, and their scientific spirit led them to form large collections of interesting objects from the furthest reaches of travel. (See Alpers, *Art of Description*, 111). Dutch still lifes often included an exotic appeal we may not notice: even the now common lemon was "a rare and refreshing sight" in the seventeenth century. See Herbert Furst, *The Art of Still-Life Painting* (New York: Scribner's, 1927), 51.

33 Helen Vendler reads this entire poem, implausibly, as the hysterical outburst of a neurotic woman who descends into madness in the two final stanzas. See her *On Extended Wings: Wallace Stevens' Longer Poems* (Cambridge: Harvard University Press, 1969), 147–49. This uncharacteristically strained reading is the result, I think, of undervaluing the Dutch aspect of Stevens' imagination.

34 Stevens himself had some German (Pennsylvania Dutch) blood, and he probably thought of the German and Dutch characters as similar in some respects. He certainly admired in German painting some of the same qualities he associated with Dutch art. See L, 117–18, 127.

35 In 1933 Stevens copied a long passage on "the normal" into his commonplace book, including such observations as "It is seldom that the normal is sought with excited zeal, yet it is the normal that is good, and it is the normal that fortunately can most easily be gained." The passage is

from A. R. Powys, review of *The Revival of Christian Architecture* by A. Welby Pugin, *London Mercury* 28 (May 1933): 63–64. See Bates, *Sur Plusieurs Beaux Sujects,* 25–29.

36 Kahr, *Dutch Painting,* 60–66. There is a distinct kind of Dutch genre painting, the *buiten partijen,* or "outdoor feast," which exactly matches the sort of scene Stevens imagines. See Peter C. Sutton, ed., *Masters of Seventeenth-Century Dutch Genre Painting* (Philadelphia: Philadelphia Museum of Art, 1984), xxix-xxx. Two paintings reproduced in this book might easily illustrate Stevens' vision of "the normal": David Vinckboons' *The Garden Party* (fig. 28) and Frans Hals' *Banquet in the Open Air* (destroyed in 1945) (fig. 29). I wish to thank Cathy Levesque for pointing this out to me.

37 The phenomenon of the middle-class collector first appeared in seventeenth-century Holland. Stevens' awareness of this probably helped shape his image of himself as an art collector. As J. H. Huizinga writes, "Foreign visitors [to Holland] were taken aback by the widespread desire to own works of art. Good paintings could be bought in Rotterdam fairground booths, and were wont to grace the walls of even the humblest houses. You will not find a cobbler, an English traveller wrote, who does not own a painting" (*Dutch Civilization in the Seventeenth Century and Other Essays* [New York: Frederick Ungar, 1968], 45).

In this new situation, paintings were seldom commissioned but were produced instead for the marketplace: "We have little information from the commissioning of works since the great majority were made for the market or, better, the markets. They were sold either out of the painter's shop, from kermis stalls, or, if they took the form of prints, at a bookseller dealing in maps, books, and prints" (Alpers, *Art of Description,* 1). The close relation between business and art that prevailed in this market was congenial to the Dutch collectors, who were generally businessmen themselves. Stevens would naturally have been drawn to a time and place where the love of art could be a normal part of the ordinary businessman's daily life.

38 Alpers, *Art of Description,* xxv.

39 Cornelis Veth, *The Fine Arts,* vol. 20 of *A General View of the Netherlands* (The Hague: Netherlands Ministry of Agriculture, 1915), 6.

40 Arthur K. Wheelock, Jr., "Still Life: Its Visual Appeal and Theoretical Status in the Seventeenth Century," in *Still Lifes of the Golden Age: Northern European Paintings from the Heinz Family Collection* (Washington, D.C.: National Gallery of Art, 1989), 12.

41 Lawrance Thompson records a conversation between Frost and Stevens that took place in Key West in February 1940. Frost reportedly said to Stevens, "Your trouble, Wallace, is that you write poems about bric-a-brac." See Thompson, *Robert Frost: The Years of Triumph, 1915–1938* (New York: Holt, Rinehart and Winston, 1970), 666.

42   Jarrell, *Poetry and the Age,* 141.

43   Kahr, *Dutch Painting,* 126–27.

Chapter 3. "The Man with the Blue Guitar" and Surrealism

1   John C. Burnham, *Paths into American Culture: Psychology, Medicine, and Morals* (Philadelphia: Temple University Press, 1988), chap. 6, "The Influence of Psychoanalysis upon American Culture," 98.

2   The best account of "Owl's Clover" as an important but failed experiment is in A. Walton Litz, *Introspective Voyager: The Poetic Development of Wallace Stevens* (New York: Oxford University Press, 1971), 203–28.

3   Latimer was a mysterious figure who used various pseudonyms and apparently disappeared in the late 1930s. See L, 256–57.

4   André Breton, *Manifestoes of Surrealism,* trans. Richard Seaver and Helen R. Lane (1969; rpt. Ann Arbor: University of Michigan Press, 1972), 14.

5   Another aspect of Stevens' correspondence with Latimer during the mid-1930s that shows traces of surrealism is Stevens' readiness to admit unconscious influences in his poetry: "The pseudo-primitive of which you speak is . . . unconscious" (L, 207); "If there are any literary relations between my things and those of other writers, they are unconscious" (L, 290). References to the unconscious are rare at other times in Stevens' career. Here they reflect, I think, the currency of the term in the contemporary art world.

6   Quoted in Russell Lynes, *Good Old Modern: An Intimate Portrait of the Museum of Modern Art* (New York: Atheneum, 1973), 142–43.

7   Peter Quennell, "The Surrealist Exhibition," *New Statesman and Nation,* June 20, 1936: 967.

8   Ibid.: 968.

9   Stevens' fear of being classified as a surrealist was well founded. Even so sympathetic a spirit as Henry Church, who was perhaps his closest friend and whose opinions he greatly respected, considered that Stevens' group of poems "A Thought Revolved" (1936) was "tainted with surréalisme" (letter from H.C. to W.S., dated April 17, 1939, in the Huntington Library, San Marino, Calif.). The novelist Bryher observed his surrealist

tendencies more diplomatically: "Why has no one seen that he was fore-
runner of all surrealistes, throwing an absurd but apt comparison,
snatched from candy tray or poster, into the midst of beautiful and abstract lines?" ("My Introduction to America," in *Life and Letters Today*
26 [September 1940]: 238).

10 Edward Alden Jewell, "Proteus of Modernism," *New York Times*, Nov. 1,
1936, sec. 10, p. 9.

11 For details about this exhibition, and for a history of the Atheneum during
its modernist heyday in the 1930s, see Eugene R. Gaddis, ed., *Avery
Memorial, Wadsworth Atheneum: The First Modern Museum* (Hartford,
Conn.: Wadsworth Atheneum, 1984).

12 Clive Bell, "Picasso," *New Statesman and Nation*, May 30, 1936: 857.

13 I cite canto numbers rather than page numbers for quotations from "The
Man with the Blue Guitar," so that the reader may easily consult either CP
or *Palm*.

14 This transcript of Picasso's conversation is reprinted in English in Dore
Ashton, ed., *Picasso on Art: A Selection of Views* (New York: Viking,
1972), 6–13.

15 Susan Brown Weston, "The Artist as Guitarist: Stevens and Picasso,"
Criticism 17 (1975): 111–20.

16 See especially Judith Rinde Sheridan, "The Picasso Connection: Wallace
Stevens's 'The Man with the Blue Guitar,'" *Arizona Quarterly* 35 (1979):
77–89. See also Rajeev S. Patke, *The Long Poems of Wallace Stevens: An
Interpretative Study* (New York: Cambridge University Press, 1985) and J.
V. Brogan, *Part of the Climate: American Cubist Poetry* (Berkeley: Univer-
sity of California Press, 1991).

17 Alfred H. Barr, Jr., *Fantastic Art, Dada, Surrealism* (New York: Museum
of Modern Art, 1936), 217.

18 André Breton, *Surrealism and Painting*, trans. Simon Watson Taylor
(1965; rpt. New York: Harper & Row, 1972), 7. The phrase "even the
'surrealist' label" is added as a footnote in Breton's text. For convenience I
have included it here in parentheses instead.

19 André Breton, "Picasso poète," *Cahiers d'art* 10 (1935): 185.

20 James Thrall Soby, *After Picasso* (New York: Dodd, Mead, 1935), 98.

21 Quennell, "Surrealist Exhibition," 967.

22 William Rubin, ed., *Pablo Picasso: A Retrospective* (New York: Museum
of Modern Art, 1980), 308–09.

23 Christian Zervos, "Fait social et vision cosmique," *Cahiers d'art* 10
(1935): 145.

24 For a thorough discussion of the significance of the term "pure poetry" for

Stevens in the 1930s, see A. Walton Litz, "Wallace Stevens' Defense of Poetry: La Poésie Pure, the New Romantic, and the Pressure of Reality," in George Bornstein, ed., *Romantic and Modern* (Pittsburgh: University of Pittsburgh Press, 1977), 111–32.

25 Breton, "Picasso poète," 186.

26 Susan B. Weston quotes a few excerpts from this article. But she quotes them in French without translating them, and her comments reveal a number of basic misunderstandings of Breton's difficult prose. Other critics, such as Patke, have followed suit.

27 Breton, "Picasso poète," 186. I wish to thank Virginia Middleton of the University of Connecticut and Mortimer Guiney of Antioch College for helping me to translate this essay accurately. Any awkwardness and errors in the final translation are entirely my own.

28 The deliberate symbolism of this gesture is partly obscured by Breton's elliptical prose. According to Lydia Gasman, in the actual event the woman who had just given birth was Breton's wife, Jacqueline, and Picasso placed the miniature guitar directly on her pudendum. (Telephone conversation with Lydia Gasman, Dec. 10, 1985; also see her "Mystery, Magic, and Love in Picasso, 1925–1938: Picasso and the Surrealist Poets" [Ph.D. diss., Columbia University, 1981], p. 61, n. 4.)

29 Breton, "Picasso poète," 188.

30 Breton, *Anthologie de l'humour noir,* rev. ed. (Paris: Editions du Sagittaire, 1950).

31 Breton, "Picasso poète," 186.

32 Anne d'Harnoncourt and Kynaston McShine, eds., *Marcel Duchamp* (Museum of Modern Art and Philadelphia Museum of Art, 1973), 21; Breton, *Surrealism and Painting,* 280.

33 Breton, *Surrealism and Painting,* 277.

34 Breton, "Picasso poète," 186. "On saisit par là le besoin d'expression totale qui le possède et lui impose de remédier de la sorte à l'insuffisance relative d'un art par rapport à l'autre."

35 Ibid.

36 Renato Poggioli, ed., *Matino domenicale ed altre poesie* (Turin: Giulio Einaudi, 1954), 179.

37 Zervos, "Fait social," 150.

38 Quoted in Peter Brazeau, *Parts of a World: Wallace Stevens Remembered* (New York: Random House, 1983), 118.

39 A. Everett Austin, *Newer Super-Realism* (Hartford, Conn.: Wadsworth Atheneum, November 1931).

Chapter 4. *Parts of a World* and the Abstraction/Surrealism Debate

1 Joseph N. Riddel, *The Clairvoyant Eye: The Poetry and Poetics of Wallace Stevens* (Baton Rouge: Louisiana State University Press, 1965), 150. One later poem that invokes "the world of the art gallery"—specifically, the Durand-Ruel Gallery—is "Holiday in Reality" of 1944 (CP, 312–13). Barbara Fisher's sensitive reading of this poem takes into account the significance of the gallery setting. See her *Wallace Stevens: The Intensest Rendezvous* (Charlottesville: University Press of Virginia, 1990), 129–32.

2 Joseph Carroll, *Wallace Stevens' Supreme Fiction: A New Romanticism* (Baton Rouge: Louisiana State University Press, 1987), 106.

3 Eleanor Cook, *Poetry, Word-Play, and Word-War in Wallace Stevens* (Princeton: Princeton University Press, 1988), 160.

4 We cannot doubt that Stevens intended this grotesque pun. He himself had been considering the purchase of several "hangings" in New York art galleries not long before he wrote "Parochial Theme": "We have about reached the saturation point [in regard to home furnishings] and need very little more except some hangings here and there. August, as I remember it, is the month when they almost give hangings away on 57th Street"(L, 321).

5 *Southern Review* 4, no. 2 (Autumn 1938): 382–95.

6 The analogy applies to *any* display of selected works of art—not only in a museum or art gallery, but also in the home of a private art collector. I limit the discussion here to the example of an "art exhibition" for the sake of clarity and convenience, though the example of the private art collection is even more appropriate in some ways. The important point is that Stevens imagines himself in the position of a man who chooses to acquire particular artworks and determines how they will be displayed. The art collector, the curator, and the museum director are all possible alter egos in this respect.

7 Michel Benamou, *Wallace Stevens and the Symbolist Imagination* (Princeton: Princeton University Press, 1972), 13.

8 Diane Middlebrook's perceptive comment on "Notes" as a "collection" is apropos in this context: "*Notes* as a whole and in its parts seems to be an exalted version of the junk-shop of 'Dezembrum' (CP, 218) or the Blue Guitarist's patchings: a collection of odds and ends that represents the collector's range of interests" (*Wallace Stevens and Walt Whitman* [Ithaca: Cornell University Press, 1974], 142). We may think of "Notes" as an *art* collection that serves the same purpose.

9 John Russell, "A Fine Scottish Hand," *New York Times Magazine,* July 22, 1990: 24.

10 The exhibition ran Jan. 25 through Feb. 15, 1938.

11 Clement Greenberg, review of an exhibition of John Marin, *The Nation,* Dec. 25, 1948; rpt. in John O'Brian, ed., *Clement Greenberg: Collected Essays and Criticism* (Chicago: University of Chicago Press, 1986), 2: 268.

12 Frank Doggett and Robert Buttel, eds., *Wallace Stevens: A Celebration* (Princeton: Princeton University Press, 1980), 101.

13 George L. K. Morris, "Art Chronicle: Miró and the Spanish Civil War," *Partisan Review* 4, no. 3 (February 1938): 33.

14 Ibid., 32, 33. *Still Life with Old Shoe* was included in the Miró exhibition at the Pierre Matisse Gallery, April 18 through May 7, 1938. See Barbara Rose, *Miró in America* (Houston: Museum of Fine Arts, 1982), 137. It seems likely that Stevens saw the painting there, and that he remembered it when he told Charles Henri Ford in August 1938 that he found Miró "miraculous."

15 Norman Bryson, *Looking at the Overlooked: Four Essays on Still Life Painting* (Cambridge: Harvard University Press, 1990), 13–14.

16 Ibid., 13.

17 This cryptic signature stands for the two authors of the Foreword, both of whom were "Juniors": A. Everett Austin and Henry-Russell Hitchcock. They signed their full names to the essay when it appeared as a separate article in *Art News.* See "Aesthetic of Still Life over Four Centuries: Dead Nature, Caravaggio to Picasso," *Art News* 36 (Feb. 5, 1938): 12–13ff.

18 Harry Holtzmann and Martin S. James, eds., *The New Art—The New Life: The Collected Writings of Piet Mondrian* (Boston: G. K. Hall, 1986), 295. Quoted from Mondrian's essay "Plastic Art and Pure Plastic Art," in J. L. Martin, Ben Nicholson, Naum Gabo, *Circle: An International Survey of Constructive Art* (London: Faber and Faber, 1937).

19 It is by no means necessary to see still life as related to surrealism, with its representational values and other "literary" qualities. Roger Fry emphasizes precisely the opposite aspects of still life: its value as "pure" art, uncontaminated by "humanity," that encourages appreciation of strictly formal, abstract qualities: "It is in still-life that we frequently catch the purest self-revelation of the artist. In any other subject humanity intervenes. . . . The still-life . . . guards the picture itself from the misconstruction of those whose contact with art is confined to its effect as representation" (*Cézanne: A Study of His Development* [1927; rpt. New York: Noonday Press, 1970], 4).

20 See "Twenty Years: Some Aspects of English Glass," *Apollo* 26 (1937): 10–11. Stevens read *Apollo* regularly between 1936 and 1940. See L, 368; and Milton Bates, *Sur Plusieurs Beaux Sujects: Wallace Stevens' Commonplace Book* (Stanford and San Marino: Stanford University Press and The Huntington Library, 1989), 57, 63, 73.

21 The word *object* entered Stevens' poetic vocabulary in the 1930s. Its first appearance was in "The Man with the Blue Guitar," in a passage clearly related to the notion of surrealist objects: "A dream (to call it a dream) in which / I can believe, in face of the object" (xviii; see chap. 2). Thereafter, Stevens nearly always used the term to make some point about art theory, as in the titles "Prelude to Objects," "A Completely New Set of Objects," "Desire and the Object," and "Local Objects." His use of the word may derive from the critical discourse surrounding the abstraction/surrealism debate. The "crisis of the object" (André Breton's phrase) was at the heart of this debate. Pure abstraction sought to eliminate objects entirely from art. Surrealism, on the contrary, insisted on the object as the central concern of art.

22 Julien Levy, *Surrealism* (New York: Black Sun Press, 1936), 9.

23 Salvador Dalí, *The Conquest of the Irrational* (New York: Julien Levy, 1936), 19; his and Miró's remarks are both quoted by George L. K. Morris in "Sweeney Soby and Surrealism," *Partisan Review* 9, no. 2 (March–April 1942): 125.

24 Maurice Raynal, review of Cercle et Carré exhibition in *L'Intransigeant*, April 29, 1930: 7; quoted in *Kandinsky in Paris, 1934–1944* (New York: Guggenheim Museum, 1985), 44.

25 From a conversation recorded in the Artists Club, New York, March 28, 1952; quoted in William C. Seitz, *Abstract Expressionist Painting in America* (Cambridge: Harvard University Press, 1983), 55–56.

26 The artist George McNeil recalls that Alfred Barr disliked expressionistic art. Barr refused to look at Hans Hofmann's canvases at the Samuel Kootz Gallery, for example, and he did not attend the opening of Hofmann's first exhibition at MOMA in 1963 (interview with McNeil, March 10, 1989).

27 Herbert Read, *Art Now: An Introduction to the Theory of Modern Painting and Sculpture*, rev. ed. (New York: Harcourt, Brace, 1936), 146. I am grateful to the late Holly Stevens for allowing me to examine Stevens' copy of the 1933 edition of this book when it was still part of her personal library. It has since been acquired by the Huntington Library.

28 Peter Brazeau, *Parts of a World: Wallace Stevens Remembered* (New York: Random House, 1983), 130.

29 It is worth emphasizing, because noted critics have sometimes thought

otherwise, that Stevens' political views did not interfere with his appreciation of *Partisan Review*'s superior quality. On the contrary, he remained a loyal reader of and contributor to *PR* till the end of his life, describing its editors as "a group well worth helping although I do not share that group's politics" (L, 620). It seems likely that he found *PR* so exhilarating at least partly *because* its political views so challenged his own. As he once remarked about a review of *Ideas of Order* in the Marxist *New Masses,* "Merely finding myself in that *milieu* was an extraordinarily stimulating thing" (L, 296).

30 Stewart Buettner, *American Art Theory, 1945–1970* (Ann Arbor: UMI Research Press, 1981), 28.

31 In 1940, Morris retold for his readers the history of the AAA and its conflict with MOMA. See "The Museum of Modern Art (as Surveyed from the Avant-Garde)," *Partisan Review* 7, no. 3 (May–June 1940): 200–203.

32 For Morris's aesthetic views, see especially these articles in *Partisan Review*: "Some Personal Letters to American Artists" (4, no. 4 [March 1938]: 36–41), "American Abstract Artists: Third Annual Exhibition" (4, no. 3 [Spring 1939]: 63–64), and "On the Mechanics of Abstract Painting" (8, no. 5 [September–October 1941]: 403–17).

33 Melinda A. Lorenz, *George L. K. Morris: Artist and Critic* (Ann Arbor: UMI Research Press, 1982), 21.

34 Copied from "A note in *Apollo* for November, 1938, p. 266 on Picasso's 'Guernica,' exhibited at the New Burlington Galleries in London," in Stevens' notebooks *Sur Plusieurs Beaux Sujects* in the Huntington Library. I am grateful to Milton J. Bates for providing me with a typewritten transcript of these notebooks while he was editing them for publication. Stevens heads this entry "A just placing of Picasso" (Bates, *Sur Plusieurs Beaux Sujects,* 61–63). He echoed this judgment in a letter a few years later: "A man who depends on his intelligence like Picasso . . . can never be anything but intelligent" (L, 478).

35 Robert Motherwell, "Painter's Objects," *Partisan Review* 11, no. 1 (Winter 1944): 93–97.

36 Stevens' use of the term *abstraction* in so positive a sense in 1942 naturally brought him under attack by writers sympathetic to New Critical standards. The best example is that of Randall Jarrell, because he is a critic otherwise sympathetic to Stevens. See his "Reflections on Wallace Stevens" in *Poetry and the Age,* 133–48.

37 Robert M. Coates, "Abstractionists, and What about Them?" *The New Yorker,* March 18, 1939: 57.

38 Levy, *Surrealism*, 26–27.

39 Helen Vendler, *On Extended Wings: Wallace Stevens' Longer Poems* (Cambridge: Harvard University Press, 1969), 144.

40 Hilton Kramer, "The Two Henry Moores," *The New Criterion*, October 1986: 2–3.

41 Stevens owned a painting by Jean Marchand entitled *Les Oliviers*, now in the collection of Holly Stevens. It is a landscape painted in a fairly impressionistic style. It is neither abstract nor surrealist. Stevens' engagement with advanced art theory did not affect his taste for conventional painting.

42 A. Walton Litz, *Introspective Voyager: The Poetic Development of Wallace Stevens* (New York: Oxford University Press, 1972), 264–76.

43 Like most of Stevens' books, the poems of *Parts of a World* are arranged roughly in chronological order. The poems of 1938–39 are in the first half of the book; the poems of 1940–42 are in the second half.

44 This reflects not a radical change but a gradual shift of emphasis. Stevens had been interested in the concept of the hero since "Owl's Clover" and "The Man with the Blue Guitar." This interest is evident throughout *Parts of a World*. The "Canonica" sequence, for instance, which I have characterized according to its relation to still-life painting, also contains the poem entitled "Idiom of the Hero."

Chapter 5. "Notes toward a Supreme Fiction" and Abstract Art

1 B. J. Leggett, *Wallace Stevens and Poetic Theory: Conceiving the Supreme Fiction* (Chapel Hill: University of North Carolina Press, 1987), 17.

2 For an account of abstract expressionism as the "triumph" of American art, see Irving Sandler, *The Triumph of American Painting: A History of Abstract Expressionism* (New York: Harper & Row, 1970).

3 By the late 1940s Stevens recognized a more general "momentum toward abstraction" in all the arts. Two letters of 1948 use this phrase (L, 601–02, 608), and in the same year Stevens wrote in his notebook: "The momentum of the mind is all toward abstraction" (OP, 204). In all three instances, his exact point of reference is ambiguous. The phrase may be read either as a reference to the contemporary state of the arts (and the intellectual life) or as a more general rule that would apply at any time. In either case, his use of the phrase is related to contemporary trends in the art world.

4 *Art News* 40 (Feb. 15, 1941): 34–35; *Art Digest* 15 (March 15, 1941): 8–9.

5 Edward Alden Jewell, "Abstraction Lays Siege to Us Anew," *New York Times,* March 9, 1942, sec. VIII, 5:1.

6 George L. K. Morris, "Recent Tendencies in Europe," *Partisan Review* 6, no. 5 (Fall 1939): 31–32.

7 George L. K. Morris, "On the Mechanics of Abstract Painting,"" *Partisan Review* 8, no. 5 (September–October 1941): 414.

8 William Plomer, "Surrealism To-Day," *New Statesman and Nation,* June 29, 1940: 794.

9 Jerome Mellquist, "Art and Disorder," *New Republic,* March 23, 1942: 405.

10 Descartes' *Regulae ad directionem ingenii* were much in Stevens' thoughts in the 1930s. He alludes to them in his poem of 1935 "Winter Bells" (CP, 141; see L, 348), and they were the model for the Captain's *Regulae Mundi* in his poem of 1939 "Life on a Battleship" (OP, 107). The Captain's three "rules" in the latter poem were, in turn, a trial run for Stevens' prescriptive subtitles in "Notes." We may not be far wrong if we think of "Notes" as Stevens' attempt to write his own "Rules for the Direction of the Mind."

11 Stevens' deliberate focus on the rational aspects of the supreme fiction in "It Must Be Abstract" is also evident in his use of the word *idea.* It appears only in this section of "Notes," where it is used sixteen times.

12 Luigi Grassi and Mario Pepe, *Dizionario della critica d'arte* (Torino: Unione Tipografico–Editrice Torineae, 1978).

13 Citations for "Notes" give subsection and canto rather than page numbers, so that the reader can refer to either CP or Holly Stevens, ed., *The Palm at the End of the Mind* (New York: Alfred A. Knopf, 1971).

14 Wilhelm R. Valentiner, *The Art of the Low Countries* (New York: Doubleday, Page, 1914), 6–7.

15 This observation helps to explain the appearance of Descartes in "Notes" (I.iv). The French philosopher appears not only as the epitome of rationalism but also as the inventor of analytical geometry. In this context, too, it is surely not irrelevant that Descartes settled in Holland, where he was a contemporary of Frans Hals, who painted his best- known portrait.

16 Germany invaded the Netherlands on May 10, 1940. The Dutch government surrendered four days later.

17 See H. L. C. Jaffe, *De Stijl, 1917–1931: The Dutch Contribution to Modern Art* (Cambridge: Harvard University Press, 1986).

18 Helen Searing, "From the Fogg to the Bauhaus: A Museum for the Machine Age," in Eugene R. Gaddis, ed., *Avery Memorial, Wadsworth Atheneum: The First Modern Museum* (Hartford, Conn.: Wadsworth Atheneum, 1984), 21.

19 *Hartford Courant,* "New Avery Memorial Building," Nov. 18, 1933: 20; in the director's scrapbook, Wadsworth Atheneum (microfilm).

20 The centrality of architecture in the De Stijl movement helps to explain, I think, the appearance of Viollet-le-Duc in "Notes" (I.viii). In the catalogue of the "Modern Architecture" exhibit, the essay on Oud begins: "Oud was born at Purmerend in 1890. His artistic heritage leads back to Cuijpers, an exponent of medieval rationalism like Pugin in England or Viollet-le-Duc in France" (Alfred H. Barr, Henry-Russell Hitchcock, and Philip Johnson, *Modern Architecture: International Exhibition* [New York: Museum of Modern Art, 1932], 91). Viollet-le-Duc was a major figure in the nineteenth-century movement that reinterpreted Gothic architecture as rational and functional rather than decorative and mystical. In his view, every element of medieval architecture had a structural purpose. This rationalist approach to design established the basic principles of De Stijl and of the International Style. Thus Stevens' reference to Viollet-le-Duc invokes modern rationalism rather than wistful medievalism. I wish to thank Douglas Brenner for clarifying this point for me.

21 The Atheneum showed five of Mondrian's abstractions in its "Abstract Art" exhibition in 1935 and three others in a selection of works from the Société Anonyme collection in 1940. In 1936, the Atheneum became the first American museum to purchase a Mondrian painting for its permanent collection: *Composition in Blue and White* of 1935 (Gaddis, *Avery Memorial,* 52 [fig. 15]). Holly Stevens recalled that in her father's visits to the Atheneum, the Mondrian works were "among the things that he liked there" (conversation with the author). Stevens could also have viewed works by Mondrian at A. E. Gallatin's Gallery of Living Art on Washington Square, near the house of his friend Walter Pach.

22 Shows that featured Mondrian's paintings in 1942 were: the American Abstract Artists annual exhibition in March (Mondrian had joined the AAA shortly after his arrival in New York in 1940), "Abstract Art" at MOMA, "Artists in Exile" at the Pierre Matisse Gallery, "Masters of Abstract Art" at Helena Rubinstein's New Art Center, a selection of new acquisitions at the Gallery of Living Art, and the opening exhibition of Peggy Guggenheim's Art of This Century.

23 Harry Holtzman and Martin S. James, eds., *The New Art—The New Life: The Collected Writings of Piet Mondrian* (Boston: G. K. Hall, 1986), 338.

24 Stevens wrote to Henry Church on Jan. 28, 1942: " I am going to write a very small book for a private press which will certainly not be published until late in the summer or early autumn. As yet I have not written a word

of it" (L, 401). This is his first reference to "Notes," which he completed in May 1942.

25 Robert M. Coates, "At the Galleries," *The New Yorker* 7, no. 51 (Jan. 31, 1942): 55.

26 A. Walton Litz, "Wallace Stevens' Defense of Poetry: *La Poésie Pure,* The New Romantic, and the Pressure of Reality," in George Bornstein, ed., *Romantic and Modern: Revaluation of Literary Tradition* (Pittsburgh: University of Pittsburgh Press, 1977), 220.

27 "The Great Flight of Culture: Twelve Artists in U.S. Exile," *Fortune* 24, no. 6 (December 1941): 103.

28 Coates, "At the Galleries," 55. Stevens read the *New Yorker* regularly. He bought a subscription for a friend in 1938, describing it as "one weekly that I feel quite sure that you would like" (L, 332). Wilson E. Taylor recalls that Stevens planned his gallery visits to New York while reading this magazine: "He used to get those current exhibits from *The New Yorker.* I don't think he ever used to come down that he didn't read *The New Yorker* on the way" (Peter Brazeau, *Parts of a World: Wallace Stevens Remembered* [New York: Random House, 1983], 84).

29 Piet Mondrian, *Plastic Art and Pure Plastic Art, and Other Essays,* ed. Robert Motherwell (New York: Wittenborn, 1945), 52.

30 "Lines and Rectangles," *The New Yorker* 17, no. 3 (March 1, 1941): 9; "Great Flight of Culture," 103; "Studio," *The New Yorker* 20, no. 9 (April 15, 1944): 21.

31 "Lines and Rectangles," 9.

32 Leggett, *Stevens and Poetic Theory,* 493.

33 Alfred H. Barr, *Cubism and Abstract Art* (New York: Museum of Modern Art, 1936), ll.

34 Mondrian, "Abstract Art," in Holtzmann and James, *The New Art,* 331.

35 Mondrian's published works are listed in Holtzmann and James, *The New Art,* 398–99. There is no indication that Stevens ever read such historically important periodicals as *De Stijl, Cercle et carré,* and *Abstraction-Création,* where some of Mondrian's essays appeared. Mondrian's two pieces in *Cahiers d'art* (1931, 1935), which Stevens may have read, do not suggest parallels in his poetry.

Although Mondrian delivered one major public lecture and published three essays in English in 1942, Stevens probably did not know these works when he wrote "Notes." Two of the essays appeared after Stevens had written most or all of "Notes": "Abstract Art" was written in 1941 but not published till late 1942 in Peggy Guggenheim's *Art of This Century,* 32–33 (rpt. in Mondrian, *Plastic Art,* 27–29; see Holtzmann and

James, *The New Art,* 331); and "Pure Plastic Art" appeared in the catalogue of the exhibition "Masters of Abstract Art," held at the New Art Center in New York April 1 to May 14, 1942 (rpt. in Mondrian, *Plastic Art,* 30–36; see Holtzmann and James, *The New Art,* 342). The auto-biographical essay "Toward a True Vision of Reality" was published as a pamphlet in conjunction with Mondrian's one-man show at the Valentine Gallery in January and February 1942; there is no evidence that Stevens attended this exhibit or knew of the pamphlet (rpt. in Mondrian, *Plastic Art,* 9–15; see Holtzmann and James, *The New Art,* 338). "A New Real-ism" was delivered (by Balcomb Greene) on Mondrian's behalf as a lec-ture before the American Abstract Artists on Jan. 23, 1942; but this lecture was not reported in the press, so far as I can tell, and the essay was not published till 1945 (Mondrian, *Plastic Art,* 16–26; see Holtzmann and James, *The New Art,* 345).

It seems probable, however, that Stevens was familiar with "Plastic Art and Pure Plastic Art" in the book *Circle,* edited by the English abstract group and published in 1937 (J. L. Martin, Ben Nicholson, and Naum Gabo, eds., *Circle: An International Survey of Constructive Art* [London: Faber and Faber, 1937]). George L. K. Morris reviewed this book in the December 1937 issue of *Partisan Review,* singling out Mondrian's essay as "the most lucid key to a painter's intentions that this reviewer has encoun-tered." ("Modernism in England," *Partisan Review* 4, no. 1: 70). Stevens saved this issue because his poem "The Dwarf" appeared in it. The pub-licity about Mondrian in the winter of 1941–42 may have reminded Stevens about *Circle* and inspired him to seek out this "lucid key" to Mondrian's aesthetic theory just as he was about to develop his own theory in "Notes."

Charles Altieri points out several general parallels between this essay and "Notes," but does not elaborate and misleadingly equates Mondrian's views with those of Stevens' painter friend Walter Pach ("Why Stevens Must Be Abstract, or What a Poet Can Learn from Painting," in Albert Gelpi, ed., *Wallace Stevens: The Poetics of Modernism* [New York: Cambridge University Press, 1985], 90–91). I am grateful to Nancy J. Troy for helping me to determine what Stevens could have known of Mondrian's theory in early 1942.

36 Mondrian, *Plastic Art,* 50. Page references for quotations from "Plastic Art and Pure Plastic Art" refer to this edition.

37 A possible source for Stevens' "Weather by Franz Hals" is the painting *A Man with a Beer Keg,* reproduced in color in Thomas Craven, *A Treasury of Art Masterpieces: From the Renaissance to the Present Day* (New York:

Simon & Schuster, 1939). It is one of Hals' few outdoor portraits, showing a sky "Brushed up by brushy winds . . . , / Wetted by blue, colder for white."

38 Craven, *Treasury*, 282.

39 Mondrian's aesthetic theory was deeply influenced by his interest in theosophy (see Robert P. Welsh, "Mondrian and Theosophy," in *Piet Mondrian, 1872–1944: Centennial Exhibition* [New York: Guggenheim Museum, 1971]). For most of the pioneers of abstract painting (Kandinsky, Malevich, Pollock, et al.), abstraction had a spiritual significance. See Maurice Tuchman et al., *The Spiritual in Art: Abstract Painting, 1890–1985* (New York: Abbeville, 1986); and Roger Lipsey, *An Art of Our Own: The Spiritual in Twentieth-Century Art* (Boston: Shambhala, 1988).

40 For the best recent discussion of the supreme fiction as a "religious surrogate" (203), see Milton Bates, *Wallace Stevens: A Mythology of Self* (Berkeley: University of California Press, 1985), chap. 6.

41 Letter from Mondrian to Winifred Nicholson, Sept. 4, 1936, quoted in Holtzmann and James, *The New Art,* 288.

42 Stevens' insistence that "in projecting a supreme fiction, I cannot imagine anything more fatal than to state it definitely" (L, 863–64) helps to explain, I think, why he avoided any direct reference in "It Must Be Abstract" to abstract art. Any concrete analogy for his method would be as "fatal" to it as any definition would be to the supreme fiction itself. The only chance of success, therefore, lay in remaining utterly silent about possible equivalents: "I have no idea what form the supreme fiction would take. The NOTES start out with the idea that it would not take any form: that it would be abstract" (L, 430); "Let us . . . not say that our abstraction is this, that or the other" (L, 438). Ironically, this restriction meant that Stevens could not mention his chief analogy for the kind of abstraction he had in mind.

43 James Thrall Soby, *Paintings, Drawings, Prints: Salvador Dalí* (New York: Museum of Modern Art, 1941), 30.

Chapter 6. Rival Doctrines Harmonized

1 Frank Doggett, *Wallace Stevens: The Making of the Poem* (Baltimore: Johns Hopkins University Press, 1980), 112.

2 The phrase "rival doctrines harmonized" comes from B. J. Leggett, *Wallace Stevens and Poetic Theory: Conceiving the Supreme Fiction* (Chapel

Hill: University of North Carolina Press, 1987), 35, where it refers to the reconciliation of opposites in I. A. Richards' *Coleridge on Imagination.*

3 Jerome Mellquist, "Art and Disorder," *New Republic* 106, no. 12 (March 23, 1942): 405.

4 Reprinted in Franklin Rosemont, ed., *André Breton: What Is Surrealism?* (New York: Monad, 1978), 245.

5 *View* 2, no. 3 (October 1942): 28. The shift from "to *invent* [is] not to discover" in this notebook entry to "to *impose* is not / To discover" in the poem probably indicates no more than Stevens' greater attention to verbal accuracy in his poetry. "To invent" *is* strictly "to discover," as any dictionary will show.

6 Compare this passage from a book Stevens later owned: "The charge that can be made against the Surrealists, and the subtle cause of their final failure to carry through their 'revolution,' is that they have tried to *force* the unconscious, to conquer by violence secrets that might be revealed more readily to more artless minds." Marcel Raymond, *From Baudelaire to Surrealism* (New York: Wittenborn, Schultz, 1950), 299.

7 See OP, 226; L, 871; and Frank Doggett and Robert Buttel, eds., *Wallace Stevens: A Celebration* (Princeton: Princeton University Press, 1980), 51.

8 Werner Haftmann, *Painting in the Twentieth Century,* vol. 1 (1965; rpt. New York: Praeger, 1976), 267–80.

9 Haftmann would "occasionally" count Miró's friend André Masson, too, as an exemplar of absolute surrealism (*Painting,* 268). Although Stevens is entirely silent about Masson, it is worth noting that his friend Henry Church was acquainted with Masson and saw a good deal of the French artist while he was living in the United States during the Second World War. (Church mentions seeing Masson in letters to Stevens dated Nov. 14, 1943, Nov. 15, 1944, and April 24, 1945, in the Wallace Stevens Archive of the Huntington Library.) The American sculptor David Hare, who was friendly with many of the expatriate surrealist artists, recalls that "Masson had heard of Wallace Stevens" (telephone interview, Dec. 22, 1987).

10 Barbara Rose, *Miró in America* (Houston: The Museum of Fine Arts, 1982), 21. The catalogue to the Dalí exhibition, but not to the Miró exhibition, was in Stevens' library. Perhaps Stevens acquired it because it was written by James Thrall Soby, whom he knew and respected. He did not become acquainted with James Johnson Sweeney, the author of the Miró catalogue, until about 1950 (see L, 669–70).

11 Robert M. Coates, "Had Any Good Dreams Lately?" *The New Yorker* 18, no. 42 (Nov. 29, 1941): 58–59.

12 Robert Motherwell, "The Significance of Miró," *Art News* 58, no. 4 (May 1959): 32–33ff.; rpt. in Rose, *Miró in America,* 122.

13 Robert Motherwell, exhibition catalogue (New York: Kootz Gallery, 1947); quoted in William C. Seitz, *Abstract Expressionist Painting in America* (Cambridge: Harvard University Press, 1983), 94.

14 Another aspect of surrealist automatism may be related to Stevens' poetic practice. The Surrealist artists often sought imagery charged with unconscious associations by practicing free association while contemplating the artistic medium they were using. Here is Miró: "What is most interesting to me today is the material I am working with. It supplies the shape which suggests the form just as cracks in a wall suggested shapes to Leonardo" (Rose, *Miró in America,* 118).

The example of Leonardo was frequently cited in contemporary discussions of automatism. Haftmann records that Max Ernst invented the method of *frottage* "recalling Leonardo's admonition that the images suggested to our fantasy by spots, smouldering coals, or drifting clouds should be taken seriously (they are, says Leonardo, 'like the ringing of bells in which we hear what is in our minds')" (Haftmann, *Painting,* 269). Stevens does not refer to the Leonardo passage, but he had in mind a similar analogy for his own poetic method when he admonished his friend William Carlos Williams that "one has to keep looking for poetry as Renoir looked for colors in old walls, woodwork and so on" (letter dated April 9, [1918?], printed in William Carlos Williams, *Imaginations* (New York: New Directions, 1970), 15.

15 Stevens might just as well be compared to his favorite painter, Paul Klee, in terms of his use of automatism. "Klee was a pioneer in automatic drawing, one of the facets of his art which particularly recommended him to the Surrealists, on whom he had a considerable influence. Though hardly known in France at the time, Klee was championed by the Surrealists. He is one of the few modern painters mentioned in the Surrealist manifesto and, despite the fact that he was not then, and never would become, a member of the movement, his work figured in the first exhibition of Surrealist painting at the Galerie Pierre, Paris, 1925" (William S. Rubin, *Dada, Surrealism, and Their Heritage* [New York: Museum of Modern Art, 1968], 190). Klee's relation to the Surrealists—that of an outsider but a kindred spirit—was similar to Stevens'.

16 This question may be intended to suggest Descartes, to whom Stevens alludes in lines 17–18 of canto viii, thereby recalling all his references to the French philosopher in "It Must Be Abstract." The standard biography of Descartes at the time Stevens was writing describes the watershed in the philosopher's thinking: "The decision had once for all to be made; the question, 'What am I to believe?' had to be answered; and Descartes met the question bravely. Let us get rid of the old tradition altogether, he boldly said, and build up for ourselves a new system from the foundation. . . . Descartes asks what is the essential in all this reasoning and questioning, and he replies, all is founded on the knowledge of Self, on what we afterwards learned to call Self-consciousness. . . . He expressed his principle in the well-known phrase *cogito ergo sum*" (Elizabeth S. Haldane, *Descartes: His Life and Times* [1905; rpt. New York: American Scholar Press, 1966], 173–75). So Stevens begins his canto viii with the question "What am I to believe?" and in the sixth stanza gives his own revision of Descartes' dictum: "I have not but I am and as I am, I am." The phrase "majesty is a mirror of the self" (line 17) recalls I.iv, in which Adam was "the father of Descartes" and Eve "made air the mirror of herself."

17 Eleanor Cook, *Poetry, Word-Play, and Word-War in Wallace Stevens* (Princeton: Princeton University Press, 1988), 189–213.

18 Wine is suggested in the "ruddy pulses" of the grape leaves (ii) and appears as the sacred "marriage wine" at the wedding of the Captain and Bawda (iv); as the Canon Aspirin's Meursault (v); the wine in a wood (vi); and as the "twelve wines" with which the soldier returns home in the Epilogue.

19 André Breton, *Manifestoes of Surrealism,* trans. Richard Seaver and Helen R. Lane (1962; rpt. Ann Arbor: University of Michigan Press, 1972), 14.

20 Ibid., xi.

21 Herschel B. Chipp, *Theories of Modern Art: A Source Book by Artists and Critics* (Berkeley: University of California Press, 1968), 509.

22 "The Great Flight of Culture," *Fortune,* December 1941: 102.

23 Robert M. Coates, "War and the Artist," *The New Yorker* 18, no. 4 (March 14, 1942): 70.

24 Sidney Janis, "School of Paris Comes to U.S.," *Decision* 2, nos. 5–6 (November–December 1941): 95.

25 John Peale Bishop,"The Arts," in "The American Culture: A Symposium," *Kenyon Review* 3, no. 2 (Spring 1941): 188.

26 Aline B. Saarinen, *The Proud Possessors: The Lives, Times and Tastes of Some Adventurous American Art Collectors* (New York: Random House, 1958), 336.

27 Michel Seuphor, *Dictionary of Abstract Painting* (New York: Tudor, 1958), 77.

28 This photograph is reproduced courtesy of the Philadelphia Museum of Art. Anne d'Harnoncourt, the director of the Philadelphia Museum of Art, recalls that the photograph was titled after the exhibition "Artists in

Exile" at the Pierre Matisse Gallery in 1942, and that the probable location is the New York house of Peggy Guggenheim and Max Ernst at that time (letter to the author, Aug. 30, 1989).

29 Sidney Janis, *Abstract and Surrealist Art in the United States* (San Francisco Museum of Art, 1944), 16; quoted in Jeffrey Wechsler, *Surrealism and American Art: 1931–1947* (Rutgers University Art Gallery, 1977), 49. This new attitude naturally met with some resistance in more conservative quarters. Reviewing Janis' exhibition catalogue, *Art Digest* commented: "Abstract and Surrealist art were once two well-understood and theoretically opposed schools of expression. Here they are interchanged so that the terms that were intended originally . . . as a guide to understanding the painters' intention, are used to confound the public" (Dec. 1, 1944: 8).

30 Stevens' love of aphorism exemplifies this cavalier attitude toward abstract theoretical statements: "When you first feel the truth of, say, an epigram, you feel like making it a rule of conduct. But this one is displaced by that, and things go on in their accustomed way. There is one pleasure in this volatile morality: the day you believe in chastity, poverty and obedience, you are charmed to discover what a monk you have always been—the monk is suddenly revealed like a spirit in a wood; the day you turn Ibsenist, you confess that, after all, you always were an Ibsenist, without knowing it. So you come to believe in yourself, and in your new creed" (L, 91). Beverly Coyle thoroughly explores Stevens' love of aphorism in *A Thought to Be Rehearsed: Aphorism in Wallace Stevens' Poetry* (Ann Arbor: UMI Research Press, 1983).

31 Robert Motherwell and Ad Reinhardt, eds., *Modern Artists in America* (New York: Wittenborn, Schultz, 1951), 40. The Stevens passage is from NA, 22.

Chapter 7. Stevens and the Abstract Expressionists

1 *The New Yorker* 45 (Dec. 23, 1944): 51; quoted in Paul Schimmel, "Images of Metamorphosis," in his *The Interpretive Link: Abstract Surrealism into Abstract Expressionism, Works on Paper 1938–1948* (Newport Beach, Calif.: Newport Harbor Art Museum, 1986), 17.

2 Interview with George McNeil, March 10, 1989.

3 William C. Seitz, *Abstract Expressionist Painting in America* (Cambridge: Harvard University Press, 1983), 104.

4 Quoted in ibid., 103.

5 Mark Rothko, "Personal Statement" in the exhibition catalogue for "A Painting Prophecy—1950" (February 1945), David Porter Gallery, Washington, D.C. Quoted in Schimmel, "Images," 25.

6 Dore Ashton, *The New York School: A Cultural Reckoning* (1972; rpt. New York: Penguin, 1979), 87.

7 See Charles Henri Ford, "Verlaine in Hartford," *View* 1, no. 1 (September 1940): 1.

8 Ashton, *New York School,* 135.

9 Quoted by Ashton in Schimmel, *The Interpretive Link,* 29.

10 Interview with George McNeil, March 10, 1989.

11 Ashton in Schimmel, *The Interpretive Link,* 30.

12 Letter from Francis V. O'Connor to the author, Feb. 5, 1989.

13 "Mondrian and New York Painting," in *Six Painters,* exhibition catalogue, (Houston: University of St. Thomas Art Department, February–April 1967), n.p. Michel Seuphor confirms Hess' observation that Mondrian was unappreciated in Paris: "Although [Mondrian] had been a resident of Paris from 1911 to 1914 and from 1919 to 1938—painting there a number of canvases recognized everywhere else as masterpieces of twentieth-century art—Paris remained indifferent" (*Abstract Painting: Fifty Years of Accomplishment, from Kandinsky to the Present* [New York: Abrams, 1965], 129).

14 Interview with George McNeil, March 10, 1989.

15 In the 1950s, as part of an impromptu diagram done for the benefit of William Seitz, Motherwell went so far as to label Mondrian the "Moral Ideal" of the Abstract Expressionists. (This diagram, handwritten in pencil, is reproduced in Seitz, *Abstract Expressionist Painting,* 168.) Years later, Motherwell objected to this label as far too simplistic. (Conversation with Robert Motherwell, Storrs, Conn., March 23, 1988.)

16 Thomas B. Hess, *Barnett Newman* (New York: Museum of Modern Art, 1971), 35. For the full essay, see John P. O'Neill, ed., *Barnett Newman: Selected Writings and Interviews* (New York: Alfred A. Knopf, 1990), 20–29.

17 This unpublished letter was brought to my attention by Annalee Newman. It is part of her collection and is reprinted with her permission. Although it reads as if it might be a form letter, there is no record of Barnett Newman's sending it to anyone else.

18 Ashton, *New York School,* 134, 193.

19 Ibid., 134.

20 Interview with Annalee Newman, Nov. 12, 1988.

21 Quoted in Ashton, *New York School,* 126.

22 Quoted in Irving Sandler, *The Triumph of American Painting: A History of Abstract Expressionism* (New York: Harper & Row, 1970), 33.

23 Edward Alden Jewell, "End-of-the-Season Melange," *New York Times,* June 6, 1943: sec. II, p. 9; quoted in Bonnie Clearwater, "Shared Myths: Reconsideration of Rothko's and Gottlieb's letter to the *New York Times,*" in *Archives of American Art Journal* 24, no. 1 (1984): 23.

24 Quoted in Ashton, *New York School,* 127.

25 André Breton, "The Legendary Life of Max Ernst, Preceded by a Brief Discussion on the Need for a New Myth," *View* 2, no. 1 (April 1942): 5; and "Prolegomena to a Third Manifesto of Surrealism or Else," in *VVV* 1 (June 1942): 26. Harold Rosenberg took Breton's idea of a new myth as the leading idea of his "Breton—A Dialogue" in *View* 2, no. 2 (May 1942): n.p.

26 "Art in New York City," WNYC radio broadcast, Oct. 13, 1943; quoted in Ashton, *New York School,* 129.

27 Interview with W. Jackson Rushing, quoted in his "The Impact of Nietzsche and Northwest Coast Indian Art on Barnett Newman's Idea of Redemption in the Abstract Sublime," *Art Journal* 47, no. 3 (Fall 1988): 189.

28 See Howard Baker, "Wallace Stevens," in Ashley Brown and Robert S. Haller, eds., *The Achievement of Wallace Stevens* (New York: Lippincott, 1962), 81–96; Frank Doggett, "Variations on a Nude," chap. 3 of his *Wallace Stevens' Poetry of Thought* (Baltimore: Johns Hopkins University Press, 1966), 34–54; Susan B. Weston, *Wallace Stevens: An Introduction to the Poetry* (New York: Columbia University Press, 1977); and Leonora Woodman, *Stanza My Stone: Wallace Stevens and the Hermetic Tradition* (West Lafayette, Ind.: Purdue University Press, 1983).

29 Joseph Carroll, *Wallace Stevens' Supreme Fiction: A New Romanticism* (Baton Rouge: Louisiana State University Press, 1987), 7–8.

30 Quoted in Rushing, "Impact of Nietzsche," 192.

31 Carroll, *Stevens' Supreme Fiction,* 9.

32 Barnett Newman, catalogue essay for "The Ideographic Picture" (Betty Parsons Gallery, New York, 1947), n.p.; rpt. in O'Neill, *Barnett Newman,* 107–08.

33 Harold Rosenberg, "Oh This Is the Creature that Does not Exist," *View* 3, no. 2 (April 1943): 62; rpt. in Harold Rosenberg, *The Tradition of the New* (Chicago: University of Chicago Press, 1959, 1982), 121–25.

34 Quoted in Ashton, *New York School,* 128.

35 Robert Motherwell and Ad Reinhardt, eds., *Modern Artists in America* (New York: Wittenborn, Schultz, 1951), 9.

36 Milton Bates, *Wallace Stevens: A Mythology of Self* (Berkeley: University of California Press, 1985), 240.

37 Sidney Janis, *Abstract and Surrealist Art in America* (New York: Reynal and Hitchcock, 1944), 118; quoted in Sandler, *Triumph of American Painting*, 175.

38 *Tiger's Eye* 1, no. 6 (Dec. 15, 1948): 46–60.

39 Stevens frequently referred to poetry as a "sanction" of life. See L, 299; OP, 309; NA, 173.

40 Letter from Diane Waldman to the author, March 22, 1986.

41 Ronald Sukenick, *Wallace Stevens: Musing the Obscure* (New York: New York University Press, 1967), 30.

42 Letter from Roger Fry to G. L. Dickinson, 1913; quoted in Virginia Woolf, *Roger Fry: A Biography* (1940; rpt. New York: Harcourt, 1976), 183.

43 Quoted in Ashton, *New York School*, 128.

44 Marjorie Perloff does use Stevens' categories in her provocative essay "Pound/Stevens: Whose Era?," *New Literary History* 5, no. 13 (Spring 1982): 485–514; rpt. in her *The Dance of the Intellect: Studies in the Poetry of the Pound Tradition* (New York: Cambridge University Press, 1985), 1–32.

45 Stevens was apparently aware that the relation between subject and form was a contentious issue in the contemporary art world, and he used that fact in "The Relations between Poetry and Painting" to make a point about his own poetry. This is another example of Stevens expressing his "relation to contemporary ideas" in terms of the art world, while continuing to go his own way in terms of contemporary poetry.

46 J. Hillis Miller, *Poets of Reality: Six Twentieth-Century Writers* (Cambridge: Harvard University Press, 1966), 227. Miller also compares Stevens' use of nonsense language to the Abstract Expressionists' interest in the artistic medium itself (pp. 251–53). James Baird (*The Dome and the Rock: Structure in the Poetry of Wallace Stevens* [Baltimore: Johns Hopkins University Press, 1968], 176–77) strongly disagrees with Miller's comparison. I side with Baird on this issue. Neither Stevens' poetry nor abstract expressionism can usefully be discussed as "nonsense."

47 "Modern Poetry: The Flat Landscape," *trans/formation* 1, no. 3 (1952): 152–55.

48 John O'Brian, ed., *Clement Greenberg: The Collected Essays and Criticism* (Chicago: University of Chicago Press, 1986), 1: 32.

49 Interview with Paul Cummings, June 6, 1968, in John Ashbery and Kenworth Moffett, eds., *Fairfield Porter: Realist Painter in an Age of Abstraction* (Boston: Museum of Fine Arts, 1982), 56.

50 Thomas Hess, "Artists/Writers: An Impure Excursion," *Art News* 44, no. 8 (December 1955): 28, 59.

51 Fairfield Porter papers, Archives of American Art.

52 See my "Fairfield Porter and Wallace Stevens: Kindred Spirits of American Art," *Archives of American Art Journal* 24, no. 1 (Fall 1984): 2–12.

53 Rackstraw Downes, letter to the author, Sept. 22, 1983. See his *Fairfield Porter: Art in Its Own Terms: Selected Criticism, 1935–1975* (New York: Taplinger, 1979).

54 Paul Cummings, interview with Fairfield Porter, in Ashbery and Moffett, *Fairfield Porter,* 53.

55 Downes, *Fairfield Porter,* 168–69.

56 Quoted in Downes, *Fairfield Porter,* 22. This letter from Porter to Downes is dated Dec. 16, 1972 (letter from Downes to the author, Sept. 22, 1983).

57 Quoted from a review of an exhibition of John Marin in the *Nation* (Dec. 25, 1948); rpt. in O'Brian, *Clement Greenberg,* 2: 268.

58 Hayden Carruth, "Stevens as Essayist," *The Nation* 174, no. 24 (June 14, 1952): 584–85; rpt. in Charles Doyle, ed., *Wallace Stevens: The Critical Heritage* (London: Routledge and Kegan Paul, 1985), 353–56. Edward Honig noted the "virile" quality of Stevens' critical essays in "Three Masters," *Voices* 148 (May–August 1952): 34–35; rpt. in Doyle, *Wallace Stevens,* 357–58.

59 Winfield Townley Scott, "Stevens and the Angel of Earth," *Providence Journal,* Dec. 2, 1951: sec. VI, p. 8; rpt. in Doyle, *Wallace Stevens,* 347–48.

60 Doyle, *Wallace Stevens,* 354.

61 "A Statement," in Motherwell and Reinhardt, *Modern Artists,* 7; rpt. in Ann Eden Gibson, *Issues in Abstract Expressionism: The Artist-Run Periodicals* (Ann Arbor: UMI Research Press, 1990), 313.

62 Motherwell and Reinhardt, *Modern Artists,* 40; rpt. in Gibson, *Issues,* 375–76. *Modern Artists in America* also includes a transcript of "The Western Round Table on Modern Art," held in San Francisco April 8–10, 1949. On the topic of art as magic, focusing particularly on the enigmatic, spiritual aspect of art objects, the cultural anthropologist Gregory Bateson commented astutely: "Could I put on record the name of Wallace Stevens, the poet who has made works of art, poems, dealing specifically with this problem" (p. 32; rpt. in Gibson, *Issues,* 361).

63 Ashton, *American Art since 1945* (New York: Oxford University Press, 1982), 132.

64 The quoted words are from John Gruen, *The Party's Over Now* (New York: Viking, 1972), 261. Pavia recalled discussion of Wallace Stevens at the Club in a telephone interview with me on Nov. 24, 1987. He remembers in particular that Emmanual Navaretta—one of his closest friends and a founding member of the Club—often spoke of Stevens' poetry with great enthusiasm.

65 Quoted in Gruen, *Party's Over,* 178.

66 Sandler, *Triumph of American Painting,* 270.

67 Rosenberg, *Tradition,* 35, 39. For my understanding of Rosenberg's critical stance, I am particularly indebted to Elaine O'Brien, who is completing a book on him. See her master's thesis "Art as Tragedy: An Investigation of Harold Rosenberg's Ethical Aesthetic" (San Diego State University, 1988).

68 Rosenberg, *Tradition,* 25.

69 Ibid., 31.

70 Ibid., 31, 26.

71 Rosenberg glosses Newman's painting with quotations from "Notes toward a Supreme Fiction" in "Icon-Maker: Barnett Newman," *The New Yorker* 47 (Jan. 1, 1972): 43–46, rpt. in his *The De-Definition of Art* (Chicago: University of Chicago Press, 1972), 92–94; and in *Barnett Newman* (New York: Abrams, 1978), 32, 38.

72 Stevens' personal index to Henri Focillon's *The Life of Forms in Art* (New Haven: Yale University Press, 1942), which he wrote on the dust jacket of the book, includes this notation: "Art is action 66." See B. J. Leggett, *Wallace Stevens and Poetic Theory: Conceiving the Supreme Fiction* (Chapel Hill: University of North Carolina Press, 1987), 149.

73 Rosenberg, *Tradition,* 28, 26, 38, 27, 29.

74 Milton Bates, *Sur Plusieurs Beaux Sujects: Wallace Stevens' Commonplace Book* (Stanford and San Marino: Stanford University Press and The Huntington Library, 1989), 53–55.

75 Rosenberg, *Tradition,* 28.

76 Donald Kuspit, *Clement Greenberg: Art Critic* (Madison: University of Wisconsin Press, 1979), 130.

77 Ashton, *New York School,* 195.

78 Sandler, *Triumph of American Painting,* 271.

79 Jackson Pollock, "My Painting," *Possibilities* 1 (Winter 1947–48): 79. For Baziotes' love of boxing, see Barbara Cavaliere, "An Introduction to the Method of William Baziotes," *Arts Magazine* 51, no. 8 (April 1977): 128.

80 These are the first two points in a numbered agenda for modern art that the artists included as part of their letter. I have omitted the numbers in my transcription.

81 Adolph Gottlieb and Mark Rothko, "The Portrait of the Modern Artist," radio broadcast on WNYC, New York, Oct. 13, 1943; quoted in Sandler, *Triumph of American Painting*, 64.

82 Quoted in Ashton, *New York School*, 163.

83 "Oh This Is the Creature That Does Not Exist"; rpt. in Rosenberg, *Tradition*, 124–25.

84 New York: Wittenborn, 1950. Stevens cites this book in "The Relations between Poetry and Painting" (NA, 173). His personal copy is in the Huntington Library.

85 Rosenberg, *Tradition*, 93, 91, 93–94.

86 Ibid., 88, 91, 93.

Chapter 8. *The Auroras of Autumn* and Jackson Pollock

1 An alternative approach would be to use as an analogy a painter or painters who had a documented interest in Stevens, as Pollock did not. William Baziotes is perhaps the most interesting example since, as his friend Robert Motherwell recalled, "Baziotes was deeply interested in Stevens, partly because both were born in Reading, Pa." (letter to the author, Sept. 21, 1983). There is the additional irony in this case that Baziotes is the only Abstract Expressionist mentioned—with frank revulsion—by Stevens. (See L, 574, 579.) But Baziotes' paintings are not really typical of the whole movement. Irving Sandler prefers to classify them as "an original variant of Abstract Surrealism" (*The Triumph of American Painting; A History of Abstract Expressionism* [New York: Harper & Row, 1970), 78).

Unlike Baziotes, the majority of the Abstract Expressionists were not "literary" at all. It was the more intellectual painters among them, however, who tended to be interested in Stevens. For example, in 1946 Motherwell made a painting and a collage that were related to "The Man with the Blue Guitar." Philip Guston knew and discussed the essays in *The Necessary Angel* in the mid-1950s. Jack Tworkov engaged in discussions about Stevens while he was teaching at Black Mountain College in 1952; and he annotated his own copy of *The Necessary Angel* in the mid-1970s. But such direct evidence is scarce and fragmentary, and none of these painters is as representative as Pollock.

2 Pollock did not read much, though his library contains evidence that he subscribed to or read periodicals that sometimes contained Stevens' work, such as the *Nation, Horizon, Partisan Review,* and *View.* He and Lee

Krasner also owned a copy of *The New Pocket Anthology of American Verse: From Colonial Days to the Present,* edited by Oscar Williams (New York: Pocket Books, 1955), which contained a large selection of Stevens' poetry (pp. 464–96). This book was a gift of their poet-friend Parker Tyler; it appeared in the year of Stevens' death, only one year before Pollock himself died. For a catalogue of Pollock's library, see Francis V. O'Connor and Eugene V. Thaw, eds., *Jackson Pollock: A Catalogue Raisonné of Paintings, Drawings, and Other Works* (New Haven: Yale University Press, 1978), 4: 187–99.

Stevens may never have seen any of Pollock's paintings, but he probably saw reproductions of his pourings in such well-publicized articles as "A Life Round Table on Modern Art" *(Life,* Oct. 11, 1948: 56–79); and "Jackson Pollock: Is He the Greatest Living Painter in the United States?" *(Life,* Aug. 8, 1949: 45ff.). Stevens was also friendly, during the late 1940s and early 1950s, with James Johnson Sweeney, who was one of Pollock's early champions.

3 For the facts of Pollock's life I have relied upon Francis V. O'Connor's "The Life of Jackson Pollock, 1912–1956: A Documentary Chronology," in O'Connor and Thaw, *Pollock,* 4: 201–80.

4 Pollock's close relationship with the painter Lee Krasner, beginning in 1942, assured his education in the cubist-abstract tradition. "A former student of the European-trained modernist Hans Hofmann, Krasner was already well versed in Fauvism, Cubism and the latest trends of the School of Paris when she met Pollock. . . . An active member of the American Abstract Artists group, she socialized with the internationally famous Dutch de Stijl movement pioneer Piet Mondrian, who had escaped the threat of Fascist oppression in Europe and was living in New York" (Ellen Landau, *Jackson Pollock* [New York: Abrams, 1989], 84).

5 O'Connor and Thaw, *Pollock,* 4: 232.

6 B. J. Leggett has shown that Henri Focillon's *The Life of Forms in Art* (New Haven: Yale University Press, 1942) contributed to Stevens' thinking while he was writing "The Auroras of Autumn." Focillon treats artistic forms as if they have a life of their own that is in a state of constant change, like life itself. His view of art as a realm of continual flux, parallel to the continual flux of life, is obviously close to the ideas in Stevens' poem. See Leggett, *Wallace Stevens and Poetic Theory: Conceiving the Supreme Fiction* (Chapel Hill: University of North Carolina Press, 1987), 173–201.

7 J. Hillis Miller, "Wallace Stevens' Poetry of Being," in Pearce and Miller, *The Act of the Mind,* 143–62; rpt. in slightly different form in Miller's

Poets of Reality: Six Twentieth-Century Writers (Cambridge: Harvard University Press, 1966), 217–84.

8 Jackson Pollock, statement in *Possibilities* 1 (Winter 1947–48): 79; rpt. in O'Connor and Thaw, *Pollock*, 4: 241.

9 Ibid.

10 Pollock made this statement in response to Hans Hofmann's suggestion that he should work from nature. See Francis V. O'Connor, *Jackson Pollock* (New York: Museum of Modern Art, 1967), 26.

11 Landau, *Pollock*, 169.

12 Stephen Polcari, *Abstract Expressionism and the Modern Experience* (New York: Cambridge University Press, 1991), 254.

13 William Rubin, *Dada, Surrealism, and Their Heritage* (New York: Museum of Modern Art, 1968), 178.

14 It is commonplace to compare the physicality in the poetry of William Carlos Williams and his protégés (like Charles Olson and the Beats) with the "gestural" aspect of abstract expressionism. Williams' emphasis both on the body and on the material form of the poem obviously link him with Pollock's very physical method of painting, for example. For a comparison of Williams and Pollock, see Joan Burbick, "Grimaces of a New Age: The Postwar Poetry and Painting of William Carlos Williams and Jackson Pollock," *Boundary 2* 10, no. 3 (1982): 109–23; and Terence Diggory, "The Blue Nude and Mrs. Pappadopoulos," *William Carlos Williams Review,* Fall 1992.

The poet Stanley Kunitz, who knew many of the New York painters, remarks that their achievement has so much to do with getting the *body* into art that it seems to have nothing to do with Stevens' very cerebral kind of poetry (conversation with the author, Storrs, Conn., March 23, 1988). The painter Elise Asher, Kunitz's wife, concurs in finding Stevens' poetry too intellectual, not sensual enough to be a fitting analogy for abstract expressionism (interview with the author, Dec. 2, 1987). One purpose of this book is to challenge this way of interpreting the relation between Stevens and abstract expressionism.

15 Jackson Pollock, statement of 1951, in O'Connor and Thaw, *Pollock,* 4: 262.

16 For Stevens' composing while walking, see Brazeau, *Parts of a World,* 34, 38, 239.

17 Paul Mariani, *William Carlos Williams: A New World Naked* (New York: McGraw-Hill, 1981), 148.

18 Polcari, *Abstract Expressionism,* 256.

19 I think Harold Bloom is wrong to claim that "Farewell to an idea . . . ," the phrase that opens cantos ii-iv, refers to Stevens' concept of the First Idea

(*Wallace Stevens: The Poems of Our Climate* [Ithaca: Cornell University Press, 1977], 254–55). It is rather the idea of God to which it refers, since, as Stevens often repeated, "the major poetic idea in the world is and always has been the idea of God" (L, 378). Far from abandoning the concept of the First Idea, the first six cantos of "The Auroras of Autumn" *exemplify* it by stripping the auroras themselves of any projected feeling. The climax of this process is the sublime terror of canto vi, which Bloom justly admires.

20 That the "father" of canto iv and the "enthroned imagination" of canto vii are two versions of the same mythic material is suggested by the fact that they share a common "throne" and "crown," and that their most characteristic movement is to "leap."

21 Daniel P. Tompkins, "'To Abstract Reality': Abstract Language and the Intrusion of Consciousness in Wallace Stevens," *American Literature* 45, no. 1 (March 1973): 86.

22 Thomas F. Walsh, *Concordance to the Poetry of Wallace Stevens* (University Park, Pa.: Pennsylvania State University Press, 1963).

23 This point—like many in this chapter—applies only to the branch of Abstract Expressionism usually labeled "gestural" abstraction, which includes, in addition to Pollock, Willem De Kooning, Franz Kline, Jack Tworkov, Philip Guston, James Brooks, George McNeil, and others. It does not apply to the Abstract Expressionist painters usually classified as "meditative" or "color-field," such as Mark Rothko, Adolph Gottlieb, William Baziotes, Clyfford Still, and Barnett Newman.

24 Joseph Riddel, *The Clairvoyant Eye: The Poetry and Politics of Wallace Stevens* (Baton Rouge: Louisiana State University Press, 1965), 235.

25 O'Connor and Thaw, *Pollock*, 4: 241.

26 For a full analysis of Pollock's black paintings of 1951–53, see Francis V. O'Connor, *Jackson Pollock: The Black Pourings, 1951–1953* (Boston: Institute of Contemporary Art, 1980).

27 Quoted in Charles Doyle, *Wallace Stevens: The Critical Heritage* (London: Routledge and Kegan Paul, 1985), 405.

28 Harold Rosenberg, "Lights, Lights!," *The New Yorker* 43 (Oct. 21, 1967): 189–92ff.; rpt. in *Artworks and Packages* (1969; Chicago: University of Chicago Press, 1982), 132–43 (quote on p. 136).

29 Barbara Rose, "Jasper Johns, 'The Seasons,'" *Vogue,* January 1987: 198–99ff. The special edition to which Rose refers is *Wallace Stevens: Poems,* selected and with an introduction by Helen Vendler, with a frontispiece etching by Jasper Johns (San Francisco: Arion Press, 1985).

30 Ward Jackson, archivist at the Guggenheim Museum, recalls Johns speaking of Stevens as one of his favorite poets (interview with the author, Nov. 19, 1987); the poet David Shapiro also confirms that Johns knows and particularly likes Stevens' poetry (telephone conversation, June 20, 1990).

Index

Index